Capturing Expressivity

Capturing Expressivity

*Contexts, Methods, and Techniques
for Linguistic Research*

Edited by
JEFFREY P. WILLIAMS

OXFORD
UNIVERSITY PRESS

Great Clarendon Street, Oxford, OX2 6DP,
United Kingdom

Oxford University Press is a department of the University of Oxford.
It furthers the University's objective of excellence in research, scholarship,
and education by publishing worldwide. Oxford is a registered trade mark of
Oxford University Press in the UK and in certain other countries

© editorial matter and organization Jeffrey P. Williams 2025
© the chapters their several contributors 2025

The moral rights of the author have been asserted.

All rights reserved. No part of this publication may be reproduced, stored in a retrieval system,
transmitted, used for text and data mining, or used for training artificial intelligence, in any form or
by any means, without the prior permission in writing of Oxford University Press, or as expressly
permitted by law, by licence or under terms agreed with the appropriate reprographics rights
organization. Enquiries concerning reproduction outside the scope of the above should be sent
to the Rights Department, Oxford University Press, at the address above.

You must not circulate this work in any other form
and you must impose this same condition on any acquirer.

Published in the United States of America by Oxford University Press
198 Madison Avenue, New York, NY 10016, United States of America

British Library Cataloguing in Publication Data

Data available

Library of Congress Control Number: 2024946830

ISBN 9780192858931

DOI: 10.1093/oso/9780192858931.001.0001

Printed and bound by
CPI Group (UK) Ltd, Croydon, CR0 4YY

Links to third party websites are provided by Oxford in good faith and
for information only. Oxford disclaims any responsibility for the materials
contained in any third party website referenced in this work.

The manufacturer's authorised representative in the EU for product safety is
Oxford University Press España S.A. of El Parque Empresarial San Fernando de Henares, Avenida
de Castilla, 2 – 28830 Madrid (www.oup.es/en or
product.safety@oup.com). OUP España S.A. also acts as importer into Spain
of products made by the manufacturer.

Contents

List of Figures	vii
List of Tables	ix
The Contributors	x

1. Introduction *Jeffrey P. Williams*	1

PART I. CONTEXTS

2. Ideophones: How the world speaks to us *Christa Kilian-Hatz*	17
3. Expressives in Kammu singing *Håkan Lundström and Jan-Olof Svantesson*	33

PART II. METHODS

4. Eliciting ideophones in the field: The IdEus-Psylex collection of stimuli *Iraide Ibarretxe-Antuñano*	53
5. A multi-methods toolkit for documentary research on ideophones *Bonnie McLean and Mark Dingemanse*	74
6. Detecting and analysing expressives in a language corpus *Nicolau Dols and Pere Garau*	108
7. Empathy and indirect methods for fieldwork with ideophones in Pastaza and Upper Napo Kichwa *Janis Nuckolls and Tod Swanson*	122
8. Documenting stealth lexicon: Field methods to collect the use of ideophones in Yucatec Maya *Olivier Le Guen and Rodrigo Petatillo Chan*	145

vi CONTENTS

9. Studying Japanese mimetics 169
   Kimi Akita

PART III. TECHNIQUES

10. Is there an aesthetic component of language? 189
    Harshit Parmar and Jeffrey P. Williams

11. Learning to learn expressives: Finding cultural salience in
    linguistic fieldwork 215
    Nathan Badenoch

Index 236

List of Figures

2.1. Presentation of descriptive content as in comics	24
2.2. Spoken (verbal) quote presented as in comics	25
2.3. Ideophones presented as in comics	26
2.4. Kinds of utterances	30
4.1. The geographical area inhabited by speakers of Basque and Basque dialects	59
4.2. *Dizdiz* across Basque dialects	60
5.1. A multi-methods toolkit for documentary research on ideophones	76
5.2. Unidimensional shape stimuli	81
5.3. Multidimensional shape stimuli	83
5.4. MDS plot showing relationships between Siwu ideophones	85
5.5. Lexical entry for *sa*	91
5.6. Example sentence for *sa*	91
5.7. Lexical entry for *nosonoso*	92
5.8. Lexical entry for *bhux*	96
5.9. Searching for the tag 'curve'	97
5.10. Top-level structure in the Siwu ideophone lexicon	98
5.11. Network representation of Siwu ideophones	99
6.1. An example of an annotated segment	111
6.2. Flow diagram of a Praat script	113
6.3. Praat script form for the edition of variable values	114
7.1. A toucan's fruit	123
7.2. A forest spirit's cry	126
7.3. A rustling sound	127
7.4. Sprinkling ashes	128
7.5. An agouti snake's sound	138
7.6. An agouti snake's whistle	139
7.7. A baby rising up	141
8.1. Gestures used with ideophones in a multimodal performance	147
8.2. Schematization of the possible derivations of a CVC root in an ideophone in Yucatec Maya	149

viii LIST OF FIGURES

8.3. The speaker uses character perspective to represent how the remedy should be put in one's eye 150

8.4. The speaker uses character perspective to represent how the cow felt on the ground 154

8.5. Gesture accompanying the ideophone *che'eh* 'shake' 157

8.6. 'and he pulled it, *hóohts'o'on*' 158

8.7. The speaker showing how the deer fell into the sheep's enclosure 160

8.8. Spectrogram of the sentence encompassing the ideophone 161

9.1. Log10 frequency of 801 mimetics per million words in BCCWJ 176

10.1. Graphic representation for the experiment design 194

10.2. (A) Spatial clusters for contrasted E vs NE (reading + translation) for combinations of different languages. (B) Spatial clusters of E vs NE contrast for reading and translation separately. (C) Spatial cluster for contrasted R>T and T>R 198

10.3. Visualization of design matrix for first-level analysis. The columns correspond to regressors while the rows correspond to time points. Higher amplitudes are represented with a lighter shade of grey, while lower amplitudes are represented using darker shades of grey. 206

10.4. Reaction times for reading and translation 209

10.5. Correlation between reading speed and response time 210

10.6. Comparison of response times for reading and translation 211

11.1. Mapping thematization of expressive salience 231

List of Tables

2.1.	Verbal direct speech vs ideophonic direct speech	22
2.2.	Sound-symbolic techniques with ideophones	28
3.1.	Regular expressive morphology	34
3.2.	Size and vowel quality	35
3.3.	Expressives in the Kammu dictionary and in Kammu songs	43
3.4.	Context categories of expressives	44
4.1.	Linguistic characterization of Basque ideophones	56
4.2.	Variables for IdEus-Psylex stimuli	62
5.1.	Strategies for representing ideophone meanings	94
6.1.	Examples of the resulting data	119
10.1.	Cluster level information for all the contrasts shown in Figure 10.2	199
10.2.	Weights for regressors corresponding to different contrasts	207
10.3.	Subject level p-value for paired t test	209

The Contributors

Kimi Akita is Associate Professor in the Department of English Linguistics at Nagoya University. He has published numerous articles on ideophones in Japanese and other languages in major journals, such as *Cognitive Linguistics, Cognitive Science, Journal of Linguistics, Linguistics*, and *Studies in Language*. He also edited *Ideophones, Mimetics and Expressives* (2019).

Nathan Badenoch works in South-east and South Asia on linguistic performance, multilingualisms, and language as ecological knowledge. He has conducted extensive ethnographic research on languages of Laos, with recent work focused on expressives in the Austroasiatic language Bit, as well as Mundari, spoken in Eastern India. He co-edited *Expressives in the South Asian Linguistic Area* (Brill) and *A Dictionary of Mundari Expressives* (Tokyo University of Foreign Studies). He is currently Associate Professor of Global Interdisciplinary Studies and Director of Asian Studies at Villanova University and editor of *Southeast Asian Studies* (Kyoto University).

Rodrigo Petatillo Chan is a PhD student at CIESAS, in Mexico. His is a native speaker of Yucatec Maya from Quintana Roo. His work deals with multimodal expressivity with a focus on how gestures complement complex predicates and ideophones in Yucatec Maya.

Mark Dingemanse is Associate Professor in Language and Communication at the Centre for Language Studies, Radboud University Nijmegen. His PhD thesis on the meaning and use of ideophones in Siwu won the AVT/Anéla dissertation award (2012) and the Max Planck Society's Otto Hahn Medal (2013), and his subsequent work on ideophones and iconicity, much of it collaborative, has combined observational, experimental, and typological perspectives. In another line of work, he investigates how language is shaped by and for social interaction.

Nicolau Dols is a full professor of Catalan at the Universitat de les Illes Balears (Majorca), and a member of Institut d'Estudis Catalans, whose Philological Section (the official academy for Catalan language) he currently chairs. His research interests lie mainly in the fields of phonology and, more generally, of grammar. He co-authored (with Max W. Wheeler and Alan Yates) *Catalan. A Comprehensive Grammar* (Routledge, 1999) and (with Richard M. Mansell) *Catalan. An Essential Grammar* (Routledge, 2017). His research has also addressed issues in sociolinguistics, language standardization, translation, and constructed languages. His contribution to this volume has been partially funded by research projects PID2021-128381NB-I00 (Ministerio de Ciencia e Innovación, Spain) and PROMETEO/2023/006 (Generalitat Valenciana).

Pere Garau (Selva, Majorca, 1997) is an associate lecturer at the Universitat de les Illes Balears. His research primarily focuses on the metre of Catalan poetry, exploring its computational and phonological dimensions. Beyond this, he has delved into the language of

THE CONTRIBUTORS xi

the media—particularly subtitling—and a range of topics in linguistics, sociolinguistics, and poetry. He is also a member of the research team for the Corpus Oral de la Llengua Catalana (Oral Corpus of the Catalan Language) project led by the Institut d'Estudis Catalans.

Iraide Ibarretxe-Antuñano is Professor of General Linguistics at the University of Zaragoza and researcher at the Institute for Heritage and Humanities (IPH-U. Zaragoza). She is also an elected Fellow of The Academy of Europe (Linguistics Section). Her research focuses on the relation between language, cognition, and communication from a typological and psycholinguistic perspective. She has published on topics related to semantic typology (lexicalization, polysemy), ideophones and sound symbolism, and the relationship between metaphor, embodiment, and culture.

Christa Kilian-Hatz is applied professor of linguistics at Goethe University Frankfurt am Main. Her fascination with African languages and linguistics began in 1986 when she was a literacy development worker with the Baka pygmies in Southern Cameroon; during this time she was already collecting and translating their myths. She followed this by studying linguistics at the University of Cologne and working on various research projects on typology, grammaticalization, and ideophones, as well as the documentation and analysis of a Khoisan language. In 2005 she moved to the Goethe University in Frankfurt, where she focuses specifically on the reconstruction of a proto-Pygmy language.

Olivier Le Guen is a professor-researcher at CIESAS (Mexico City). Ha has been conducting research for the last twenty years on the Yucatec Maya culture and language in Mexico. His research lies in the field of linguistic-anthropology and psycholinguistics, with a multidisciplinary orientation integrating the methods of anthropology, linguistics, and cognitive psychology. He has published on expressivity, expressive morphology, and also gesture and multimodality.

Håkan Lundström, Professor Emeritus, Malmö Faculty of Fine and Performing Arts, Lund University, has worked with Kammu musical tradition within the Kammu research project at Lund University, most recently in the interdisciplinary study *In the Borderland Between Song and Speech*. He was involved in a long-term exchange and development programme between Malmö and Hanoi that included documentation of music of ethnic groups in Vietnam. His other research interests include Japanese and Alaskan Native American musics.

Bonnie McLean is a doctoral candidate in the Department of Linguistics and Philology at Uppsala University. She is interested in the roles of iconicity in language change, with a doctoral project that involves quantifying the iconicity of words and exploring how this affects their transmission over time. Before coming to Uppsala, she studied linguistics and Japanese at the Australian National University, where she wrote her honours thesis on the phonological and semantic development of ideophones in Japonic. She is also interested in the linguistic typology of ideophone systems.

Janis Nuckolls is a professor in the department of linguistics at Brigham Young University. She is an anthropological linguist with wide-ranging interests in sound symbolism, grammar, evidentiality, discourse, ideophones, and gesture. Much of her published work has focused on ideophone use in Pastaza Kichwa, a dialect of the Quechua family of languages spoken in Amazonian Ecuador, and it includes numerous articles spanning a range of topics, including ideophones' phonology, semantics, pragmatics, and gestural usage. An article on the neurolinguistics of ideophones is forthcoming. She has developed an extensive audiovisual archive devoted to ideophones, *Quechua Real Words* http://quechuarealwords. byu.edu. Her most recent book, co-authored with Tod Swanson, is *Amazonian Quichua Language and Life: Introduction to Grammar, Ecology, and Discourse from Pastaza and Upper Napo Quichua*.

Harshit Parmar is a distinguished researcher specializing in biomedical signal processing, with a focus on functional neuroimaging. His expertise lies in the design and application of machine-learning techniques for fMRI data analysis, image processing, time series analysis, and data visualization. Demonstrating his proficiency through impactful publications, Dr. Parmar excels in designing and training sophisticated deep-learning algorithms tailored for MRI data. His methodological contributions extend to enhancing preprocessing, interpretation, and visualization of diverse high-dimensional biomedical data sets. Notably, his research goes beyond algorithmic development, delving into the extraction and visualization of cognitive spatial–temporal relationships from neuroimaging data, offering valuable insights into decision-making processes.

Jan-Olof Svantesson, Professor Emeritus, Centre for Languages and Literature, Lund University, is an expert on Yùan Kammu and the long-term coordinator of linguistic research on Kaṁmu. He was awarded his PhD in General Linguistics in 1983 for a dissertation on Kammu phonology and morphology. He has subsequently worked on different aspects of the Kammu language, including a dictionary of Yùan Kammu. His other research interests include Mongolian phonology.

Tod D. Swanson is Associate Professor of Religious Studies and Senior Sustainability Scholar in the Global Institute for Sustainability at Arizona State University. His research draws on anthropological linguistics and comparative religion to interpret the Amazonian Kichwa social relation to nature and indigenous thinking about the environment in the western Amazon. For the last twenty years he has directed the Andes and Amazon Field School, a Summer FLAS (Foreign Language and Area Studies) Kichwa language programme on the Napo River in Ecuador. In that context he applies his research to seek solutions for a more sustainable future in Ecuador's Amazonia region. His most recent publication, 'Feeling with the land: Llakichina and the emotional life of relatedness in Amazonian Kichwa thinking', is published in the *Journal of the American Academy of Religion*.

Jeffrey P. Williams is Professor of Ethnology and Linguistics at Texas Tech University in Lubbock, Texas, US. His research covers lesser-known varieties of English, expressivity, language endangerment, and language contact. His field research has been in the West Indies, Australia, Papua New Guinea, and Menorca (Balearic Islands, Spain). He has published books with Cambridge University Press, John Benjamins, and Routledge. His most recent edited book, published by Cambridge University Press, is entitled *Expressivity in European Languages* and appeared in autumn 2023.

1

Introduction

Jeffrey P. Williams

Expressivity can take a number of grammatical paths to manifestation in speech. Expressivity is no different from other properties of human language that find articulation in grammar through principles, rules, and representations. All languages exhibit expressivity in both grammar and usage. Expressivity punctuates discourse in meaningful ways.[1]

All of these statements are non-controversial in twenty-first-century linguistics, as the study of expressivity has gradually grown in stature among the disciplines of the language sciences, over the last decade in particular.[2] While there are much earlier accounts of expressivity, especially within descriptive traditions of African, East Asian, and European linguistics, modern linguistic theory has been rather slow to incorporate information regarding these forms and processes into contemporary dialogue. In fact, in the case of most earlier grammars, expressivity in the forms of expressives, ideophones, mimetics, and onomatopoeic forms is often relegated to the margins and footnotes at best. As the contributors to this volume make clear in their chapters, this situation no longer holds in modern linguistic documentation and description.

Expressivity can best be defined as the grammaticalization of sensory qualities: it is used to characterize the way things are perceived through the senses and are then articulated and conveyed in a linguistic message. Expressivity is a form of linguistic pointing in which the common ground is utilized by a speaker to highlight a perception, an attitude, an emotive state, or otherwise make some sort of descriptive metacommentary in which s/he expresses particulars about a word but not the meaning of the word itself. It is about the perception of a culturally based reality that is at stake in expressivity.

The linguistic enquiry into sensory perception and linguistic beautification as manifested in grammar can be referred to as grammatical aesthetics (after Williams 2014). Grammatical aesthetics is not about transmitting truth or facts, but about transmitting perception based on interpretation. From the perspective of interpretive anthropology, expressives are forms in search of meanings.

---

[1] This process and its products should not be confused with mere decoration, which some have claimed expressivity in language can be attributed to (Haiman 2018).

[2] Expressivity can be said to be coming into its own with the forthcoming 'Oxford Handbook' volume, to be entitled *The Oxford Handbook of Expressivity* (Gutzmann, ed.).

Jeffrey P. Williams, *Introduction*. In: *Capturing Expressivity*. Edited by: Jeffrey P. Williams, Oxford University Press.
© Jeffrey P. Williams (2025). DOI: 10.1093/oso/9780192858931.003.0001

2 JEFFREY P. WILLIAMS

Expressivity is emergent in discourse and grammar. Without a doubt, it is the most creative aspect of the human linguistic faculty, linking both competence and performance in a complex and novel means of expression. I contend that expressivity is governed by a **Principle of Expressivity** that is universal in human language, which states the following:

> a systematic feature of human language is the ability to articulate and communicate perception of natural and social worlds.[3]

This contributors to this volume all provide direct evidence for such a principle and also discuss the means by which it can be discerned in grammar and discourse.

1.1 Histories of expressivity

In *Timaeus*, Plato's fourth-century BCE account of the formation of the universe and his explanation of its impressive order and beauty, he argues that discourse about the natural world mimics the intelligible world. This argument foreshadows the extensive treatments that have developed to account for the class of forms in language that linguists refer to as expressives, ideophones, or mimetics. Expressives and their kind appear in discourse about the natural and social worlds to represent what is perceived in the intelligible world.

The term 'expressivity', or expressive meaning, has a long history in linguistics. In the early twentieth century, several European linguists became interested in the properties of expressives and reduplication in human language. Brandstetter (1917), Oehl (1913–14, 1917–18), and Bühler (1934) all made significant contributions to the recognition of an expressive function of language. All three saw this expressive component and its exponents in the form of 'echoic' words and reduplications as remnants of an earlier stage in human communication. Oehl's work is particularly insightful in his recognition of and attention to what he referred to as 'bildwort' in Indo-European, which captured the words in Indo-European that refer to particular animals through a novel use of linguistic resources: forms that we might refer to as onomatopoeic or mimetic.

Bühler developed the most comprehensive account, albeit evolutionary, in his 'Theory of Language'—*Sprachtheorie*—that was published in 1934. In the modern era, it was Roman Jakobson, building on an earlier insights of Bühler (1934), who coined the term 'expressive' or 'emotive' for one of the functions of language (Amaral 2018). Jakobson describes it, saying that it '... focused on the ADDRESSER [speaker], aims a direct expression of the speaker's attitude toward what he is

---

[3] This principle can apply to both expressive and prosaic language, if we are intent on maintaining that distinction (cf. Zwicky and Pullum 1987).

speaking about' (Jakobson 1960: 354) and provides interjections as the prime examples of this.

Linguistic analyses of expressivity have tended to focus on the syntax and semantics of the property. The works of Cruse (1986), Gutzmann (2019), Gutzmann and Henderson (2019), and Potts (2005, 2007) are most notable in this arena where the focus has been primarily on interjections.[4]

Morphologically centred work has followed later through the heavily debated work of Zwicky and Pullum (1987). Morphophonological strategies to expand expressivity in language—typically through processes of echo word formation—and some of the functions of reduplication are explored in the collections edited by Williams (2014), (2021), and (2023).

Since the work of Jakobson, anthropological linguists have been more keen to engage with expressivity through its various guises in language practices. This is manifest in the work of individuals such as Sherzer (1987, 2002) and Nuckolls (1996, 1999, 2010, and also represented in a chapter of this volume), Webster (2008), and Webster, Lahti, and Barrett (2014).

The present volume represents a new chapter in the history of the study of expressivity, focusing on the methods, contexts, and techniques of investigation of the process. It provides a case-study approach to how to 'capture' expressivity in language and culture.

1.2 Terminologies of expressivity

The linguistics literature is crowded with a variety of terms for the carriers of expressivity: expressives, ideophones, mimetics, onomatopoeics, and a host of other specialized terms. These terms share the property of being descriptors for a purported class of special words in a wide range of the world's languages. The structural and functional dimensions of the forms themselves do not warrant such a plethora of terms.

There is a somewhat ingrained distinction between expressives and ideophones, based on the geographical sources of the two. The term 'expressive' has wider currency in the grammars of languages from South and South-east Asia. The term 'ideophone' has its origins in the early twentieth-century writings on African grammatical categories and it is used widely to describe a class of forms in African as well as Native American languages. 'Ideophone' can also be found as a descriptor in grammars of Korean and Chinese.

---

[4] The research into this area of expressivity has been done mostly in Indo-European languages, including English, German, and Greek, with considerable attention being paid to expletive expressivity. We have little to no information about expletive expressivity in other languages.

Expressives, as a category, are an amalgam of forms and processes, some of which are independent words and some of which are derivational processes. Expressives are iconic devices that allow speakers to express certain perceptual qualities of entities, including human beings, in a discourse. They are notoriously hard to elicit in standard grammatical frames of linguistic discovery.

'Mimetic' is often used in the grammars of Japanese forms. The point of this delineation is simply to show that the variation in usage is based on historical usages (Doke for 'ideophone' in African languages in the 1930s, for example) and not on actual structural or functional differences.

In the list below I outline the key features, as designated by a range of scholars, showing the similarities and differences between the three terms and then discuss these to provide a coherent accounting of adopting a single term.

- expressives—shape-shifting forms (Williams 2014, 2021)
- expressives—convey complex meanings reduced into a single praxis (Tuvasson 2011)
- expressives—separate lexical class (Diffloth 1972)
- expressives—iconic (multiple references by many scholars)
- expressives—used especially with languages of South-east Asia (widespread)
- ideophones—more iconic than other features of language (Dingemanse 2018; Akita and Pradeshi 2019)
- ideophones—different classes of words (Doke 1935)
- ideophones—set apart from other word classes (Dingemanse 2018)
- ideophones—refer to depiction/description in language (Doke 1935)
- ideophones—tame vs wild ideophones—tame ideophones are prone to changing word class and can shift into being nouns, verbs, etc. (Rhodes 1994)
- ideophones—marked words (Dingemanse 2018, 2019)
- ideophones—create involvement between speaker and hearer (Nuckolls 1999)
- ideophones—used broadly and interchangeably but especially with languages of Africa, Central Asia, the Americas, and to some extent East Asia
- mimetics—mimic or invoke an idea (Akita and Pardeshi 2019; Akita, this volume)
- mimetics—marked words (Akita, this volume; Dingemanse 2019)
- mimetics—special class set apart from other word classes
- mimetics—used for forms in Japanese primarily

As can be easily seen, there are a wide range of opinions and characterizations regarding the features that describe expressives, ideophones, and mimetics, and yet there is considerable overlap in the characterizations as well, that needs to be resolved to develop a more tightly strung definition of the exponents of expressivity.

1.3 Exponents of expressivity: ideophones and expressives

A series of chapters in this volume all revolve around determining the repertoire of ideophones/expressives in given languages. In her contribution to this volume, **Kilian-Hatz** provides a means for determining what ideophones, or expressives, are in grammar. She provides a means to distinguish ideophones/expressives from other word classes as well as gestures in Table 2.4 (page 28). Her classification captures many astute generalizations about the relationships between various forms of expressivity. In her classification, Kilian-Hatz proposes that gestures are proximate to both ideophones and interjections, but differ in that they are non-verbal constructions. Ideophones are iconic, grammatically aloof, highly auto-semantic and clause-like. In her scheme, ideophones differ from interjections only insofar as interjections are always appellative, while ideophones, or expressives, are not. She is making a claim for differing exponents of expressivity in grammar. In contrast to these types, descriptive content words are symbolic, auto-semantic, and single clausal constituents. And finally, function words are highly symbolic and grammatically bound.

In doing so, she harkens back to one of the earliest characterizations of ideophones in the Bantu languages by Doke (1935: 119), where he states that ideophones are '... a vivid representation of an idea in sound. A word, often onomatopoeic, which describes a predicate, qualificative or adverb in respect to manner, colour, sound, smell, action, state or intensity'. But more to the point, Kilian-Hatz adopts Fortune's (1962: 6) characterization of ideophones as 'dramaturgic predicates' comparable to vocal gestures. She contends that ideophones are equivalents to complete, clausal utterances.

In their chapter, **Håkan Lundström** and **Jan-Olof Svantesson** investigate the expressive repertoire of the Yùan Kammu dialect—an Austroasiatic (Mon-Khmer) language spoken mainly in Northern Laos and also in adjacent areas of Vietnam, Thailand, China, and Myanmar—from the combined perspectives of linguistics and ethnomusicology. Their contribution highlights the necessity of the 'right' consultant in field research on expressivity. Their primary consultant, Kàm Ràw, possesses an impressive knowledge of his own culture and language and is also an accomplished singer. His knowledge and his use of expressives in singing makes it possible to understand not only the meaning of the expressives but also their emotional and associative qualities.

As the authors explicate in their chapter, expressives are particularly common in praise songs, an important part of the repertoire of songs that are sung in address of one or more individuals. They point out that it is important to consider not only the lexical meaning of the expressives, but also their meaning in the context of *trnàam*—orally transmitted poems which forms the basis of *tɔ́əm* songs—to which they belong. As the authors point out, the contextual meanings of the expressives mainly relate to praise (success/wealth and

6 JEFFREY P. WILLIAMS

beauty), deprecation (belittling of oneself/lack of respect), and sadness (lone-liness/unrequited love/poverty). Expressivity in Kammu belongs to songs that, apart from sadness, express strong inner feelings of shyness or embarrassment, reflecting an inner perceptual categorization.

1.4 What expressivity does

Expressivity, in any language, allows speakers to bring to the fore aspects of an entity or an event through the structural properties of grammar and discourse. Component parts of the utterance are given prominence through transformation, sometimes involving the rule of quantity whereby more elements are seen to demand more cognitive attention (cf. Williams 2021). Expressivity, through its iconicity, reduces the seemingly cumbersome nature of description in discourse: it allows the speaker to condense complex and multifaceted information into a single praxis.

As some have described the work of expressives, they 'inflict' meaning, they do not express it. Once one performs an expressive, it cannot be withdrawn from the inscription of the contextualized discourse. Expressives are an example of what Gärdenfors (2014) has referred to as 'fast meeting of the minds', where expressives function as an example of grammatical pointing. The fast process consists of the development of a shared world—known as a 'common ground' in the model of the geometry of meaning—during a discourse or a shared communicative act. Anthropological linguists might merely describe this shared world as 'culture'.

1.5 What characterizes expressivity?

So what characterizes expressivity in language? There are several features that have been isolated as portraying expressivity in language: performativity, immediacy, interpretation, ephemerality, interpretation, empathy, and repeatability, to name a few.

The work of Potts (2005, 2007) in particular has focused on the aspect of performativity in expressivity, linking it to its performative functionality. One performs expressives—one doesn't just say them. This is a recurrent characterization that can also be found in the work of ethnographically oriented linguists such as Badenoch (2021), Webster (2008), as well as in the pioneering writings of the late Gérard Diffloth (1976, 1995, 2021).

The meaning of expressivity is *interpretively emergent*. This perspective on expressivity echoes the semiotic interpretation of the meaning of signs being determined through interpretation. In the sense of Geertz (1974) following from

Malinowski (1922), we are attempting to capture the 'native's point of view' in the understanding and use of expressivity in culturally conditioned ways.

The *elusive, ephemeral*, and shifting quality of expressivity makes it difficult to capture through standard linguistic elicitation frames. This is due partly to the highly contextualized nature of the usage. It is often a fleeting experience or perception that evokes the use of an expressive form in grammar. While the forms that expressivity may take, such as expressives/ideophones/mimetics, can be elicited through grammatical elicitation frameworks, understanding the semantic scope of such forms and their morphosyntactic characteristics often cannot.

1.6 Tools for capturing expressivity

The overarching question that animates this book is: how do we document, or engage with, such an elusive—at times—practice as is expressivity? The contributors to this volume all possess extensive experience with exactly this task—engaging with expressivity. In each chapter, a different tack is taken in documenting, describing, and analysing expressivity.

Since many forms of expressivity do not lend themselves well to formal, structured elicitation frames, how do we as linguistically trained scholars capture it? Expressivity exists 'in the moment' and is not easily generated paradigmatically. Expressivity is difficult to study on its own because it is deeply embedded in the *immediacy* of discourse. This is one aspect that links all approaches to the types of expressivity as well as its related component of ephemerality.

Equally, and in many cases, the 'right' native speaker needs to be consulted who can reflect upon expressivity in the grammar and create scenarios where such a form might exist, as several authors in this collection stress.

There is a developing set of methodologies which are best suited to the intricacies and particularities of capturing expressivity in grammar. **Ibarretxe-Antuñano**, like the other authors in this collection, seeks to set the record straight on the centrality of expressivity to grammar in human language. Her focus in this chapter is on capturing the extensive expressivity in the Basque language. As she points out, expressivity in the form of ideophones (or expressives) is pervasive, as well as ubiquitous, being present in both oral and written contexts. Moreover, their presence is recorded in a wide range of registers and dialects. Ibarretxe-Antuñano addresses the difficulties in the elicitation of ideophones from a cross-linguistic perspective by introducing the IdEus-Psylex stimulus kit, which was designed specifically for eliciting Basque ideophones in the field.

The IdEus-Psylex stimulus kit was first tested in a field setting in 2009. Thirty-seven speakers participated in the initial study, distributed among three age groups (16–30 yrs = 17; 31–60 yrs = 12; 61–90 yrs = 8) with different educational backgrounds. All of the participants came from rural areas and they were native speakers of four main dialects: Western Basque (twelve subjects), Central Basque (six subjects), Navarrese Basque (twelve subjects), and Navarrese-Lapurdian Basque (seven subjects).

As the author makes clear, the IdEus-Psylex stimulus kit was created based on the specific characterization of the Basque language and the status of Basque ideophones. The main goal of this tool was to provide researchers with a collection of materials that would reveal the knowledge and usage of ideophones in Basque, but it might be adapted for other languages.

Further in this vein, **Bonnie McLean** and **Mark Dingemanse**, like many other authors in this collection, stress the difficulty of capturing expressivity by utilizing traditional methods for language description and documentation. In their chapter, they review some of the new and experimental techniques that have been used to elicit, describe, and analyse ideophones, and discuss how these may be used in the field to address some of the unique challenges that ideophones pose. These methods and techniques include stimulus-based elicitation; multimodal folk definitions; hybrid modes of analysis (combining images and text); and new ways of compiling and presenting multimodal corpora of ideophones. Their contribution focuses on three main challenges to capturing expressivity: collecting ideophones; unravelling their slippery semantics; and representing them in ways that accurately represent their special semiotic properties. They also review methods used in psycholinguistic research to study the sensory properties of words and the organization of the lexicon.

Crucial to their approach is the triangulation of insights from multiple sources, including the exploitation of polysemiotic resources and the integration of etic and emic perspectives. This chapter synthesizes some of the most effective techniques used to elicit ideophones and to uncover their meanings, while simultaneously producing rich, polysemiotic representations of those meanings. Importantly, in some ways complementing Akita's contribution, McLean and Dingemanse explore novel means of presenting and engaging with dictionaries of expressivity, suggesting ways to transform these from mere documentary records to a viable and dynamic tool for understanding it.

The ways in which types of data interact with methods of investigation for productive research on expressivity are explored by **Nicolau Dols** and **Pere Garau** in their chapter. They argue for the viability of using oral corpora for research on expressivity where there is a strong connection between form and meaning. Based on this characterization of expressives and a strong body of data from Catalan, they demonstrate that an oral corpus is an elegant tool for finding and collecting forms in which similar shapes convey predictable meanings, or in their words exhibit a high degree of iconicity.

They propose that a battery of types of resources is a need for the analysis of expressivity in any language, stating that the importance of acoustic data cannot be overlooked—although it typically has been. Beyond this, the authors stress the

INTRODUCTION 9

importance of textual or discourse elements in the analysis of expressivity. They present a toolkit of methodologies; namely Praat—TextGrids—and Regex (Regular Expression) devices to simplify working with expressives within audio corpora and written corpora respectively.

In their chapter **Janis Nuckolls** and **Tod Swanson** discuss what they have learned from field methods designed to record ideophones, or expressives, in eastern Amazonian Ecuador, among speakers of Upper Napo Kichwa and Pastaza Kichwa. Particularly enlightening for the field worker in expressivity, Nuckolls and Swanson also include those methods that have been less obviously successful in capturing expressivity.

They successfully argue that the special qualities of ideophones in Kichwa-speaking culture, and possibly in other cultures as well, require different approaches from traditional linguistic methods for data gathering. Some of their successful methods include: interviewing while involved in tasks which speakers find engaging and enjoyable, asking about subject matter which speakers find interesting, moving, or humorous, and allowing ideophones to emerge through conversation before attempting to ask targeted questions about their use and functionality.

Their conclusion is that the use of ideophones by Kichwa speakers frequently revolves around empathy for both humans and non-humans; not only for their interior states, but also for the minute perceptual details of their ways of being in the world. This chapter provides the initial characterization of empathy as a key feature of expressivity in grammar.

Another contribution that focuses on methods derived from the challenges of capturing expressivity is the chapter by **Olivier Le Guen** and **Rodrigo Petatillo Chan** (a native speaker of Yucatec Maya). They discuss the challenging nature of documenting the iconic and multimodal character of ideophones in Yucatec Maya. The authors, like others in the book, propose that a combination of differing methodologies can help provide a better understanding of the Yucatec Maya stealth lexicon and its formation and use in this language.

As the authors point out, many speakers and most of the modern linguistic tradition consider expressives to be not 'real words', or childish, or as having a peripheral linguistic status (Ibarretxe-Antuñano makes the same observation for Basque in her chapter). For field linguists, the characteristics of these words means that documenting them is a difficult task, both theoretically as well as practically, as often elicitation out of the blue is next to impossible. In their chapter, Le Guen and Chan present the specificity of ideophones in Yucatec Maya (Mexico), their use, and what methodologies are best suited to collect them in the field.

In 'Studying Japanese mimetics', **Kimi Akita** describes the representative methods of collecting and analysing mimetics adopted in Japanese linguistics and summarizes important findings from a general, cross-linguistic perspective. An important distinction that sets apart the study of expressivity in Japanese from that accomplished in other languages is that the vast majority of Japanese linguists are native speakers of the language and hence able to provide grammatical insights that are often difficult to elicit even from extremely reflective native speakers of other languages. Another important distinction involving methods of studying Japanese mimetics that Akita points out is the existence of mimetic dictionaries of Japanese; again something that is absent from the tools that can be used to study expressivity in other languages.

As Akita makes clear to us, the study of Japanese mimetics has a long history supported through native speaker linguists' introspection; the existence of various dictionaries and corpora; as well as the use of linguistic experimentation. All of these advanced research environments and methods have enabled Japanese linguistics to make important descriptive and theoretical contributions to research into the formal grammar of expressivity. However, as Akita points out, these advantages have also deterred Japanese linguists from natural, multimodal conversation data, which are crucial for uncovering the essential properties of mimetics as an interactional device.

Beyond the description and methods for capturing expressivity are the techniques employed by researchers to nuance expressivity in differing contexts. The two contributions by Parmar and Williams, and Badenoch, in this volume, anchor the contextual extremes of capturing expressivity: from the field to the lab.

The 'field' in 'fieldwork' in anthropology has been through a period of re-evaluation, while the same cannot be said of the place of the 'field' in linguistics. In anthropology, the critique has revolved around the static nature of participant observation and ethnographic analysis in producing descriptions that do not adequately address contemporary anthropological issues and concerns. The same could be leveled as a critique for methods of the field in linguistics—standard elicitation methods do not adequately address the needs of expanding concerns in grammatical analysis: a case in point being the study of expressivity.

In their chapter, **Harshit Parmar** and **Jeffrey Williams** employ a different type of data to investigate the considerable speculation about the nature of expressivity as a linguistic principle through neurolinguistic experimentation. They base their experimental analysis of expressivity in Gujarati and Hindi (Indo-Aryan languages of South Asia) on the observation made by many linguists (Diffloth 1972, 1976, and 1980; Dingemanse 2012, 2015, and 2018; Williams 2014; Zwicky and Pullum 1987) that expressivity is 'special' or 'unusual' vis-à-vis 'normal' or 'prosaic' morphosyntax. The authors set out to test the speculation that because of their unique traits, expressives are perceived differently in the linguistic stream of understanding, conducting a preliminary investigation to test that using a neuroimaging (fMRI) experiment.

Their study seeks to provide preliminary data to assist in answering the question 'Is there an aesthetic component of language?' that was first proposed in modern linguistics by Gérard Diffloth in 1972 in his seminal article 'Notes on

Expressive Meaning' (Diffloth 1972). If the aesthetic component exists separately from other components of grammar, then there might be some different localization for the brain activity associated with the production and interpretation of expressives. Their results suggest that there are certain regions involved in processing the expressives differently from the non-expressives in the cognitive architecture of these two languages. Furthermore, activation in some of the brain regions suggests that expressives are not processed completely in typical language-processing regions, indicating that expressives may be perceived as a more creative and aesthetic part of language by the brain.

In his chapter, **Nathan Badenoch** reflects on conversations with his primary Bit language consultant (Souler) as a consideration of how we learn about expressivity through ethnographically oriented linguistic fieldwork. Badenoch engages with the long-standing tradition of bringing the people we work with into the linguist's reflection on the grammar, with a specific interest in understanding his own framework for studying expressives. His chapter provides us with a clear window on Bit linguistic ideology through the lens of expressivity.

Badenoch points out that Bit speakers have a high awareness of the poetic play that expressives add to speech. This is a repetitive theme that field linguists who work on expressivity in natural language articulate. Badenoch recounts the multimodal nature of expressivity in Bit by stating that his consultant *explains* the meaning using words, *demonstrates* actions and states using his body and the surrounding space, and *performs* emotions and reactions using facial expressions and head movements. His contribution is a successful attempt to present an ethnographic account of his primary consultant's micro-ethnographic discourses on expressives. Badenoch concludes that the salient features that Souler emphasizes show how these words contribute to the linguistic culture of the Bit, constituting a key area of their semiotic ideology.

In recounting how speakers of Semai—an Austro-Asiatic language of Malaysia—use expressivity, Diffloth (2021) has described how the speakers characterize the use of expressive words as 'shooting', as one would shoot an arrow. In Semai, expressivity is an ephemeral act of discourse-centred grammar; one which cannot be retrieved after it has been propelled.

1.7 Conclusions

Expressivity in language, as articulated through a wide range of grammatical and lexical resources, is fleeting. It is context-sensitive and temporal. This is not to be unexpected, since expressivity is tied directly to perception. Perception itself, is fleeting, temporally bounded, and contextually determined. So the big question for linguists in general is how do we 'capture' expressivity if it is so fleeting? This volume breaks new ground in demonstrating how many successful scholars have done exactly that in using a wide range of methods and techniques, ranging across a number of different contexts.

This book collects original scholarship from a wide range of languages written by scholars with extensive research experience in the field of expressivity. Each takes a somewhat different perspective on solving the riddle of how to capture expressivity—from research in the field to more experimental environments. Expressivity has been a systematically obscured component of grammar. This has been due to a combination of factors, the first being that many linguists working in the field are not competent enough in the vernacular to participate in discourse that utilizes expressivity to a high degree. Badenoch makes this the focus of his contribution to the volume. Further, standard elicitation, as McLean and Dingemanse as well as others in this volume demonstrate, will not yield results in expressivity. A creative and non-standard toolkit is required for the special nature of expressivity in the grammatical universe.

References

Akita, Kimi and Pardeshi, Parshant (eds) (2019). *Ideophones, Mimetics and Expressives.* (Iconicity in Language and Literature 16.) Amsterdam/Philadelphia: John Benjamins.

Amaral, Patricia (2018). Expressive meaning. In Frank Liedtke and Astrid Tuchen (eds), *Handbuch pragmatik.* Berlin: Springer, 325–323.

Badenoch, Nathan (2021). Silence, cessation and stasis: animating 'absence' in Bit expressives. *Journal of Linguistic Anthropology* 32(1): 94–115.

Brandstetter, Renward (1917). *Die Reduplikation in den indianischen, indonesischen und indogermanischen Sprachen.* Luzern: Luzerner Kantonschule, 33.

Bühler (1934). *Sprachtheorie.* [Theory of language]. Jena, Germany: Gustav Fischer Verlag.

Cruse, D. Alan (1986). *Lexical Semantics.* Cambridge: Cambridge University Press.

Diffloth (1972) Notes on expressive meaning. *Chicago Linguistic Society* 8: 440–447.

Diffloth, Gérard (1976). Expressives in Semai. Oceanic Linguistics Special Publications. No. 13, *Austroasiatic Studies* Part I: 249–264.

Diffloth (1980). Expressive phonology and prosaic phonology in Mon-Khmer. In Theraphan L. Thongkum (ed.), *Studies in Mon-Khmer and Thai Phonology and Phonetics in Honor of E. Henderson.* Bangkok: Chulalongkorn University Press, 49–59.

Diffloth, Gérard (1995). *i*:big, *a*:small. In Leanne Hinton, Johanna Nichols, and John J. Ohala (eds), *Sound Symbolism.* Cambridge: Cambridge University Press, 107–114.

Diffloth, Gérard (2021). Foreword. In Nathan Badenoch and Nishaant Choksi (eds), *Expressives in the South Asian Linguistic Area.* Leiden: Brill, vii–x.

Dingemanse (2018). Redrawing the margins of language: Lessons from research on ideophones. *Glossa: A Journal of General Linguistics.* 3(1): 4. http://doi.org/10.5334/gjgl. 444

Dingemanse, (2019). 'Ideophone' as a comparative concept. In Kimi Akita and Prasant Pardeshi (eds). *Ideophones, Mimetics and Expressives.* Amsterdam: John Benjamins, 13–33.

Doke (1935). *Bantu Linguistic Terminology.* London: Longman Greens and Co.

Gärdenförs, Peter (2014). *Geometry of Meaning: Semantics Based on Conceptual Spaces.* Cambridge, MA: Massachusetts Institute of Technology.

Geertz, Clifford (1974). 'From the native's point of view:' on the nature of anthropological understanding. *Bulletin of the American Academy of Arts and Sciences* 28: 26–45.

Gutzmann, Daniel and Robert Henderson (2019). Expressive updates, much? *Language* 95(1): 107–135.

Haiman, John (2018). *Ideophones and the Evolution of Language*. Cambridge: Cambridge University Press.

Jakobson, Roman (1960). Closing statements: linguistics and poetics. In Thomas A. Sebeok (ed.), *Style in Language*. Cambridge, MA: MIT Press, 350–377.

Malinowski, Bronislaw (1922). *Argonauts of the Western Pacific*. London: G. Routledge and Sons.

Nuckolls, Janis (1996). *Sounds Like Life: Sound-symbolic Grammar, Performance, and Cognition in Pastaza Quechua*. New York: Oxford University Press.

Nuckolls, Janis (1999). The case for sound symbolism. *Annual Review of Anthropology* 28: 225–252.

Nuckolls, Janis (2010). *Lessons from a Quechua Strongwoman: Ideophony, Dialogue and Perspective*. Tucson: University of Arizona Press.

Oehl, Wilhelm (1917–18). Elementare wordschöpfung. *Anthropos XII–XIII*: 575–624.

Oehl, Wilhelm (1919–20). Elementare wordschopfung 4–9. *Anthropos XIV–XV*: 405–464.

Potts, Christopher (2005). *The Logic of Conventional Implicatures*. Oxford: Oxford University Press.

Potts, Christopher (2007). The expressive dimension. *Theoretical Linguistics* 33: 165–197.

Richard Rhodes (1995). 'Aural Images' In Hinton, Nuckolls and Ohala (eds). *Sound Symbolism*. Cambridge: Cambridge University Press, 276–292.

Sherzer, Joel (1987). Discourse-centered approach to language and culture. *American Anthropologist* 89: 295–309.

Sherzer, Joel (2002). *Speech Play and Verbal Art*. Austin: The University of Texas Press.

Tufvesson, Sylvia (2011). Analogy-making in the Semai sensory world. *The Senses and Society* 6: 86–95.

Webster, Anthony K. (2008). 'To give an imagination to the listeners': the neglected poetics of Navajo ideophony. *Semiotica* 171: 343–365.

Webster, Anthony K., Lahti, Katherine, and Barrett, Rusty (eds) (2014). Ideophones: between grammar and poetry. Special Issue *Pragmatics & Society* 5(3).

Williams, Jeffrey (ed.) (2014). *The Aesthetics of Grammar: Sound and Meaning in the Languages of Mainland Southeast Asia*. Cambridge: Cambridge University Press.

Williams, Jeffrey (ed.) (2021). *Expressive Morphology in the Languages of South Asia*. London: Routledge.

Williams, Jeffrey (ed.) (2023). *Expressivity in European Languages*. Cambridge: Cambridge University Press.

Zwicky, Arnold and Pullum, Geoffrey (1987). Plain morphology and expressive morphology. *Proceedings of the Thirteenth Annual Meeting of the Berkeley Linguistics Society (1987)*, 330–340.

PART I
CONTEXTS

2

Ideophones

How the world speaks to us

Christa Kilian-Hatz

2.1 Introduction

The study of ideophones is still young, dating back to the end of the nineteenth century only. The most important pioneers are Diedrich Westermann (1927 and 1937) and Clemens Doke (1935). Westermann creates the term *'Lautbilder'* ('sound pictures') for a striking onomatopoeic class of words in West African languages *'which describe an object or an event as a whole'* (Westermann 1937: 159). Doke (1935: 118) reports on a similar class of words in many Bantu languages and calls them 'ideophones' according to their function as *'a vivid representation of an idea in sound'*. Influenced by Westermann's and Doke's descriptions, ideophones are almost exclusively described for African languages until the 1970s. Meanwhile, the use of ideophone-like words is observed in all language families of the world; so their existence is clearly a universal feature of human language (cf. Kilian-Hatz 1999).

The term 'ideophone' is used to describe word-like elements of the speech act that differ formally and functionally from conventional lexemes. They are treated in most individual languages either as a separate word class or as a special class of nouns, verbs, adverbs, adjectives, and/or interjections. These striking words are also found in German or English, as the following word examples (1,2) show:

(1)   German
      boing, zack, rummms, piff-paff-poff, buuuuum

(2)   English
      pop, wiggle-waggle, tick tock, ding-dang-dong, ptt ptt ptt

But such examples from Indo-European languages do not cover the whole range of what is denoted under the term 'ideophone'. The following selection (3a–g) of examples from Zulu demonstrates the semantic diversity of words subsumed under the term 'ideophone'; they are representative of ideophones in many languages of the world, as shown in the typological survey of Kilian-Hatz (1999):

Christa Kilian-Hatz, *Ideophones*. In: *Capturing Expressivity*. Edited by: Jeffrey P. Williams, Oxford University Press.
© Christa Kilian-Hatz (2025). DOI: 10.1093/oso/9780192858931.003.0002

(3) Zulu

    a. Lomntwana u-sa-thi   bhada-bhada uma e-hamb-e.
       this.child   it-always-say bhada-bhada when it-walk-SBJ

      'This child is still unsteady when walking' (Fivaz 1963: 141).

    b. Ngi-the   ngi-zi-hlal-el-e,   memfu abantu.
       I-say.SBJ I-REFL-sit-there-PERF memfu people

      'As I was sitting by myself, suddenly appeared people' (Fivaz 1963: 157).

    c. Intshe ye-thuk-e   bheka bhabha amaphiko.
       ostrich he-get.a.fright-SBJ look   bhabha wings

      'The ostrich got a fright, look at its wings flapping' [doing bhabha]
      (Fivaz 1963: 157).

    d. Ba-thi   be-sa-dobha   gumbuqu isikebhe umoya.
       they-say they-already-fish gumbuqu boat   sqall

      'As they were fishing, the boat was suddenly capsized [lit. gumbuqu']
      by a squall' (Fivaz 1963: 156).

    e. W-e-fika   emnyango w-a-thi   aga ukungena.
       he-PAST-arrive LOC.door he-TAM-say aga enter

      'He arrived at the door, and hesitated [lit. 'he said aga']
      to go in' (Fivaz 1963: 146).

    f. Se-l-a-thi   khelekehle izwe lakithi nga-manzi.
       still-it-TAM-say khelekehle land our   it is-water

      'Our land has been deeply eroded by the water' (Fivaz 1963: 146)
      [lit. It says 'blub blub', our land is (under) water].

    g. Indlu i-gcwel-e   ciki   abantu.
       house it-be full-PERF ciki/very people

      'The house is [very] full of people' (Fivaz 1963: 153).

And almost exclusively in African languages, ideophones may even denote shades of colour:

(4) Yoruba

    a. pán wèè   'be red everywhere'
       pán kankan   'be very pale red'
       pán ròbè   'be attractively red'
       pán tòtò   'be unattractively red' (Awoyale 1983–84: 16)

b. dúdú <u>fafa</u>   'be very deep, inpleasant black'
  dúdú <u>yòyò</u>   'be very rich, uniform black'
  dúdú <u>sìsì</u>   'be very unevenly black'
  dúdú <u>kele</u>   'be deeply blue (of liquids)'
  dúdú <u>woí</u>   'be deep and rich black' (Awoyale 1983–84: 16).

2.2 Expressivity in ideophones

Most authors focus on the special expressive function of ideophones as part of an expressive register. They name them 'expressive adverbs' e.g. in the Mande language Bambara (cf. Dumestre 1981), 'expressive onomatopes' in the Amerindian Guarani language Urubu-Kaapor (cf. Kakumasu 1986), or simply 'expressives' e.g. in the Mon-Khmer language Semai (cf. Diffloth 1976) or 'expressives' and 'quasi expressives" in Malay (cf. Carr 1966). The characterization of a whole group of words as particularly expressive is based on mainly three observations:

(a) Intonational-prosodic accentuation:

Already Fortune (1971) states that

> ideophones in particular, are very prone to the addition of expressive features. A narrator using this dramatic style, and wishing to convey an exact impression of the individual event or situation he is describing, will want to use the features of stress, pitch, length, tempo, constriction, voicing.
>
> (Fortune 1971: 242)

(b) Sound symbolism:

The phonetic motivation and iconicity of ideophones is considered a particularly expressive feature (cf. Carr 1966: 372 and Diffloth 1994: 108). Hence, outside Africa, ideophones are known mainly as 'onomatopes'.

(c) Gestures:

Ideophones are frequently accompanied by gestures. Moreover, gestures and ideophones are very similar in nature because both are highly iconic and thus belong to the 'affecto-imagistic dimension' (Kita 1997: 392ff.). De la Vergne de Tressan (1952: 643) therefore interprets ideophones as 'vocal gestures'. Ideophones may even be substituted by gestures, as reported e.g. for Igbo (cf. Emenanjo 1978: 50) or for Xhosa in example (5):

20 CHRISTA KILIAN-HATZ

(5) Xhosa
Ukuthi ngqe   'to do quickly, fully, entirely; run quickly'
'ngqe' may be replaced by the two forefingers, one behind the other making the same movement as when calling someone, but moving away from the body instead of towards it. Used in this way it means 'to run away quickly' (Weakley 1977: 12).

All of these expressive features are cross-linguistically more prominent and frequent in ideophones than in other parts of speech. On the other hand, expressivity is not an exclusive feature of ideophones. The same expressive techniques are also used with nouns and verbs. Expressive techniques such as gestures and prosody are often, but not necessarily, linked to ideophones. Conversely, ideophones are not an obligatory part of expressive language.

Therefore, instead of expressivity, the dramaturgical function of the ideophones comes to the fore in order to characterize them. Doke has already defined ideophones in Bantu languages as

> a vivid representation of an idea in sound. A word, often onomatopoeic, which describes a predicate, qualificative or adverb in respect to manner, colour, sound, smell, action, state or intensity.
>
> (Doke 1935: 119)

Similarly, Fortune (1962: 6) characterizes ideophones in the Bantu language Shona as part of the event level in being 'a vivid re-presentation or re-creation of an event in sound'. Ideophones qualify as 'dramaturgic predicates' comparable to vocal gestures (Fortune 1962: 6). Finally, Kunene points to the shift of participant roles in Southern Sotho (Bantu) ideophones, whereby 'the speaker becomes the actor of the ideophone event and the hearer becomes the witness' (Kunene 1978: 3ff.). Provoost and Koulifa (1987: 231) specify their complementary dramaturgical function in the Chadic language Uldeme by comparing ideophones to the staging of the action in a play while the descriptive register provides the dialogues.

Due to parallel psychological effects produced by the use of ideophones ('mimetics') in Japanese, Kita (1997) argues

> that the semantics of mimetics and that of other parts of a sentence belong to different dimensions ... . The two dimensions have different characteristics. I will call the dimension of quantification and predication the analytic dimension. It has been the main focus of formal semantic theories. I will call the dimension where the semantics of mimetics belong the affecto-imagistic dimension.

The analytic dimension includes what Lyons[1] called descriptive information ... .
It is 'about' a certain experience, but not a rendition of an experience itself'

(Kita 1997: 386f.)

So ideophones are by no means free variants or synonyms of non-ideophones, rather they are complementary in terms of the function they have in discourse.

So let's summarize: due to the role-shifting function of ideophones, the listener is assigned the role of an eyewitness to the events taking place immediately before him. This dramaturgical effect of ideophones is now described in many languages of the world as 'living', 'immediate', and 'direct'. Such information thus confirms the consensus of several linguists formulated in Voeltz and Kilian-Hatz (2001: 3), that ideophones differ cross-linguistically from other word classes essentially in their dramaturgical function of simulating an event.

The dramaturgical function of shifting narrative dimension and participant roles is therefore a crucial cross-linguistic criterion for the definition of ideophones. The use of expressive techniques such as prosody and gestures, on the other hand, is not a key feature of ideophones, even though they accompany and support them more frequently than descriptive words.

2.3 Ideophone as subtype of direct speech

Direct speech, too, is by its very nature a production of verbal utterances. And here, too, 'shifts of pragmatic properties' occur, namely a 'change of reference', which is indicated by a change of deictic elements such as adverbs, pronouns, demonstratives, tense, mode, etc. The shifts occur exactly when the narrative text turns into 'verbalization', i.e. into direct speech. The shifts compared to the normal text are, among other things, the role shift of speaker and addressee, as well as the shifts of place and time (cf. von Roncador 1988: 5, 66).

Comparable to a live broadcast on the radio, the speaker, by using ideophones or direct speech, creates the illusion that the verbalized event or situation happens simultaneously with the moment of its production/pronunciation. Ideophones and direct speech differ insofar as direct speech quotes a speech act, whereas ideophones report an extra-linguistic event like a sound, a smell, a taste, a visual impression, a movement, or a psychic emotion. Since ideophonic utterances also consist of only a single word, deictic elements that indicate the reference (such as demonstrative pronouns, other pronouns, tenses, local deictics) are missing here. The complementary nature of the two types of direct speech is summarized in Table 2.1.

[1] Lyons (1977: 52).

22 CHRISTA KILIAN-HATZ

Table 2.1 Verbal direct speech vs ideophonic direct speech

	Verbal direct speech	Ideophonic direct speech
Model of quote	speech act	extra-linguistic state or event: acoustic sound, movement, taste, feeling ...
Sensational experience	audible	audible, visible, tactile, smell, taste, psychic
Reference	+ deictic	- deictic

In addition to the functional parallels, there are also a number of formal parallels between direct speech and ideophonic speech: like direct speech, ideophones may be introduced either obligatorily or optionally into the context by a *verbum dicendi* as demonstrated in examples (3a,e,f, 5, 6, 9, 12a, 15a), a quotation marker/*complementizer*, as in (7) from Tamil and (8a) from Somali. Ideophones are also commonly introduced by so-called 'dummy-verbs' (cf. Childs 1994: 187f.) like 'to do', 'to give', 'to have', 'to be', as in (8b, 9, 15), or other language-specific elements used to introduce a quote. Common introducing elements are also perception verbs, as in (10, 11). Different environments are possible in (13, 14).

(6) Southern Sotho
bá   thóla   bá-re   <u>tú</u>. Or: bá   thóla   <u>tú</u>.
They kept quiet they say/do <u>tu</u>   they kept quiet <u>tu</u>
'They kept quiet— (they kept) <u>dead quiet</u>' (Kunene 1978: 29).

(7) Tamil
Ava <u>kupu kupu-ɳɳu</u> aʐutaa.
she QUOT   <u>kupu kupu-weep.PAST.3sg.F</u>
'She wept <u>with a sobbing sound</u>' (Asher 1982: 242).

(8) Baka
Mópipìi   à   mɛ̀ɛ̀   <u>píípíípíípíí</u>.
bird m.   IMPFV do   <u>píípíípíípíí</u>
'The *mopipi*-bird is calling [lit. does] <u>píípíípíípíí</u>' (Kilian-Hatz 1999: 102)

(9) Somali
   a. Sabuulkii   baa   <u>dhilig</u>   yiri.
      corn-cob.M.ANAPH   FOC   <u>dhilig</u>   said.3.M
      'The corn-cob <u>broke off</u>' (Dhoorre and Tosco 1998: 141).

IDEOPHONES: HOW THE WORLD SPEAKS TO US   23

b. Gacantiisa   ayaan   <u>dhilig</u>   siiyay.
   arm.F.3.M.art   FOC.1sg   <u>dhilig</u>   gave.3.M

   'I <u>broke</u> his arm' (Dhoorre and Tosco 1998: 141).

(10) Baka
      Bùku   à   gɔ.   ɓà   sià: <u>bukuluuu</u>.
      ball   IMPFV   go   IMP   see   <u>bukuluuu</u>

      'The ball is rolling away, look: <u>bukuluuu</u>' [i.e. rolling and rolling]
      (Kilian-Hatz 1999: 101).

(11) Southern Sotho
      Ka-utlwa   <u>swahlaswahla</u>.

      'I heard   a <u>rustle-rustle</u>' (Kunene 1965: 38).

(12) English
      a.   The cork cried <u>pop</u>.

      b.   'The cork went <u>pop</u>' (Oswalt 1994: 302).

(13) Southern Sotho
      a.   Ya-re   <u>phótsɛ</u>.
            it-say/do   <u>phótsɛ</u>

            'It <u>shot out like a bullet</u>' (Kunene 1978: 17).

      b.   <u>Phótsɛ</u>.

            '<u>Shot out like a bullet</u>' (Kunene 1978: 17).

(14) German
      a.   <u>Peng!</u>   Da   knallt   die   Tür.
            <u>bang</u>   there   bang.3sg.PRES   the   door

            '<u>Bang</u>! There's the door banging.'

      b.   Da   knallt   – <u>peng</u> –   die   Tür.
            there   bang.3sg.PRES   <u>bang</u>   the   door

            'There the door bangs: <u>Bang</u>'.

      c.   Da   knallt   die   Tür: <u>Peng!</u>
            there   bang.3sg.PRES   the   door   <u>bang</u>
            'There the door bangs: <u>Bang</u>'.

Beside the kinds of embedding above, ideophones may also substitute a predicate,
as in (15).

(15) The ideophone as substitute for a verb in Baka:
Kùnda ndiandìàndiandìà.
turtle ndiandìàndiandìà

'The turtle [is staggering] ndiandìàndiandìà' (Kilian-Hatz 1999: 119).

The most frequent positions of the ideophone in a sentence, or sometimes more likely their translations, may have led to idephones being classified as subcategories of adverbs, nouns, or predicates in individual languages. However, some languages allow a variety of positions that at first seem arbitrary. But it is precisely this syntactical mobility of ideophones that leads Kunene (1978) to reject purely syntactical definitions as misleading:

> Because of its syntactical aloofness, we cannot properly speak of the syntax of the ideophone. We can, however, describe the collocations in which it is found and thus, by categorizing its juxtapositions with other parts of speech, 'know it by the company it keeps', and how it behaves in that company.
>
> (Kunene 1978: 16)

Like direct speech, ideophones are independent of the position which they occupy in a clause. They are syntactically independent *because* they are grammatically and pragmatically different from the major word classes.

Comics are a good illustration of how information is presented at the event level. Descriptive information as defined by Lyons is presented in boxes and is always graphically separated from the event level of the drawing, as shown in Figure 2.1.

Figure 2.1 Presentation of descriptive content as in comics

In contrast, direct speech and ideophones belong to the event level. They deviate graphically in comics from the descriptive context in that they are an integral part of the image.[2]

Figure 2.2 shows a purely spoken (verbal) quote—quotes are generally presented in comics in speech bubbles connected to their speakers:

Figure 2.2 Spoken (verbal) quote presented as in comics

Figure 2.3 shows a series of combat noises expressed by ideophones depicting various details of the combat.

But ideophones can also appear completely detached and isolated from any other context, thus providing all the information about the ongoing story. This is the case in example (16), from a Baka fairy tale in which a complex storyline is rendered solely with ideophones.

2.4 Semantics and sound symbolism of ideophones

The utterances in Figure 2.2 consist of individual words, but each of the words is only part of the clause; they denote only one single aspect of the whole event being described in a clause. In contrast, a single ideophone has a more complex

---

[2] For copyright reasons, we cannot use original drawings from comics—the illustrations in Figures 2.1–2.3 are therefore our own drawings, based on similar representations in comics.

26 CHRISTA KILIAN-HATZ

Figure 2.3 Ideophones presented as in comics

(16) Series of ideophones in spoken text in Baka (Ubangian)
<u>Wòàwòàwòàwòà</u>,   <u>pɔ́ɔ́</u>,
the hunters are discussing   the chimpanzee interrupts eating

<u>kung</u>,   <u>wóoò</u>,
a spear strikes the chimpanzee   the chimpanzee falls down

<u>pao</u>,
the chimpanzee breaks a branch.

<u>tung</u>.
hard falling the chimpanzee arrives on the ground (Kilian-Hatz 1999: 29).

meaning. Each ideophone e.g. in (16) contains information about the actor as well as about its performed action or its state. Therefore, ideophones are equivalents to complete, clausal utterances. Their clause-like character is finally reflected in that they form an intonation unit of their own apart from the context where they may be embedded. Here, too, the ideophonic 'dialogue' is parallel to the embedded direct speech.

Whereas descriptive words form single constituents that are combined analytically in a clause to denote an event, an ideophonic clause-like utterance consists in one word only. Consequently, there aren't further grammatical relations and morphological marking known otherwise from constituents in a descriptive sentence. Ideophonic one-word-utterances are therefore *simplicia* wherein the whole information is bundled synthetically.

Their special performative function of verbalized dramatization is achieved by their inherent sound-symbolic nature. Information is encoded in sound-symbolic, 'sub-morphemic units'. Ideophonic phonetic symbolism means that the phonetic components of the ideophones are not only differentiating in meaning, but also carrying meaning at the same time. Sub-morphemic units may consist of a syllable, a sound, or a tone that follow each other iconically, according to the sequence of single components of an event (cf. Weakley 1977). According to Rhodes (1994), such sub-morphemes may be phonetically realized in either a 'wild' or merely a 'tame' manner, i.e. a speaker-dependent preference to express only one ('tame') or more than one ('wild') nuance of an event in one sub-morpheme. Most of the ideophones found across languages are rather 'tame' realizations. The wild implementations are observed almost exclusively with sound imitations.

There are some cross-linguistic principles in the formation of ideophones that seem to be universal. They are summarized as follows (see Kilian-Hatz 1999: 179):

- The complex semantics of an ideophone results from the sum of its sound-symbolic, sub-morphemic parts, as demonstrated in (17).

(17)   Ewe

      [i]   =   tight, dense, narrow, impenetrable, deep, dark, gloomy
      [m] =   veiled, closed, dark

      → *mimi* 'squeeze', 'press' (Westermann 1937: 171)

- Ideophones are invariable *simplicia*.
- A single ideophonic event is encoded in a syllable.
- The linear order of the syllables symbolizes the chronological sequence of the ideophonic partial events.
- The phonological length of the ideophone represents the complexity and duration of the event.
- The meaning of sub-morphemic units of an ideophone is language-specific and conventionalized.

Especially the latter principle may be surprising. In fact, ideophones are fairly arbitrary phonetically. There does not appear to be an absolute sound–meaning relationship in ideophones. Rather, the meaning is only relative and dependent on certain semantic fields,

The arbitrary becomes clear when trying to derive the meaning from the phonetic form of ideophones in a foreign language: In a test with French students, neither the meaning 'gun bang' of the Japanese ideophone *zudon* nor the 'clock ticking' *kachi-kachi* could be recognized. Only those ideophones were recognized that sound similar in the foreign and native languages—such as *nyao* for the cat's meow (French 'miaou') or *kokekokko* for the rooster's crow (French 'cocorico') (cf. Frei 1970). This makes it clear that there are no pure icons in ideophones, only learned, iconic symbols. Sound-symbolic contrasts or gradual differences are subject to specific individual language patterns. At the vowel level, such patterns exist according to the distinction of high and low, front and back, or round and unround. This also includes the tonal contrasts high/low, which lead to antonymous word pairs as in vowel alternation. Sound variation in ideophones generally occurs through pairs of either vowels, or consonants, or tones, but not through the replacement of a vowel by a consonant or tone.

Nevertheless, there are some universal sound-symbolic techniques. They concern the ongoing process of the ideophonic event. They are summarized in Table 2.2.

Table 2.2 Sound-symbolic techniques with ideophones

	syllable-initial	syllable-final
Plosive (unvoiced) (voiced)	Abrupt, sudden, hard onset of an event or part of an event (see (18a-b)). Sudden, soft onset of an event or part of an event (see (19)).	Abrupt, sudden, hard termination of an event or part of an event (see (20)).
Fricative	Gradual onset of an event or part of an event (see (21) with an initial bilabial fricative, (22)).	Gradual cessation or phasing out of an event or part of an event (see (18b), (22)).
Nasal	Gradual soft onset of an event or part of an event (see (23)).	Reverberation of a sound or persistence of a state/action (see (25)).
Liquid	Continuity of a smooth, flowing event (esp. a movement) (see (26)).	
Reduplication of the syllable or word	Iteration of an event or part of an event (iconic to the number of reduplications)	
Lengthening of a single vowel or single consonant	Duration of a part of an event	

IDEOPHONES: HOW THE WORLD SPEAKS TO US   29

(18) a. Zulu

UManthombi   wamuthi   <u>thási</u>   umntwana   wagijima   naye.
M.   he.said   <u>thási</u>   child   he.disappeared with him.

Mathombi made <u>thasi</u> [i.e. he grabbed] the child and disappeared
with him'
(Voeltz; personal communication).

b. German

puff   'sudden onset or waning of magic power' (Havlik 1991: 14)

(19) German
bum(m ...)   'faint', 'swoon' (Havlik 1991: 60)

(20) German

sklik   'single dropping tear' (Havlik 1991: 124)

(21) Baka
<u>Poò poò poò poò</u>   'é   à   'uù   a   wà.
<u>poò poò poò poò</u>   3sg.H IMPV   blow   LOC   fire
,Poò poò poò poò, he blows into the fire embers' (Kilian-Hatz 1999: 170).

(22) Khwe

wuuuhhh   'The hippo dives into the water' (Kilian-Hatz 1999: 170).

(23) Baka

ngɛngɛmu ngɛngɛmu ngɛngɛmu 'waving a flashlight back and forth'
(Kilian-Hatz 1999: 170).

(24) Zulu

mónyu   'pull out' (Voeltz, personal communication)

(25) Baka
wuuum   'a herd of elephants is passing' (Kilian-Hatz 1999: 171).
kinginging 'stay in one place'

(26) a. German
lapse   'glide back to reality from a dream world' (Havlik 1991: 100)

b. Khwe
vlll   sound and movement of flames in the wind
(Kilian-Hatz 1999: 171)

2.5 Conclusion

In order to distinguish ideophones from other word classes and gestures we can use the features listed in Figure 2.4. Gestures are very near to ideophones and interjections, but they are non-verbal utterances, because both are immediate parts of the event-level. Ideophones are iconic, grammatically aloof, highly auto-semantic, and clause-like. They differ from interjections only insofar as interjections are always appellative, but not ideophones. In contrast, descriptive content words are symbolic, auto-semantic, and single clausal constituents. Functional words, finally, are highly symbolic, and grammatically bound.

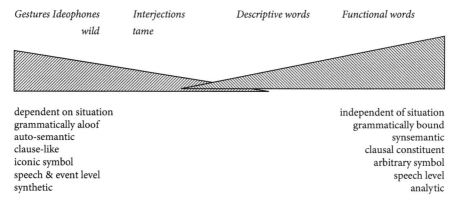

Figure 2.4 Kinds of utterances

Furthermore, it was shown that ideophones are formally and functionally very near to direct speech so that they even qualify as a subtype of direct speech in a broader sense. Languages differ herein typologically in (a) how ideophones are embedded into the context: with or without an introducing element?, as parataxis, as paraphrase or both?, (b) their language-specific sound symbolism, and (c) the range of sensations they may quote.

An ideophone is not a verbal utterance but a verbalized event. Here the extra-linguistic events 'have their say directly'. This is how the world around us speaks to us. In this sense, Doke's term 'ideophone'—derived from Greek 'self-sounding'—comes into its own to the full extent.

References

Asher, R. E. (1982). *Tamil.* (LDS Lingua descriptive Studies 7). Amsterdam: North-Holland Publishing Company.
Awoyale, Yiowola (1983–84). On the semantic fields of Yoruba ideophones. *Journal of the Linguistic Association of Nigeria* 2: 11–22.

Carr, Denzel (1966). Homorganicity in Malay/Indonesian expressives and quasi expressives. *Language* 42(2): 370–377.

Childs, Tucker G. (1994). African ideophones. In Leanne Hinton Johanna Nichols, and John J. Ohala (eds), *Sound Symbolism*. Cambridge: Cambridge University Press, 178–204.

De la Vergne de Tressan, M. (1952). Du langue descriptif en Peul. *Bulletin de l'Institut Français d'Afrique Noire* 14: 636–659.

Dhoorre, Cabdulqaadir Salaad and Tosco, Mauro (1998). Somali ideophons. *Journal of African Cultural Studies* 11(2): 125–156.

Diffloth, Gerard (1976). Expressives in Semai. *Austroasiatic Studies 1, Oceanic Linguistics.* Special Publication 13: 249–264.

Diffloth, Gerard (1994). *i*: big, *a*: small. In Leanne Hinton, Johanna Nichols, and John J. Ohala (eds), *Sound Symbolism*. Cambridge: Cambridge University Press, 107–114.

Doke, Clement. M. (1935). *Bantu Linguistic Terminology*. London: Longmans.

Dumestre, Gérard (1981). Idéophones et adverbes expressifs en Bambara. *Afrique et Langage* 15: 20–30.

Fivaz, Derek (1963). *Some Aspects of Ideophones in Zulu.* (Hartford Studies in Linguistics 4). Hartford, CT: Hartford University Foundation.

Fortune, G. (1962) *Ideophones in Shona. An Inaugural lecture.* London: Oxford University Press.

Fortune, G. (1971). Some notes on ideophones and ideophonic constructions in Shona. *African Studies* 30(3–4): 237–257.

Frei, Henri (1970). Cinquante onomatopées japonais. In David Cohen (éd.). *Mélanges Marcel Cohen.* (Janua Linguarum, Series Maior 27). The Hague / Paris: Mouton, 359–367.

Havlik, E. J. (1991). *Lexikon der Onomatopöien: Die lautimitierenden Wörter im Comic.* Frankfurt am Main: Zweitausendeins.

Kakumasu, James (1986). Urubu-Kaapor. In Desmond C. Derbyshire and Geoffrey K. Pullum (eds), *Handbook of Amazonian Languages*, Vol. 1. Berlin: Mouton de Gruyter, 326–403.

Kilian-Hatz, Christa (1999). *Ideophone: Eine typologische Untersuchung unter besonderer Berücksichtigung afrikanischer Sprachen.* Dr. Habil. Dissertation, University of Cologne.

Kita, Sotaro (1997). Two-dimensional semiotic analysis of Japanese mimetics. *Linguistics* 55(2): 379–415.

Koch, Peter and Wolf Oesterreicher (1985). Sprache der Nähe—Sprache der Distanz: Mündlichkeit und Schriftlichkeit im Spannungsfeld von Sprachtheorie und Sprachgeschichte. *Romanistisches Jahrbuch* 36: 15–43.

Kunene, Daniel P. (1965). The ideophone in Southern Sotho. *Journal of African Languages* 4: 19–39.

Kunene, Daniel P. (1978). *The Ideophone in Southern Sotho.* (Marburger Studien zur Afrika- und Asienkunde, Serie A: Afrika, Band 11). Berlin: Dietrich Reimer.

Lyons, John (1977). *Semantics*, vol. 1. Cambridge: Cambridge University Press.

Oswalt, Robert L. (1994). Inanimate imitations in English. In Leanne Hinton, Johanna Nichols, and John J. Ohala (eds), *Sound Symbolism*. Cambridge: Cambridge University Press, 293–324.

Provoost, D. Pierre and S. Pierre Koulifa. (1987). *Essai sur la langue Uldeme.* (Archives d'Anthropologie 30.). Tervuren, Belgique: Musée Royale de l'Afrique Centrale.

Rhodes, Richard A. (1994). Aural images. In Leanne Hinton, Johanna Nichols, and John J. Ohala (eds), *Sound Symbolism*. Cambridge: Cambridge University Press, 276–292.

Voeltz, F. K. Erhard and Christa Kilian-Hatz (eds) (2001). *Ideophones*. (Typological Studies in Language 44). Amsterdam / Philadelphia: John Benjamins.

Von Roncador, Manfred (1988). *Zwischen direkter und indirekter Rede: Nichtwörtliche direkte Rede, logophorische Konstruktionen und Verwandtes.* (Linguistische Arbeiten 192). Tübingen: Niemeyer.

Weakley, Alastair James (1977) [1973]. *An Introduction to Xhosa Ideophone Derivation and Syntax.* Grahamstown: Rhodes University, Department of African Languages, Communication 2.

Westermann, Diedrich (1927). Laut, Ton und Sinn in westafrikanischen Sudansprachen. In Franz Boas (ed.), *Festschrift Meinhof.* Glückstadt—Hamburg: J. J. Augustin, 315–328.

Westermann, Diedrich (1937). Laut und Sinn in einigen westafrikanischen Sprachen. *Archiv für die gesamte Phonetik*, Bd. 1, erste Abteilung, Heft 4: 154–172, 193–212.

3

Expressives in Kammu singing

Håkan Lundström and Jan-Olof Svantesson

The Kammu people are one of the ethnic groups in South-east Asia that live in northern Laos and adjacent areas in Vietnam, Thailand, and China. Traditionally they live on mountain slopes, where they grow rice and other crops and also hunt. The material in this chapter comes from the Yùan area, located in the Nalè district in northern Laos. Starting in the early 1970s the 'Kammu Language and Folklore' project at Lund University has focused on the Yùan Kammu. Kàm Ràw (also known as Damrong Tayanin, 1938–2011) has been a main informant and collaborator in the roles of language consultant, assistant, and researcher. He was born and grew up in the village of Rmcùal in the Yùan area and came to Thailand and eventually to Sweden as a young man. Like many other mountain villages, Rmcùal has been abandoned and the villagers have moved to nearby communities (Évrard 2012). Kàm Ràw's cultural experience was based in the village life before these changes took place, but he also developed his knowledge of the Kammu culture throughout his life.

In this article, the expressives of the Yùan Kammu dialect are studied from the combined perspectives of linguistics and ethnomusicology. Kàm Ràw had an impressive knowledge of his own culture and language and was also a good singer. His knowledge and his use of expressives in singing made it possible to understand not only the meaning of the expressives but also their emotional and associative qualities. He was crucial to the realization of the *Dictionary of Kammu Yùan language and culture* (Svantesson, Ràw, Lindell, and Lundström 2014) and *Kammu songs. The songs of Kam Raw* (Lundström and Tayanin 2006), which are frequently referred to in the following.

3.1 The Kammu language

Kammu is an Austroasiatic (Mon-Khmer) language spoken mainly in Northern Laos and also in adjacent areas of Vietnam, Thailand, China, and Myanmar. There are at least 500,000 speakers. The Kammu variant dealt with in this chapter, the Yùan dialect spoken in northern Laos, is a tone language with two tones, high and low, denoted ´ and ', respectively. Like many Austroasiatic languages, Kammu has two kinds of syllables, usually called major and minor syllables. Major syllables

Håkan Lundström and Jan-Olof Svantesson, *Expressives in Kammu singing*. In: *Capturing Expressivity*. Edited by: Jeffrey P. Williams, Oxford University Press. © Håkan Lundström and Jan-Olof Svantesson (2025). DOI: 10.1093/oso/9780192858931.003.0003 have a phonemic vowel; minor syllables are unstressed and lack a phonemic vowel. Most words are either monosyllabic, consisting of one major syllable (e.g. *táañ* 'to weave'), or sesquisyllabic, consisting of a major syllable preceded by a minor syllable (e.g. *kṁ-mú* 'human being'). In careful speech, a minor syllable can be pronounced with a schwa vowel: [kə̀m-mú] (here and elsewhere, a word-internal syllable boundary is marked by a hyphen). There are also words with more than two syllables. Most of them are derived morphologically, including many expressives like *ŋàk-rŋ-ŋàk* (see Table 3.1 below). See Svantesson and Holmer (2015) for a short overview of the Kammu language.

3.2 Kammu expressives

Like many other languages in South-east Asia, Kammu has a separate word class of expressives (or ideophones), words which depict the speaker's impression of how something sounds, looks, smells, tastes, or feels, or his/her state of mind. Syntactically they are usually adverbs giving a more precise or intense meaning to the verb. Kammu expressives have an unusually rich regular morphology where the expressives are derived from monosyllabic roots, which carry the general meaning of those expressives that are derived from the root. Most of these roots do not occur as free words (in which case they are marked with an asterisk, e.g. **ŋàk*), but for some expressives, the root forms a momentaneous expressive, describing a sound heard once.

The morphological processes involved in the derivation of expressives are reduplication, prefixation, and infixation. As shown and exemplified in Table 3.1,

Table 3.1 Regular expressive morphology

1	R	momentaneous (sound)
2	R-R	dynamic durative
3	R-*kn*-R	dynamic durative successive
4	R-*rŋ*-R	dynamic durative plural
5	C-R	punctual
6	*r*-R	punctual plural
7	C-R-C-R	iterated
8	*r*-R-*r*-R	iterated plural
9	CC$_c$-R	static
10	*r*C$_c$-R	static plural
11	C*l*-R$_1$-C*l*-R	irregular

R = root; C (in 5, 7, 9, 11) is a lexically determined consonant; C$_c$ (9, 10) is the coda consonant of the root; R$_1$ (11) is a variant of the root with a different vowel.

eleven different expressives can, in theory, be formed from a root by the regular morphology. We have found no root from which all eleven forms can be formed, however, and quite often only a small subset of them is used. Whether or not an expressive can be formed by a given morphological operation from a given root is determined both lexically and semantically, and there seems to be some space for individual creativity.

Examples:
root: *ŋàk

3	ŋàk-kn-ŋàk	'one being keeps nodding downwards'
4	ŋàk-rŋ-ŋàk	'many beings keep nodding downwards'
5	c-ŋák	'one being nods once'
6	r-ŋàk	'many beings nod once at the same time'
7	c-ŋák-c-ŋák	'one being nods at intervals'
8	r-ŋàk-r-ŋàk	'many beings nod simultaneously at intervals'
9	ck-ŋàk	'one being whose head is bent down'
10	rk-ŋàk	'many beings whose heads are bent down'
11	cl-ŋùk-cl-ŋàk	'many beings keep nodding here and there'

root: *króp*

1	króp	'clanking sound heard once'
2	króp-króp	'clanking sound heard many times (in one place)'
4	króp-rŋ-króp	'clanking sound heard many times (in many places)'
7	c-króp-c-króp	'clanking sound heard at intervals'
11	sl-krúp-sl-króp	'clanking sound heard here and there'

Many expressive roots occur in series with different vowels, which express the relative size of the entities involved in the event. For example, the root *ŋàk exemplified above is a member of a series *ŋùk, *ŋòk, *ŋàk, *ŋèk (Table 3.2).

Table 3.2 Size and vowel quality

ŋùk-kn-ŋùk	ŋòk-kn-ŋòk	ŋàk-kn-ŋàk	ŋèk-kn-ŋèk	'keep nodding'
ŋùk-rŋ-ŋùk	ŋòk-rŋ-ŋòk	ŋàk-rŋ-ŋàk	ŋèk-rŋ-ŋèk	'keep nodding (of many beings)'
c-ŋúk	c-ŋók	c-ŋák	c-ŋék	'nod once'
r-ŋùk	r-ŋòk	r-ŋàk	r-ŋèk	'nod once (of many beings)'
c-ŋúk-c-ŋúk	c-ŋók-c-ŋók	c-ŋák-c-ŋák	c-ŋék-c-ŋék	'nod at intervals'
r-ŋùk-r-ŋùk	r-ŋòk-r-ŋòk	r-ŋàk-r-ŋàk	r-ŋèk-r-ŋèk	'nod at intervals (of many beings)'
ck-ŋùk	ck-ŋòk	ck-ŋàk	ck-ŋèk	'downbent head'
rk-ŋùk	rk-ŋòk	rk-ŋàk	rk-ŋèk	'downbent head (of many beings)'
–	cl-ŋùk-cl-ŋòk	cl-ŋùk-cl-ŋàk	cl-ŋùk-cl-ŋèk	'nod here and there'

The expressives formed from *$\eta\grave{u}k$ describe large beings (perhaps human), those formed with *$\eta\grave{e}k$ describe small beings (perhaps mice), and those formed from *$\eta\grave{o}k$ and *$\eta\grave{a}k$ describe beings of intermediate size, maybe a dog or a dove (as in Appendix 3.1): *$\eta\grave{u}k$ > *$\eta\grave{o}k$ > *$\eta\grave{a}k$ > *$\eta\grave{e}k$. The sizes are relative rather than absolute, however. See further Svantesson (1983, 2017) and Svantesson and Holmer (2015) for Kammu expressives.

3.3 Expressives in the Kammu vocabulary

The Kammu-English dictionary compiled by the Kammu Language and Folklore project (Svantesson et al. 2014) contains about 14,000 words, almost 4,000 of which are expressives. Most of them are morphologically derived from about 600 roots.

The first basis for the dictionary was folk tales that were recorded in the 1970s by Kristina Lindell in northern Thailand from several Kammu speakers who originally lived in Laos. They were transcribed by her and by Kàm Ràw, an eminent storyteller who then moved to Lund and became our main language consultant. He also cooperated with Håkan Lundström on Kammu songs and music. Our dictionary is based on folk tales and songs and also on vocabulary related to other aspects of traditional Kammu life, such as agriculture, plants, animals, and the life cycle of Kammu people. Rites and ceremonies relating to the agricultural year, to childbirth, marriage, and funerals also provided words for the dictionary, as well as prayers and spells used by shamans and laymen. Since most Kammu are at least bilingual and have learnt the majority language Lao at school or earlier, virtually all modern words that do not relate to traditional Kammu life are taken over directly from Lao. They are not included in the dictionary since it is more or less impossible to decide which Lao words can be used by the Kammu, and which, if any, cannot.

When I (JOS) started the dictionary work by going through the folk-tale material with Kàm Ràw in 1974, we encountered expressives from time to time. Like many other linguists at that time I was not aware of the existence of this word class, and the few existing descriptions of Kammu, such as Smalley (1961), did not mention them. Kàm Ràw thought that they were 'not real words' and difficult to translate. After some time I read Gérard Diffloth's (1976) article about Semai, an Austroasiatic language spoken in Malaysia, where he coined the word 'expressive' for this word class, and understood that these mysterious words in Kammu also were expressives. Examples of different expressives appeared from time to time in the folk tales and also in the songs that Kàm and Håkan Lundström worked with. Kàm could complement these with many other existing forms and he started to hunt for expressives in his own speech and in the speech of other Kammu. After some time we realized that they had a complicated morphology and finally, the

EXPRESSIVES IN KAMMU SINGING   37

system of morphologically derived expressives described above emerged, more complicated and regular than in any other described language.

3.4 Kammu singing

In Kammu culture the singing that takes place in social situations, *tɔ́əm*, makes up a large part of the musical and poetical repertoire. People engage in alternating singing and in that situation a singer will expect a reply in singing. A *mono-melodic* system provides a musical base, which means that all singing that takes place in a given situation may be done by use of the same melody template. There are personal as well as regional variations of these templates.

When a pre-existing orally transmitted poem, *trnə̀əm*, is combined with the melody template of a vocal genre, the singer re-creates the song while singing. The poem itself contains much parallelism and is often very rich in rhymes. In the process of singing the singer may develop the poem by combining different poems or by adding words and lines. The poetic contents of the *trnə̀əm* have been studied in some detail (Lundström 2010). Sung poetry is basically syllable-counting. In singing, major and minor syllables are treated in the same way with regard to duration and reduplication.

The following discussion is based on Kàm Ràw's repertoire of *trnə̀əm* (Lundström and Tayanin 2006). It contains 140 *trnə̀əm* that span from songs belonging to ceremonial or formal situations to those of casual situations. Of these, 34 (24%) contain expressives and some of these have more than one expressive. The interpretations of the songs were done by Håkan Lundström in collaboration with Kàm Ràw and in communication with Jan-Olof Svantesson. Though we experimented with the translations for many years the main work with Kàm's repertoire was done during the 1990s. Håkan Lundström recorded his singing, Kàm transcribed the Kammu words and made a word-for-word translation into English. When necessary we discussed the process with Jan-Olof Svantesson, who at that time was working on the dictionary. Lundström made an English interpretation of the song and discussed it with Kàm. When he felt that the interpretation agreed with the feeling he got from the original Kammu version we decided that it was right.

Since Kammu *tɔ́əm* singing involves rather a lot of variation of the *trnə̀əm* the individual performances of one song can be rather different. The performances were therefore reduced with the help of a descriptive model that made it possible to construct a basic *trnə̀əm* that was used for the translation and interpretation.

Expressives may be translated and given a general meaning, but the interpretation varies with the context. In the glossing of the songs this was marked with '*exp*' and a category, for example '*exp look*' or '*exp sound*', and sometimes also a further description, for example '*exp look* nodding' or '*exp sound* rumble'. In the interpretation of the songs the expressives are generally described using one word and a synonym or a word of a related character, like 'nods and coos' or 'rolls and rumbles'. Sung poetry also includes other poetic principles than expressives, particularly rhythm, parallelism, rhymes, and sound-play on vowels or consonants. Sometimes some of these factors would be prioritized over the expressive contents. All this is exemplified below.

3.5 Expressives in songs

When singing is done in communication with one or more persons, rhymed words of address are often added. In their second part these words of address mention the addressed person's relation to the singer. It may be visitors in general, another clan, elder brother, elder brother's wife, son-in-law, grandson, male villagers, female villagers, etc. In the following case the singing is directed towards members of the wife-giving group, *èem*, which means the father-in-law and his relatives. The relation between wife-giving and wife-taking groups is an important one in Kammu culture (Lindell, Samuelsson, and Tayanin 1979).

1	2	3	4	5	6
Plàaŋ	lm-trèem,		èem	r-màaŋ	
silvergrass	*exp look* long, fine		wife-givers	wealthy	

Interpretation:

'Silvergrass so long and fine; wife-givers so wealthy.'

This phrase consists of two parts, each of three syllables. Syllables 1–3 serve as a metaphor for syllables 4–6. It is common in Kammu poetry that the first part is a symbolic double of the second part (Lundström 2010: 16–17). Syllables 3–4 connect the two parts with a rhyme: *trèem/èem*. This kind of rhyme is also common in sayings and proverbs and has been called *pivot rhyme* (Lindell 1988). Syllables 1 and 6 also rhyme: *plàaŋ/màaŋ*. Syllables 2 and 5 are both unstressed minor syllables: *lm/r*. The two parts thus have the same rhythm and are, so to speak, mirrored around the pivoting point. This is characteristic of words of address even though the number of syllables in each part may be more than three.

When singing to one's wife-givers it is important to address them with respect and to praise them. They are portrayed as successful, prosperous, and wealthy. The symbolic likeness to silvergrass or elephant grass, *plàaŋ* (*Miscanthus sinensis*), is strengthened by the disyllabic expressive *lm-trèem* that describes how it looks. It is built on the expressive root **trèem* with the general meaning 'level' or 'even'. It refers to a long, straight, and perfectly grown cluster of silvergrass, evoking a picture of wealth, fertility, and success. A synonymous expressive in these words of address is *lm-nèem*.

EXPRESSIVES IN KAMMU SINGING   39

A similar rhyme that often is combined with the previous one has the rhyme *plàaŋ/màaŋ*. In this case another disyllabic expressive is used for the pivot rhyme *yía/cìa*. The expressive root *yía* may express a tall and slim person or something well-grown and beautiful in general.

plàaŋ	lìa-yía,	cìa	r-màaŋ
silvergrass	*exp look* beauty	ancestry	wealthy

Interpretation:

'Silvergrass so beautiful; ancestry so wealthy'

The following *trnàəm* belongs to a traditional drum feast, when a male person of more than sixty years of age, who was also considered prosperous, was presented with a drum as a sign of his high status (Lundström and Tayanin 1981). The stanza has four lines, but owing to repetition and parallelism it consists of only two sentences, lines 1+2 and 3+4. The rhymes are an extended form of the above-mentioned pivot rhyme. They are called *cross-rhymes*, since they rhyme cross-wise when written out as below: *pír/chír, ŋàk/làk, crì/tì, táaŋ/kàaŋ, lɔɔŋ/tòoŋ*

tm-pír	ŋàk-kn-ŋàk	crì	k-táaŋ
turtle dove	*exp look* nodding	ficus	glade

Interpretation:

'The turtle dove nods and coos in the fig tree in the glade'

tm-pír	ŋàk-kn-ŋàk	crì	c-lɔɔŋ
turtle dove	*exp look* nodding	fig tree	riverbank

Interpretation:

'The turtle dove nods and coos in the fig tree by the river'

kr-làk	chír-tn-chír	kàaŋ	tr-tì
slit drum	*exp sound* rumble	house	centre

Interpretation:

'The slit drum rolls and rumbles in the central house of the village'

kr-làk	chír-tn-chír	tòoŋ	tr-tì
slit drum	*exp sound* rumble	village part	centre

Interpretation:

'The slit drum rolls and rumbles in the central part of the village'

It will be noted that the expressives *ŋàk-kn-ŋàk* and *chír-tn-chír* (*exp looks* and *exp sounds*, respectively) are trisyllabic words each consisting of one major syllable, which is repeated with a minor syllable in the middle. The dynamic durative expressive *ŋàk-kn-ŋàk* built on the root *ŋàk* (Table 3.1–3.2) expresses how it looks when a turtle dove keeps on nodding continuously and has been interpreted 'nods and coos'. The expressive *chír-tn-chír* relates to the resonant echoing sound of a good drum and is interpreted 'rolls and rumbles'. As can be seen, these trisyllabic expressives also function as rhyme-words and add to the sound-play of the poem.

Expressives are particularly common in praise songs, which is an important part of the repertoire of songs that are sung in address of one or more persons. In this particular case a long wooden drum was made by the wife-giving group, *èem*, and ceremonially presented to a successful male in the wife-taking group, *khɔ́ɔy*. The song would be sung by the receiver in praise of the drum and would include words of address directed to the wife-giving group. Furthermore, in actual singing the words of the song and words of address would be fitted into the musical template of the Yùan area, which also includes some words of exclamation, particularly *həəəy*, *eeee*, *sáh* ('I say'), and *kàay sáh* ('this I say') (Karlsson, Lundström, and Svantesson 2022: 84–88). In performance these words may be organized as follows, with the expressives in italics.

> Həəəy sáh
> tm-pír *ŋàk-kn-ŋàk*   crì   k-táaŋ
> tm-pír *ŋàk-kn-ŋàk*   crì   c-lɔ́ɔŋ
> plàaŋ *lm-trèem*, plàaŋ *lìa-yía* kàay sáh

'Hey I say
The turtle dove *nods and coos* in the fig tree in the glade
The turtle dove *nods and coos* in the fig tree by the river
Silvergrass *so long and fine*, silvergrass *so beautiful*, this I say.'

> Eee sáh
> kr-làk *chír-tn-chír*   kàaŋ   tr-tì
> kr-làk *chír-tn-chír*   tòoŋ   tr-tì
> èem r-màaŋ, cìa r-màaŋ kàay sáh

'Eee I say
The slit drum *rolls and rumbles* in the central house of the village
The slit drum *rolls and rumbles* in the central part of the village
Wife-givers so wealthy, ancestry so wealthy, this I say.'

Songs of sadness, loneliness, and longing may be sung in communication with others, but they are also sung while alone. The first rhyme-word of a pair often refers to nature. It may be birds, insects, plants, fruits that suggest the context of a being alone away from the village, guarding the rice in the fields or walking through the forest in order to empty traps. In the following song the expressive *cɔ́ɔc-cɔ́ɔc* illustrates the sad sound of a single *cáŋ-cáŋ* grasshopper in the forest where traps are set, some distance away from the village. The trisyllabic *càŋ-kn-càŋ* illustrates the feeling of loneliness and sadness. This word is also part of the rhyme pattern, *cáŋ/càŋ*. In this case the two words differ only by lexical tone, high and low respectively. It is also integrated in the prominent consonant rhyme '*c*'.

cáŋ-cáŋ	yàam	cɔ́ɔc-cɔ́ɔc	pràay	páam
grasshopper	cry	*exp sound*	trap	set up

'Where the grasshopper cries "cɔ́ɔc-cɔ́ɔc", I set my trap'

cáŋ-cáŋ	yàam	cɔ́ɔc-cɔ́ɔc	pràay	klə́əm
grasshopper	cry	*exp sound*	trap	prop up

'Where the grasshopper cries "cɔ́ɔc-cɔ́ɔc", I propped up my trap'

s-lóh	càŋ-kn-càŋ	yàam	kàay
walk	*exp feeling* lonesome	cry	return

'I walk back all by myself and crying'

s-lóh	càŋ-kn-càŋ	tə́əm	kàay
walk	*exp feeling* lonesome	sing	return

'I walk back all by myself and singing'

The grey-headed parakeet, *péɛt* (*Psittacula finschii*) that sings *péɛt-péɛt*, feeds on nuts, rice, fruits, and berries, and people would catch it with birdlime or shoot it with a gun or a crossbow in order to cook stew. In certain situations it was seen as a bad omen. It is a large, light green bird with a bright underside. When a flock flies, turning over and over, it will shift colour from dark to bright and back again. In the following song this serves as a picture of a girl's changing mind. The trisyllabic *lòom-rŋ-lòom* means many moving beings staying together, in this case the parakeets, and *r-lìak* means animals or people turning around repeatedly.

Péɛt lèɛ	lòom-rŋ-lòom
parakeet	*exp look* many fly together

'A wavering cloud of parakeets'

tòom	tèɛ	kók	r-lʌʌy.
alight	on	hog plum	*exp* [?]

'Turning over, alighting on the hog plum'.

péɛt lèɛ	lòom-rŋ-lòom
parakeet	*exp look* many fly together

'A wavering cloud of parakeets'

tòom	tèɛ	ráay	r-lìak
alight	on	tree	*exp look* flock of birds turning over

'Turning over, landing on the ráay tree.'

nàaŋ	lìak	yɔ̀h	lìak	kàay
dear	choose	go	choose	return

'Dear, choosing to leave, choosing to return,'

pìp   tèe   tè   r-wàay   tr-tɔ̀
find   yourself marry tiger   double

'You'll end up married to a bad tiger spirit.'

nàaŋ   lìak   yɔ̀h   lìak   kàay
dear   choose go   choose return

'Dear, choosing to leave, choosing to return,'

pìp   tèe   tè   róoy   kìn   tr-tɔ̀
find   yourself marry spirit vampire double

'You'll end up married to a vampire spirit.'

Reduplicated verbs and simile are used to depict similar experiences as expressives in songs, and they are therefore interesting in a comparative perspective. In the song material, five reduplicated verbs (Appendix 3.2) are used in a way that is more or less identical to that of expressives. All of them depict sounds, and all of them have a basic meaning like 'hit', i.e. a movement that produces a sound, for instance: *pát pát* based on the verb *pát* 'to swat' or *téñ téñ* from *téñ* 'to knock'. Reduplication of a verb usually means that the action denoted by the verb is intensified or is going on for some time, just like the dynamic durative expressives (2 in Table 3.1). Their form, consisting of a repetition of a monosyllabic form, is also identical to that of the dynamic expressives. Thus, they are most probably interpreted as expressives although they formally are reduplicated verbs.

Simile (Appendix 3.3) is constructed with the verb *mían* 'to look like, to resemble', with effect similar to English (*be*) *like*, for instance: *làm mían òm ká* 'delicious like fish soup'. Like reduplicated verbs, similes are often integrated parts of the rhyme pattern and occasionally they are used in combination with expressives: *r-ʔàaŋ mían màt prì* 'shining like the sun', where *r-ʔàaŋ* is an expressive describing a red sky.

3.6 Categories of expressives

We have divided the expressives, and also the other techniques used in the song material, into five categories depending on what they depict: sound, move, look, touch, or inner feeling. In a survey of recent research on expressives (ideophones), Mark Dingemanse (2012) compared expressives in languages from different parts of the world and formulated a hierarchy of what they depict:

sound > movement > visual patterns > other sensory perceptions > inner feelings

This means that if a language has, for example, expressives depicting visual patterns, it normally also has ideophones depicting movement and sound.

Dingemanse's categories correspond rather closely to ours (sound, move, look, touch, and inner feeling), 'touch' being the only 'other sensory perception' found in our material. The approximately 600 expressive roots recorded in the Kammu dictionary were compared to Dingemanse's hierarchy in Svantesson (2017). The result is shown here in Table 3.3, where the distribution (number of occurrences and percentages) of the expressives found in songs over the five categories is shown as well. In addition, the results for all three expressive techniques (expressives, verb reduplication, and simile) taken together are shown there.

Table 3.3 Expressives in the Kammu dictionary and in Kammu songs

Dingemanse's hierarchy	Kammu dictionary	Kammu songs	
		expressives	all techniques
sound	31%	8 (13%)	17 (22%)
movement	31%	13 (21%)	14 (18%)
visual patterns/looks	24%	32 (52%)	36 (46%)
other sensory perceptions/touch	9%	3 (5%)	4 (5%)
inner feelings	5%	5 (8%)	7 (9%)

Table 3.3 shows that the dictionary frequency basically agrees with the hierarchy, which thus can be given a frequency interpretation: a higher category has higher lexical frequency. The expressives occurring in songs show quite another pattern, however. The relative frequency of the category 'sound' is much smaller and the frequency of 'visual patterns/looks' is much higher in the song material than in the dictionary. This tendency remains, but is a bit weaker if verb reduplication and simile are added as expressive techniques.

3.7 Contents within the categories

In many cases the meaning of an expressive is obvious and clearly agrees with the main meaning of the song. In some cases the meaning of the expressives is more far-fetched. This depends on a characteristic of rhymes in Kammu *trnǝǝm*, namely that the first word of a rhyme-pair also serves as a metaphor for the second rhyme-word even though their lexical meanings may be completely different. The first rhyme-word thus has one lexical meaning and another meaning in the context of the *trnǝǝm*, where it by analogy takes over the meaning of the second rhyme-word (Lundström and Tayanin 2006: 13–15).

Therefore it is meaningful to consider not only the lexical meaning of the expressives, but also their meaning in the context of *trnǝǝm* to which they belong. When the categories of expressives are compared to context categories based on the contents of the songs that the expressives belong to, it turns out that the context categories recur in each category (Table 3.4). The most consistent ones are: praise (30), deprecation (12), and sadness (12). Four expressives belonging to songs of other contents have been left unclassified. A comparison with reduplicated words and simile shows a similar profile though these are much fewer in number. Expressives that relate to praise come from songs praising success/wealth and beauty. Those of deprecation generally relate to belittling of oneself or absence of respect, and those of sadness are about loneliness, unrequited love, and poverty.

Table 3.4 Context categories of expressives

| | Praise | | Deprecation | Sadness | | |
	Success	*Beauty*	*Belittling oneself*	*Loneliness*	*Unrequited love*	*Poverty*
Looks	7	12	2	2	4	–
Moves	5	–	6	–	–	1
Sounds	5	–	–	2	1	–
Inner feeling	–	–	2	2	–	–
Touch	1	–	2	–	–	–
Total	**18**	**12**	**12**	**6**	**5**	**1**

The song type *tə́əm* is the most complex form of song in Kammu culture, musically as well as poetically. No other song form makes use of so many poetical techniques (Karlsson, Lundström, and Svantesson 2022: 28–30). This probably explains why expressives are more common than reduplicated vowels and simile in the repertoire at hand. The expressives are very effective and, as shown, they have poetical potential and are highly useful as rhyme-words.

The song of the drum-giving ceremony quoted above contains some interesting information. That the expressive *ŋàk-kn-ŋàk*, meaning '(dove) nods and coos', rhymes with *krlàk*, meaning 'slit drum', is of particular interest. The drum that was used in the villages where Kàm Ràw grew up is called *prìŋ wàaŋ*, meaning 'long drum'. It was made of a hollowed log and had one skin at either end. The *krlàk* is a different kind of drum, a so-called slit drum, that was made of a hollowed-out log where both ends were closed. It had no membranes, but a slit was made on one side and the slit drum produced a resonant sound when struck on the side or on the inside as a pestle. Kàm Ràw had heard of the *krlàk* from the elders who said that it had existed generations earlier. What we have here is a song of a traditional drum-giving ceremony that mentions a drum that no longer exists and where the name of the drum rhymes with an expressive. Because of this rhyme the word *krlàk* could not be easily exchanged for *prìŋ wàaŋ*. It can be concluded that the expressive *ŋàk-kn-ŋàk* is old and has been preserved as a rhyme-word.

In most cases the expressives are integrated in the rhyme pattern and since many songs with expressives belong to ceremonial or formal situations, it is likely that they represent an older layer in the singing tradition. The fact that all expressives except one are unique to a specific song may also be explained by their function as rhyme-words.

Looking at the context categories, the meanings of the songs with expressives may explain the low proportion of the category 'inner feelings' discussed above (Table 3.3). That 'sadness' relates to inner feelings is rather obvious, but also praise and deprecation involve feelings of shyness or embarrassment—in the case of praise, on the part of the listener and in the case of deprecation, on the part of the singer.

3.8 Conclusions

Expressives (or ideophones) depict the speaker's impression of how something sounds, looks, smells, tastes, or feels, or his/her state of mind. Kammu expressives are derived from monosyllabic roots, which normally do not occur as free words, but carry the general meaning of those expressives. The morphological processes involved in the derivation of expressives are reduplication, prefixation, and infixation. A comparison shows that the main differences between expressives in the Kammu dictionary and in the song repertoire of Kàm Ràw are:

- visual patterns are more common in the songs,
- sound is rather less common,
- movement is slightly less common,
- one might perhaps expect inner feelings to be more strongly represented in the songs.

The song genre *tɔ́əm* is built on the orally transmitted poems *trnɔ̀əm* and is the most complex form of song in Kammu culture. Most expressives occur in songs of ceremonial or formal content and are integrated in their poetical structure, which may explain why expressives are more common in the songs than reduplicated vowels and simile. As the first of two rhyme-words an expressive has one lexical meaning and another meaning in the context of the song, where it takes over the meaning of the second rhyme-word by analogy.

The contextual meanings of the expressives mainly relate to praise (success/wealth and beauty), deprecation (belittling of oneself/absence of respect), and sadness (loneliness/unrequited love/poverty). They belong to songs that, apart from sadness, express strong inner feelings of shyness or embarrassment.

It is obvious that expressives have important functions in the songs, and in some cases they may be unique to particular songs. The fact that they occur in songs that belong to traditional ceremonial or formal occasions like the harvest feast or wedding feast suggests that some of these expressives may be of a considerable age, but this remains to be studied in detail.

3.9 Appendix 3.1

Categories of expressives in songs

Expressive	General meaning (in dictionary)	Specific meaning (in song)
Sound		
bíap-bíap (5a2)	—	I grope my way weeping
chír-tn-chír (3a2)	sound of the long wooden drum heard repeatedly at long intervals	drum rolls and rumbles
cɔ́ɔc-cɔ́ɔc (9a6)	sound of the *cáŋ-cáŋ* grasshopper heard in one place	the grasshopper cries 'cɔ́ɔc-cɔ́ɔc'
pə̀r-pə̀r (7a9)	a lot of water in one place	bamboo tube so full, so full
súut-súut (9a5)	crying of one person	sob, sob, locked-up bamboo rat
tɨ̀in-tɨ̀in (3a2)	sound of people stamping in one place	tramping feet on the covered bridge
yàay-yàay (3b4)	—	the barbet cries 'yàay yàay'
yɔ̀ɔk-yɔ̀ɔk (3b4)	Cf. ʔyɔ́ɔk-ʔyɔ́ɔk one bird chattering	the swallow cries 'yɔ̀ɔk yɔ̀ɔk'
Movements		
àam-cràam (5a2)	fumbling	feel my way fumbling
c-lèk (4a1)	—	don't exaggerate so much
kɔ́h-lr-kèh (4c1)	—	swaying and turning over
kr-kɩ̀a (6f6)	many beings getting stuck on or clinging to something	don't fear that it will stick to you
lk-pɩ̀k (3: 1c)	things or people scattered everywhere	crowd under the roof beam
lñ-kàañ (3: 1c)	many beings staying in one place	crowd under the roof beam
nʌ́ʌr-nʌ́ʌr (9a7)	one object hanging down, swaying	duckweed flows, slowly swaying
ŋàk-kn-ŋàk (3a2)	one being nodding downwards many times	dove nods and coos
ràa-làp (6c2)	—	hog plum will split wide open
ràa-lèey (6c2)	—	hog plum will split completely
ròm-cŋ-ròm (5d1)	crouching [in songs]	the bewitched dog is crouching
tàan-tàk (6f6)	—	that it will come to the *chía* tree
tràan-tràan (6g1)	moving unevenly (of one object)	squeeze into the little bumblebee's/bird's hole

EXPRESSIVES IN KAMMU SINGING   47

Expressive	General meaning (in dictionary)	Specific meaning (in song)
Look		
cɔ́ɔ-ŋɔ́ɔ (7a6)	one beautiful person	beautiful sweetheart
dát-rŋ-dát (1a1, 2d1:1)	trembling in many places	trembling all over
hùaŋ-kl-hùaŋ (2e1)	—	looks like the clouds are getting low
ìi-lìaŋ (6c1)	—	beautiful words
kl-trɔ́ (2a1)	—	tiny frog
kə̀t-rŋ-kə̀t (7d3)	—	lizards go 'cackle cackle'
léem-cɔ́ɔn-cà (3: 6a)	—	sweet and fair
léem-cɔ́ɔn-kɔ̀ɔŋ (3: 6b)	—	sweet and fair
lìa-yía (3: 4a)	one tall, slim person	silvergrass so beautiful
lm-nèem (3: 3b)	level, even	silvergrass so long and straight
lm-trèem (3: 3a)	level, even	silvergrass so long and fine
lŋ-kìaŋ (3b3)	large body of water	–
lŋ-yɛ́ɛŋ (2a1, 7a6)	long and slim	small and thin; beautiful and slender
lòom-rŋ-lòom (10a6)	many moving beings staying together	wavering cloud of parakeets
l-trèeŋ (9a5)	one bird seen soaring by quickly	flap, flap, flying buttonquail
ɔ́ɔn-crɔ̀ɔn (7a3)	—	beautiful and tall
rk-ŋɔ́ɔk (3a2)	looking upwards (of many beings)	countless tied elephants bobbing their heads
r-lʌ̀ʌy (10a6)	many long, flat object|s floating away, seen briefly	cloud of parakeets turning over
r-lìak (10a6)	many objects turning around	cloud of parakeets turning over
rùut-cŋ-rùut (2e1)	—	looks like an epidemic is getting near
rt-ˀyɔ́ɔt (3b4)	glittering, unmoving objects	long, hanging bamboo strips
ry-ñàay (3b4)	many long, straight objects hanging down without moving	striped lattice
r-ʔàaŋ (2b1)	red light which lights up the sky	shining
sk-yàak (7a6)	—	large moon hanging
sñ-tùuñ (7a3)	rosy and fair face	rosy and fair
st-ˀyúut (7a3)	rosy, beautiful face	rosy and sweet

Continued

Continued

Expressive	General meaning (in dictionary)	Specific meaning (in song)
sy-pòoy (10a5)	round and small	beautiful dear; lovely dear
tàan-tàk (7a8)	—	[graceful] like a swallow
tàan-tèñ (7a8)	—	[swaying] like a swallow
thn-ʔwán (6f5)	slim, beautiful person	taro still is beautiful
tl-ʔəəl (4a2)	—	seem big like a branch
ʔyét-ʔyét (7a9)	slender, glittering, beautiful objects in one place	sweetheart so sweet, so sweet
Touch		
trùu-lm-trɔɔ (4a3)	—	an elastic hairpin
mùt-lr-màt (4a3)	soft, weak	fragile like me
wàay-wɔɔt (3b2)	—	touch the liver of the tadpole/cicada
Inner feeling		
càŋ-kn-càŋ (9a6, 7d14)	lonesome	feeling helpless at the sound of insects
c-ʔíar (4a1)	shy, embarrassed	embarrassed and uneasy
l-ŋ̀ìc (4a1)	suddenly feel fear of one person	embarrassed and unworthy
ŋʌʌy-kn-ŋʌʌy (5d3)	avoid looking at, dislike	the millipede is disgusting
rèet-cŋ-rèet (7d14)	longing for	feeling forlorn at the sound of insects

3.10 Appendix 3.2

Categories of reduplicated words in songs

Reduplicated verbs	General meaning (in dictionary)	Specific meaning (in song)
Sounds		
pát pát (2d1:1)	pát: to swat, to wave, to whisk	sounds like chopping leaves
plàa plàa (5a2)	plàa: to chop	sounds like chopping hard/soft leaves
póm póm (9a2)	póm: to beat	where basil leaves are beaten
pú pú (5a2)	pú: to hit, to beat with a rod	sounds like striking bamboo leaves
téñ téñ (3d1:1, 5a2)	téñ: to knock, to beat	sounds like hitting bamboo leaves; beating the top of a tree

3.11 Appendix 3.3

Categories of simile in songs

Simile	Interpretation in song
Sounds	
ìs mían síaŋ kɔ̀ɔŋ rók|háa (5a1)	resonant like a gong five|six fists wide (of bamboo clapper) [praising]
mían plàa plàa lá trú|réñ (5a2)	like chopping hard|soft leaves (of bamboo clapper) [deprecating]
mían pú pú|téñ téñ t-làa (5a2)	like striking|hitting bamboo leaves (of bamboo clapper) [deprecating]
ìs mían kír sn-tràan (6d1)	sounds like the first thunder of the year (of voice) [praising]
Movements	
plìat mían plìat mɔ̀ Cáan (10b2)	went off by mistake, like a tense crossbow
Looks	
r-ʔàaŋ mían màt prì|mòŋ (2b1)	shining like the sun|moon of a partridge [metaphor for a person; praising beauty]
ɔ̀ɔn-crɔ̀ɔn ... mían ɔ̀ɔn cùut|yòl (7a3)	beautiful and tall like a cùut plant|banana flower (of a woman)
st-ʔyúut ... mían ràaŋ rɔ̀ɔn (7a3)	rosy and sweet like a cockscomb flower (of a woman)
ñèɛl mían sə́ŋ kròh|kwáat km-làaŋ (10a4)	poor as if destroyed|swept away by a flood (of one's own house) [deprecating]
Touch	
làm mían prɔ́ɔk|òm ká (3a6)	delicious like squirrel|fish soup (of wine) [praising]
Inner feeling	
khwáay mían clɛ́ɛs|kíal kól hn-tùum (7a2)	old like a ripened clɛ́ɛs-vine|kól-melon (of one's own generation)
ʔwíat mían mà màan (10b2)	tired like a pregnant woman

References

Difloth, Gérard 1976. Expressives in Semai. In Philip Jenner, Laurence Thompson, and Stanley Starosta (eds), *Austroasiatic Studies*, vol. 1. Honolulu: University Press of Hawaii, 249–264.

Dingemanse, Mark 2012. Advances in the cross-linguistic study of ideophones. *Language and Linguistics Compass* 6: 654–672.

Évrard, Olivier 2012. Following Kàm Ràw's trail. In Damrong Tayanin and Kristina Lindell, *Hunting and Fishing in a Kammu Village: Revisiting a Classic Study in Southeast Asian Ethnography*. Copenhagen: NIAS Press, 1–28.

Karlsson, Anastasia, Håkan Lundström, and Jan-Olof Svantesson. 2022. 'Kammu vocal genres (Laos). In Håkan Lundström and Jan-Olof Svantesson (eds), *In the Borderland between Song and Speech. Vocal Expressions in Oral Cultures*. Lund: Lund University Press, 20–122.

Lindell, Kristina. 1988. Rhyme-pivot sayings in northern Kammu. In Leif Littrup (ed.), *Analecta Hafniensia: 25 years of East Asian studies in Copenhagen*. London: Curzon Press, 88–99.

Lindell, Kristina, Samuelsson, Rolf, and Tayanin, Damrong 1979. Kinship and marriage in northern Kammu villages: The kinship model. *Sociologus* 29(1): 60–84.

Lundström, Håkan 2010. *I Will Send My Song. Kammu Vocal Genres in the Singing of Kam Raw*. Copenhagen: NIAS Press.

Lundström, Håkan and Tayanin, Damrong 1981. Kammu drums and gongs 2: The long wooden drum and other drums. *Asian Folklore Studies* 40(2): 173–189.

Lundström, Håkan and Tayanin, Damrong 2006. *Kammu Songs. The Songs of Kam Raw*. Copenhagen: NIAS Press.

Smalley, William A. 1961. *Outline of Khmu? Structure*. New Haven: American Oriental Society.

Svantesson, Jan-Olof 1983. *Kammu Phonology and Morphology*. Lund: Gleerup.

Svantesson, Jan-Olof 2017. Sound symbolism: the role of word sound in meaning. *Wiley Interdisciplinary Reviews: Cognitive Science* 8(5): e1441.

Svantesson, Jan-Olof and Holmer, Arthur 2015. Kammu. In Mathias Jenny and Paul Sidwell (eds), *The Handbook of Austroasiatic Languages*, vol. 2. Leiden: Brill, 957–1002.

Svantesson, Jan-Olof, Ràw, Kàm (Damrong Tayanin), Lindell, Kristina, and Lundström, Håkan 2014. *Dictionary of Kammu Yùan Language and Culture*. Copenhagen: NIAS Press.

PART II
METHODS

4

Eliciting ideophones in the field

The IdEus-Psylex collection of stimuli

Iraide Ibarretxe-Antuñano

4.1 Introduction: are ideophones really that elusive to elicit?

Every language has ideophones. That is, every language has full-fledged iconic linguistic items that, besides abiding by the general formal rules and properties of prosaic words in a language, exhibit their own linguistic resources and characteristics: something that makes these words salient and foregrounded in their own languages.

There are, however, different types of ideophones. Those that are said to be 'direct' imitations of sound sources and events such as a bell tolling (*ding-dong* in English), a dog barking (*guau* in Spanish), or drinking water (*glou-glou* in French). And those that are considered 'sensory' depictions of entities, characteristics, and events that do not necessarily emit sounds per se, such as *brenk* 'a precipitous mountain' in Basque, *baṛaeʔ-buṛuiʔ* 'smooth, soft' in Mundari, or *du:* 'absolute silence' in Chichewa. The former are frequent in all languages and usually known as 'onomatopoeias' (Körtvélyessy and Štekauer 2024). The latter are more restricted in terms of language distribution and usually known by different names depending on the linguistic tradition: 'ideophones' in African linguistics (Doke 1935), and 'expressives' or 'mimetics' in Asian linguistics (Diffloth 1976; Hamano 1998; Iwasaki et al. 2017; Williams 2013).

All languages are, therefore, ideophonic to some extent. The difference lies in the type and number of ideophones: the wider the scope of ideophones, the more ideophonic the language is (Ibarretxe-Antuñano 2019). Thus, languages such as Basque, Mundari, or Chichewa are highly ideophonic, whereas languages such as English, Spanish, or French are (said to be) less ideophonic.

This cline of ideophonicity has important consequences for theoretical and empirical approaches to linguistics. In the case of Asian and African linguistics, these elements have always played an important role in the configuration of these languages. Seminal work by Samarin (1965), Diffloth (1976), Childs (1994), Hamano (1998), among many others, attests to this importance (see Dingemanse 2018 for a historical overview). Just the opposite happens in Standard Average European language-based linguistics. Since these elements were dismissed as

Iraide Ibarretxe-Antuñano, *Eliciting ideophones in the field*. In: *Capturing Expressivity*. Edited by: Jeffrey P. Williams, Oxford University Press. © Iraide Ibarretxe-Antuñano (2025). DOI: 10.1093/oso/9780192858931.003.0004 never being 'organic elements of a linguistic system. Besides, their number is much smaller than is generally supposed' in de Saussure's (1916 [1959: 69]) *Cours de linguistique générale*, ideophones have hardly been included in mainstream general linguistics literature. This dismissal does not mean that European languages lack ideophones—Balto-Finnic or Basque languages are living proofs that this is untrue (see Mikone 2001; Williams 2023). It is just that the languages usually taken as exemplars to explain and illustrate the functioning of 'Language' (i.e. English, French, Spanish, German, etc.) in modern mainstream linguistics[1] might not have the same widely attested variety of ideophones. A picture that really hides the phylogenetic and geographical scope and distribution of ideophones and, as Diffloth (1972: 440) pointed out, their central role in the characterization of natural language in general.

This is when the catch-22 arises. Ideophones are missing from most mainstream linguistic frameworks, textbooks, and even language structure databases (e.g. Dryer and Haspelmath's (2013) WALS online). Since they are not discussed in the literature, they are taken to be 'marginal exceptions' (Hockett 1958: 677) or a 'vanishingly small' part of language (Newmeyer 1993: 758). Linguists (and, as shown later, speakers) working in less described languages follow general linguistic procedures and thus neglect, miss, or avoid these elements.

A direct consequence of this situation may be the idea that ideophones are not easy targets for eliciting purposes, especially from a typological perspective. However, ideophones share formal characteristics (they are structurally foregrounded), encode similar semantic concepts, and fulfil comparable pragmatic functions (Akita and Pardeshi 2019; Akita and Dingemanse 2019; Dingemanse 2012, 2022; Hinton et al. 1994; Ibarretxe-Antuñano 2017; in press; Voeltz and Kilian-Hatz 2001, among others).

What happens is that each ideophonic language, in turn, exploits these general typological features in its own way. For instance, as far as formal saliency is concerned, ideophones are easily identifiable in some languages because they are overtly marked by certain phonemes (e.g. labiodental flap *vb* in Mundang, Niger-Congo), tones (e.g. high tones in Emai, Edoi), morphemes (e.g. *-a(n)dala* in Numbami, Astronesian), or syntactic positions (e.g. final-clause in KiVunjo-Chaga, Bantu) that cannot happen in prosaic words (see examples in Ibarretxe-Antuñano 2017). Other ideophonic languages, on the other hand, lack this exclusive overt marking and reuse typical language resources. This is the case with palatalization and reduplication in Basque. Both mechanisms are widely employed in both prosaic and ideophonic words. Similarly, phonesthemes, that is, the iconic link between sound and meaning, are typical in ideophones. Now, the specific choices of sounds and the meanings they evoke do not necessarily correspond. A well-known example is the link between size and front/back vowels. Many

---

[1] It is important to highlight the words 'modern' and 'mainstream' in this discussion. Early work in European languages such as Nodier (1808), Grammont (1901), Zamarripa (1914), or García de Diego (1968), for example, attest to the existing interest in the role of these words in language.

languages associate front vowels with smallness, but this is not a universal association. These divergences have often been taken as signs of the unsystematic nature of ideophones. However, similar divergences are also found in the typological description of other linguistic phenomena across languages: the choice of phoneme inventories, the number and type of morphological categories and markings, the presence of accusative/ergative systems, and so on. Therefore, the question is why ideophones are required to display a universal description, while other linguistic elements are not.

On top of these preconceptions, the 'elusive' nature of ideophones is often enhanced by other factors such as dialectal variation, oral vs written usage, and sociolinguistic variables such as schooling and language standardization. It is common practice to think that languages are monolectal. There is one Spanish, one English, or one French, when the truth is that there are always several Spanishes, Englishes, and Frenches, that is, diatopic variation. The idealized monolectal language perspective is often accompanied by the idea of the 'correct' language; namely, anything that is not part of the characterization of the standard written language (i.e. diafasic or diastratic variation) is wrong or marginal.

It is in this context that the elusive nature of ideophones should be placed, and where the preliminaries for the elicitation of ideophones in the field should start from. This chapter discusses these difficulties in the elicitation of ideophones from a cross-linguistic perspective and introduces the IdEus-Psylex stimulus kit. This kit was designed for eliciting Basque ideophones in the field, but it might be adapted for other languages. The first part of this chapter offers a brief overview of Basque ideophones from a typological and historical perspective to contextualize the variables used in the design of this kit. The second part focuses on the construction of the IdEus-Psylex stimulus kit and discusses variables as well as the selection of ideophones and stimuli. The final part comments on the advantages and disadvantages of this kit when used in the field and offers further ways to expand this tool in Basque and other languages.

4.2 Basque as a highly ideophonic language and its challenges for fieldwork

Ideophones are a defining feature of the Basque language. They form an open lexical word class in this language. Three reasons justify this statement (see Ibarretxe-Antuñano 2023 for a detailed review). First, their large inventory—ideophone dictionaries[2] (Ibarretxe-Antuñano 2006; Santisteban 2007) attest around 4,500

---

[2] General dictionaries such as the *Orotariko Euskal Hiztegia* (OEH; Mitxelena 1987–2005) mark onomatopoeic ideophones with the tag 'onomat'. The current OEH 9th edition online retrieves 746 lemmas with this tag. The real number, however, is much higher, since sensory ideophones are often not marked in this dictionary and different formal and dialectal variations are subsumed under the same lemma.

lexical items—and productivity—as an open class, speakers create ideophones ad hoc to meet their needs for describing new concepts (e.g. *tita-tita* 'sound of typing') or adapt ideophones commonly used in other languages (e.g. *bum, bun,* as in English *boom*). Second, their ubiquity: ideophones turn up in all contexts (oral-written), registers, and dialects. And, third, their scope, function, and structural characterization. In this respect, Basque ideophones share most of the main typological features described for this class of words: foregrounded structural characteristics, compact and multifaceted depictive meaning, and representative as well as expressive and aesthetic functions. Table 4.1 illustrates some of the main characteristics (see Ibarretxe-Antuñano 2017, 2023, for a detailed description).

Table 4.1 Linguistic characterization of Basque ideophones

Phonetics, phonology, and prosody	Characteristics	Basque ideophones
	Specific phonemes only or mostly used in ideophones	Voiced lamino-alveolar affricate /dz/ *dz*: *dzanga* 'dive'
	Palatalization (not exclusive)	*Ñir-ñir* 'gleam, twinkling' *Tipi-tapa* 'walk in quick and short steps'→ *ttipi-ttapa* 'walk in quicker and shorter steps'
	Specific phonotactics	Diphthong /iu̯/ *iu*: *bliu-blau* 'sound of several smacks' /f-/ *f -* + liquid: *frasta frasta* 'stride'
	Mimetic vowel harmony	*Terrent-terrent* 'stubbornly'
	Syllabic structure: varied	Monosyllabic: *plaust* 'heavy object falling' Polysyllabic: *tibiribiri-tibiribiro* 'chattering away'
	Phonesthemes	Velar plosives for swallowing and gulping: *zanga-zanga, zanka-zanka*
Morphology and syntax	Repetition of morphs	Partial reduplication: *pilpil-pulpul* 'palpitation' Total reduplication: *nir-nir* 'twinkle' Triplication: *za-za-za* 'speak fast'
	Affixation	IDE + *-ada* 'action, result': *dzistada* 'spark; flash of lightning'
	Compounding	*Kirri* 'grind' → *harrikirri* '(stone.IDE) gravel'
	With light verbs such as 'make/do'	*Tart egin* (IDE make) 'snap'
	Lack of morphological marking	Bare ideophones: *triki-traku* 'mess, jumble'

	Syntactic category	Multicategorial (nouns, adverbs, verbs ...) → open lexical word class
	Syntactic integration	Aloofness: *zapla!* 'slap!' and integrated: *zapladaz* (IDE+-*ada* 'action, result'+instrumental case) 'with slaps'
	Gesture	*Plisti-plasta* 'splish-splash' synchronized with upward/downward hand movement
Semantics and Pragmatics	Onomatopeic	Bells tolling: *dulun-dulun* '(big) bells tolling'; Dog barking: *zaunk-zaunk* 'sound of a big dog (barking), woof', *ttau-ttau*, *txau-txau* 'sound of a small dog barking'
	Sensory	Heat: *gori-gori* 'red-hot' Light: *dir-dir* 'shine'
	Semasiological relations	Polysemy: *Bar-bar* 'drink in gulps; sound of bubbling water; cracking; sound of an insect's walk; jabbering, talking; rhythmic falling of a light body; in droves; noise, din'
	Onomasiological relations	Partial synonymy: boiling: *bol-bol* 'sound of internal boiling; different from *fil-fil* 'simmer' or *txir-txir* 'soft boiling, usually in oil (fry)' Antonymy: *zirimiri* 'drizzling' vs *zapar-zapar* 'raining cats and dogs'
	Figurative meaning	*Bolo-bolo* 'spreading (news, gossip ...)'
	Linguistic function 'only to denote specific meanings'	*Tipi-tapa* 'walk in small steps'
	Dramaturgic function 'expressive function'	*Zanga-zanga* 'drink in gulps'
	Stylistic function 'aesthetic input' (narrative cohesion, intertextuality)	Poetry, comics, branding, linguistic landscape

The existence and role of ideophones in Basque have been long acknowledged in the traditional literature on the Basque language written by local as well as international authors. Zamarripa (1914), Azkue (1923–25), on the one hand, and Urtel (1919) and Schuchardt (1925), on the other, are among the earliest references that discussed the linguistic description of *onomatopeiak* and noticed the sheer numbers and crucial role of *Onomatopoesis* or *Schallworten* in Basque. This interest, however, faded away in the last half of the twentieth century. Most prescriptive and descriptive grammars of Basque, which formed the basis for creating language-learning materials, hardly mentioned ideophones in their pages. This is the case with the series *Euskal Gramatika: Lehen urratsak* 'Basque grammar: First Steps' published by Euskaltzaindia, the Academy of Basque Language (1985–2011), or Hualde and Ortiz de Urbina's (2003) collective work, *A Grammar of Basque*. Such a dramatic change in interest in ideophones may be, at least partly, explained by the mainstream linguistic models in vogue at that moment, models that, as discussed in Section 4.1, dismissed the role of ideophones in language. This situation is timidly changing as of recent years with the publication of scholarly papers, dictionaries (Ibarretxe-Antuñano 2006; Santisteban 2007), and the inclusion of specialized sections in Basque grammars such as Salaburu, Goenaga, and Sarasola's (2011) *Sareko Euskal Gramatika*, an online comprehensive reference grammar of Basque (www.ehu.eus/seg/).

4.3 Challenges for researching Basque ideophones

Despite this renewed interest in ideophones and the indisputable body of linguistic evidence for open lexical word-class nature, both Basque linguistic scholarship work and speakers' collective minds still situate them, as Dingemanse (2018) would call it, at the 'margins of language'.

As Dingemanse's (2018: 19) exposes, ideophones still suffer from 'three common misconceptions that recur through the history of ideophone studies' and stem from a Standard Average European language bias. They have been wrongly considered (i) 'playthings, not tools', i.e. a childish use of language, (ii) just onomatopoeia, i.e. imitations of sound emissions, and (iii) just intensifiers, i.e. equivalent to 'very'. In the particular case of Basque, two more related misconceptions may be added: ideophones are (iv) just for rural and older speakers, and (v) just for informal oral contexts, that is, not suitable for formal registers and written contexts.

As a consequence, one of the first challenges that one has to overcome when researching Basque ideophones is to make sure that researchers understand the unsuitability of these misconceptions and to enhance the speakers' own ideophonic awareness. It is very common to hear native speakers say that they do not use ideophones (or onomatopoeia). This concept is always tainted by these misconceptions, and thus, speakers would not allow themselves to speak 'wrong' or to sound 'childish' or 'rural'. Speakers are generally aware of sound imitations for animals, instruments, or child talk. All of these semantic fields, by the way, are highly productive in Basque, but with an added twist. As happens in other highly ideophonic languages, the imitation of these sounds is not restricted to one ideophone per animal, such as cows, dogs, or pigs, or per instrument, such as drums or guitars. Basque offers a range of ideophones that capture differences in types and sizes (e.g. *zara-zara* 'sound of a big fly' and *ziri-ziri* 'sound of a small fly') and particularities of Basque environment and culture (instruments, for example the *txalaparta* makes a sound like *ttakun-ttakun* and the psaltery, *ttün-ttün*). However, when speakers are told that common words for moving (*irrist* 'slide'), ingesting (*zurrup* 'sip'), boiling (*pil-pil* 'superficial boiling'), talking (*txatxala-patxala*; *txitxili-patxala* 'speaking (non-stop); ramble; chat'), or shining (*brist* 'shine') are also ideophones, a whole new scenario opens up: they recognize these words as their own.

A related issue to the speakers' awareness of ideophones is the question of how many ideophones speakers know and consider natural in everyday contexts. It is true that ideophones are more expressive than prosaic words, and that sometimes they are used on purpose to underline this expressiveness. For instance, *haize* is the prosaic word for 'wind', but one may use *firi-fara* instead to describe 'the movement of soft and warm wind'. However, many other times the ideophonic word is the only possible native choice that exists in the language to describe a certain action or object.

The situation in Basque ideophones becomes more complicated because other (socio-) linguistic factors must be brought in. One factor is the rich and diverse dialectal variation that exists in this language. Apart from the standard variety, called *Euskara Batua* 'unified Basque', five main branches are currently distinguished: Western, Central, Navarrese, Navarrese-Lapurdian, and Zuberoan (see Zuazo 2013; Camino 2019). Figure 4.1 illustrates the geographical area where Basque and Basque dialectal variation are used.

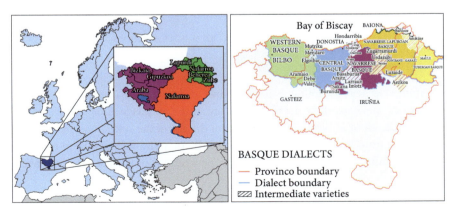

Figure 4.1 The geographical area inhabited by speakers of Basque and Basque dialects

Left: adapted from an image by Zorion, reproduced under a CC BY-SA 3.0 Creative Commons licence https://creativecommons.org/licenses/by-sa/3.0/deed.en

Right: adapted from Zuazo's http://euskalkiak.eus/en/sailkapenak.php, reproduced under a CC BY-SA 3.0 Creative Commons licence https://creativecommons.org/licenses/by-sa/3.0/deed.en

The dialectal distribution of ideophones is thus important when studying the existence and usage of these words by different speakers. Some ideophones (e.g. *tipi-tapa* 'walk in quick and short steps' or *xirimiri* (*sirimiri*) 'drizzle') are widely spread across dialects and adopted as the normative forms in Standard Basque. Others are only used in one specific local variety (e.g. *dzingua* 'sudden seawater increase' in Lekeitio (Bizkaia, Western Basque). Some others are known cross-dialectally but spelled out differently; for instance, the ideophone *dizdiz* (*dirdir, dizdir, bir-bir, sirt-sart* ...) for 'shine, dazzle', as shown in Figure 4.2.[3]

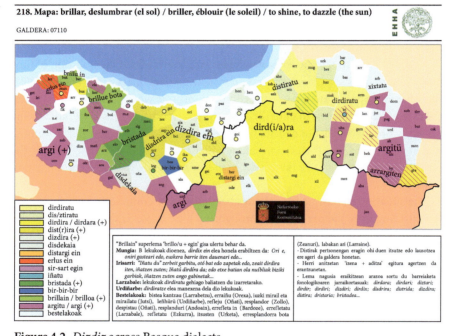

Figure 4.2 *Dizdiz* across Basque dialects
Source: EHHA (*Atlas for Basque Local Varieties*), p. 381, map 218. © Euskaltzaindia. All rights reserved.

Another crucial sociolinguistic factor has to do with the correlation between the age of speakers, their degree of literacy in the language, and their access to formal education in Basque. Depending on the age of the speaker and the region they come from, the situation with respect to literacy and formal tuition might be radically different.[4] In a nutshell, for older generations of Basque native speakers

---

[3] Maps are retrieved from Euskaltzaindia's (2005–08) *Atlas for Basque Local Varieties* (Euskararen Herri Hizkeren Atlasa (*EHHA*)). © Euskaltzaindia. All rights reserved. The interested reader can access these maps and their detailed information about dialectal variants online at www.euskaltzaindia.eus/component/ehha.

[4] The situation is much more complex than what can be covered in this section. One has to bear in mind (i) historical factors such as the dictatorship in Spain until 1975 or the banning laws in respect of the use of any other language but Spanish; (ii) the current uneven official status of the Basque

(born before the 1960s) on both *Hegoalde* (the Spanish part) and *Iparralde* (the French part) (see Figure 4.1), Basque was their language at home, but Spanish or French was the language of instruction at school. This means that they were generally illiterate in Basque. For younger generations of Basque native speakers (born after the 1980s), on the other hand, the situation was different. Basque was not only their language at home but also their language at school in those regions where Basque is an official language or where they have Basque private schools (*Ikastola*). Eventually, these younger generations were literate in Standard Basque. In fact, this is yet another sociolinguistic factor to take into account: the creation of a standard variety for Basque. Although standardization has always been on the agenda of *Euskaltzaindia*, it was not until 1968 that it was definitively launched. The normativization of Basque has been progressively developing since then. The impact of Standard Basque on ideophones is an area that needs to be investigated in more detail (see Section 4.2). Nevertheless, as discussed at the beginning of this section, language ideologies about ideophones have permeated their scholarly treatment, and, therefore, their role in the Standard Basque variety is expected to be lower-profile or less prominent than in the diatopic varieties.

All these linguistic, sociolinguistic, and even external historical factors determine the way a proper study of Basque ideophones must be designed and conducted. The following section presents the IdEus-Psylex stimulus kit, a research tool built to overcome this challenge.

4.4 Tools for investigating Basque ideophones in the field: the IdEus-Psylex stimulus kit

The IdEus-Psylex stimulus kit was created based on the specific characterization of the Basque language and the status of Basque ideophones. The main goal of this tool was to provide researchers with a collection of materials that would reveal the knowledge and usage of ideophones in Basque.

As discussed in the previous section, on the one hand, informants had to be carefully selected according to their linguistic and educational backgrounds. On the other hand, the stimulus had to be chosen to cover a wide range of meanings (entities and events), degrees of knowledge and usage (common to rare), and dialectal preferences. Section 4.4.1 describes the IdEus-Psylex stimulus kit, and Section 4.4.2 reports some results obtained in the application of this tool in the field.

---

language (official in the provinces of Bizkaia, Araba, and Gipuzkoa, and the northern part of Navarre in *Hegoalde*, not official in the provinces of *Iparralde*); and (iii) the recent and progressive standardization process of the Basque language and the development of normative rules for Standard Basque since 1968. For more information, see Gorrochategui et al. (2018).

4.4.1 The IdEus-Psylex stimulus kit

4.4.1.1 Informants

The variables at play in the selection of informants were five: (i) age: two groups: Young (18–30 years), Middle (31–60 years), and Senior (61 onwards); (ii) place: rural or urban environment; (iii) home language: Basque; (iv) language of formal education: Spanish/French or Basque; (v) degree of literacy in (Standard) Basque.

4.4.1.2 Materials

The stimulus kit is composed of three warm-ups and forty target stimuli: thirty-six short target ideophone video clips and four images. Most stimuli were specifically created for this set. These clips are designed based on the three main variables summarized in Table 4.2. The whole set of target stimuli is described in Appendix 4.1.

Table 4.2 Variables for IdEus-Psylex stimuli

Variable	Explanation
(i) Ideophone MEANING	Ten different semantic fields: CREATURES: insects, crustaceans, birds, amphibians, fish ACTIONS: motion (manner, ground), communication (chatter, gossip, impaired), light, ingestion (food/drink), destruction (cut/break), hitting, boiling, laughing, body function WEATHER MUSIC CHARACTERISTICS: physical, psychological SEX PLANT GADGET TRIFLE CHILDREN'S TALK
(ii) Ideophone TYPE	Two possibilities: If an entity/object, it is a STATIC ideophone; the stimulus is a picture If an event, it is a DYNAMIC ideophone; the stimulus is a video
(iii) Ideophone FUNCTION in language use	To test three possibilities: The ONLY choice to describe that event or entity in Basque; e.g. *karramarro* 'crab' A COMMON choice: a common, well-known ideophone, although Basque offers other possibilities to describe that event or entity either by a prosaic word or a loanword; e.g. *bor-bor* and *irakin* 'boil' a RARE choice: the ideophone exists but a prosaic word is more frequently used for describing that event or entity; e.g. *txir-txir* and *frijitu* 'fry'

4.4.1.3 Procedure

The procedure is simple. First, the informant has to complete a biographical questionnaire. Then, the experimenter explains the task. Each stimulus is shown to the informant; in the case of video clips, these are played twice and with sound. Right after that, the experimenter asks the informant: 'What is that?' for pictures and 'What is [entity] doing?' What the informant answers is considered the first answer. Since the experimenter knows the possible answers beforehand (see Appendix 4.1), s/he can prompt the informant to describe the stimuli further if necessary. For example, stimulus 39 shows a person sleeping and snoring loudly. In case the informant only mentions the verb 'sleep', the experimenter can ask them further questions such as 'How is he sleeping?'. These prompts will be classified as second answers. Additionally, the experimenter could opt for a second round of elicitation. Now, the experimenter will use the list of possible answers for the stimuli and ask the informant about the suitability of the ideophones provided for each stimulus on the basis of the variables described in Section 4.4.1.2. Sessions are to be recorded (video recorded, if possible). Raw answers are transcribed on an Excel sheet and later prepared for analysis on a second sheet.

4.4.2 The IdEus-Psylex stimulus kit in the field: some notes on data collection and results

The IdEus-Psylex stimulus kit was first tested in the field in 2009. Thirty-seven speakers participated in the study, distributed in three age groups (16–30 yrs = 17; 31–60 yrs = 12; 61–90 yrs = 8) with different schooling backgrounds. They all came from rural areas and were native speakers of four main dialects: Western Basque (twelve subjects), Central Basque (six subjects), Navarrese Basque (twelve subjects), and Navarrese-Lapurdian Basque (seven subjects).

Researchers[5] followed the procedure explained in Section 4.4.1.3. They were in charge of collecting and transcribing data. In respect to the suitability of the tool for eliciting ideophones, this stimulus kit seemed to be appropriate for this goal. Informants did not report any difficulties in performing the task. Data collectors were also positive with the procedure, but suggested two areas the kit could improve on; namely, the number of semantic fields covered and the need to add a think-aloud protocol for informants to explain more about their choice of ideophones and other possible relevant information (see Section 4.5).

As far as the research results are concerned, the IdEus-Psylex stimulus kit provided enough information to draw the following general conclusions about the use of ideophones:

---

[5] The data were collected by Ihintza Erremundeguy, Miren Ibarluzea, and Usoa Wyssenbach Ibarra. This fieldwork was part of their qualifying requirements for the optional course 'Applied Linguistics'. This subject was taught as part of the Masters in Basque Philology and Applied Linguistics at the University of the Basque Country during the 2008–09 academic year. I take this opportunity to thank them for their work and enthusiasm. Mila esker!

64   IRAIDE IBARRETXE-ANTUÑANO

(i) All informants, regardless of their sociolinguistic or dialectal background, employed ideophones in their first answers.

(ii) Older informants show a qualitative difference with respect to younger informants. They employed a higher number of items classified as RARE ideophones. For instance, *girrintzi* for the air moving by a spinning windmill (stimulus 37, Appendix 4.1). Younger informants, on the other hand, knew more recent ideophones for specialized objects, as in the case of *daratulu* 'drill' (stimulus 7, Appendix 4.1).

(iii) The degree of agreement among informants when providing an ideophone answer depends on two factors. One is the type of stimulus: ideophones categorized as the ONLY option and COMMON were the ones that attracted more ideophone answers, for instance *karramarro* 'crab' (stimulus 16, Appendix 4.1). The other is dialectal variation: informants used the dialectal form for the ideophone; for example, 'wade' (stimulus 30, Appendix 4.1) is denoted as *plisti-plasta, pitxin-patxan, txipristadak, plistin-plastan, plasta-plasta, klas-klas, laprast,* and *laban* in stimulus 30, Appendix 4.1).

(iv) The use and frequency of some ideophone variants seem to be favoured by the normativization of the language. Standard Basque ideophones are learned at school and these seem to be the preferred choices in younger speakers. For example, in the case of snowing (stimulus 36, Appendix 4.1), older speakers use *fara-fara* (or *farra-farra*), an ideophone that specifically means 'to snow profusely and softly' whereas younger speakers prefer *mara-mara,* This ideophone means 'profusely' in general but it is the normative ideophone taught for this kind of snowing at school.

Results (ii) and (iii) were expected, but results (i) and (iv) were interesting discoveries: they offered further support to confirm that ideophones are indeed used by all speakers, not just by older generations, and to show the impact of standardization in the choice and usage of ideophones.

4.5 Conclusions

Ideophones have been reported to be elusive, unsystematic, and challenging to test in the lab or in the field. However, some of these preconceptions arise from a general misunderstanding of the nature of ideophones and the crucial role they play in language, a misunderstanding that stems from mainstream linguistic models that assume that what happens in Standard Average European languages is what happens in language in general. And Standard Average European languages are low-ideophonic. Ironically enough, these languages represent a tiny percentage of the language diversity in the world, and the more cross-linguistic studies on ideophones are published, the more evident it becomes that what happens in Standard Average European languages is the exception, not the norm.

Ideophones, like any other word class, pose challenges for the researcher: cross-linguistic similarities and language-specific differences, dialectal variations, sociolinguistc variables ... However, perhaps the biggest challenge that ideophone research needs to overcome is the scarcity of well-established and standardized methodologies for their language-specific and, eventually, cross-linguistic, investigation.

The IdEus-Psylex stimulus kit, a set of forty ideophone stimuli (thirty-six video clips and four images), is a contribution aimed at filling this gap. Its goal has been to provide elicitation materials to study the usage of ideophones in Basque. This is a highly ideophonic language whose ideophone system has suffered from general misconceptions about its nature and consequently been overlooked by modern scholarship on Basque linguistics as well as by Basque speakers. This kit has already been tested in the field, and results show that it is a suitable tool for elicitation and that ideophones are indeed a crucial part of the language for all speakers, regardless of their linguistic and sociolinguistic background.

Although these results confirm the usefulness of the IdEus-Psylex stimulus kit, there is naturally room for improvement. The kit fell short in the number of semantic fields it covered, missed the possibility of letting the informants explain their choices, and was administered under similar conditions (i.e. in the same order and video clips played with sound). Considering these limitations, a new version, the IdEus-Psylex 2.0,[6] has been developed. This improved version tests a wider range of semantic fields, includes a new variable (sound vs mute stimulus), and modifies the elicitation conditions (stimuli are now randomized and organized in different orders). The kit is not just designed for eliciting Basque ideophones; it aims to become a useful tool for cross-linguistic ideophone research. Therefore, it includes materials to test semantic areas (e.g. taste, colour, or smell), which are less developed in Basque ideophones but frequent in other ideophonic languages such as Mundari (Ibarretxe-Antuñano 2021; Osada and Badenoch 2019). The IdEus-Psylex 2.0 consists of 100 stimuli. The procedure protocol includes two more tasks to be administered after the naming task with the kit: a questionnaire that addresses issues related to ideophone knowledge and usage practices ('Do you know the word [ideophone]?'; 'Have you seen this word [ideophone] being used in writing/orally?'; etc.), and a post-test where speakers are asked to explain the meaning of ideophones.

This chapter started with ideophones situated at the margins of language. There is still a long way to go before these margins are redrawn. However, the use of tools like the IdEus-Psylex Stimulus kit is the right path to follow to break those margins and use ideophones *china-chano, tipi-tapa, toko-toko, dao dao dao, cugi cugi* ..., or just 'walk step by step, quickly, steady', and reach the place where they have always belonged.

---

[6] The IdEus-Psylex 2.0 has been developed in collaboration with María Louro Mendiguren (University of Zaragoza).

4.6 Appendix 4.1

IdEus-ideophone stimulus set

STIMULUS		GOAL	IDEOPHONE	SEMANTICS	TYPE	FUNCTION
01-A-B-boilhard		Water boiling	*Bor-bor*	ACTION: BOILING	DYNAMIC	COMMON
02-W-hail2		Hail	*Txitxar, kazkabar, kiski-kaska*	WEATHER	DYNAMIC	ONLY, COMMON
03-A-D-break		Break branch	*Karaskatu, kraska*	ACTION: DESTRUCTION	DYNAMIC	COMMON
04-A-H-drops		Drops, dripping	*Tanta, tanga-tanga*	ACTION: HITTING	DYNAMIC	ONLY
05-A-L-beam8		Lighthouse light	*Zinta*	ACTION: LIGHT	DYNAMIC	RARE
06-A-M-slide-kid1		Sliding on a toboggan	*Txirrist, irrist*	ACTION: MOTION	DYNAMIC	ONLY
07-G-drill-object		Drill	*Ta(r)ratulu, daratulu, zaztagin*	GADGET	STATIC	RARE

08-A-D-cuthair		Cut hair with scissors	*Gliski-glaska*	ACTION: DESTRUCTION	DYNAMIC	RARE, COMMON
09-A-I-sip2		Sip liquid	*Hurrup*	ACTION: INGESTION	DYNAMIC	COMMON
10-A-M-roll2b		Ball rolling	*Firri-farraka*	ACTION: MOTION	DYNAMIC	RARE, COMMON
11-C-Ph-hunchback		Hunchbacked person	*Konkor*	CHARACTERISTICS: PHYSICAL	STATIC	ONLY
12-A-M-trudge2		Walk with difficulty	*Tikili-takala, hinkili-hankala*	ACTION: MOTION	DYNAMIC	RARE
13-A-D-tear		Tear cloth	*Zirrist-zarrast, zarrat*	ACTION: DESTRUCTION	DYNAMIC	COMMON, ONLY
14-A-L-sparkle1		Sparkle	*Nir-nir, dir-dir*	ACTION: LIGHT	DYNAMIC	COMMON, ONLY
15-A-M-helter-skelter		Roll down	*Pinpi-punpaka, dinbilidanbalaka*	ACTION: MOTION	DYNAMIC	COMMON

Continued

Continued

STIMULUS		GOAL	IDEOPHONE	SEMANTICS	TYPE	FUNCTION
16-Cr-C-crab-object		Crab	*Karramarro*	CREATURES: CRUSTACEAN	STATIC	ONLY
17-A-M-drag		Drag object	*Arrast*	ACTION: MOTION	DYNAMIC	ONLY, COMMON
18-A-D-hammer1		Beat with hammer	*Tauki-tauki*	ACTION: DESTRUCTION	DYNAMIC	RARE, ONLY
19-A-L-laugh		Laugh	*Kra-kra, irri*	ACTION: LAUGHING	DYNAMIC	COMMON, ONLY
20-A-B-fry		Fry bacon	*Txir-txir*	ACTION: BOILING	DYNAMIC	RARE, ONLY
21-A-M-swing-kid-1		Swinging kids	*Dintzili-dantzalaka, zanbulu*	ACTION: MOTION	DYNAMIC	COMMON
22-A-D-grind		Grind coffee	*Birrindu*	ACTION: DESTRUCTION	DYNAMIC	COMMON
23-A-I-wolfdown2		Wolf down food	*Mauta-mauta*	ACTION: INGESTION	DYNAMIC	COMMON

24-A-M-zig-zag4		Cars zig-zagging, road shape	*Sigi-saga*	ACTION: MOTION	DYNAMIC	COMMON
25-P-poppy		Poppy	*Kalikola, mitxoleta*	PLANT	STATIC	ONLY
26-A-D-pump-explode		Burst	*Zart*	ACTION: DESCTRUCTION	DYNAMIC	COMMON, RARE
27-W-drizzle7-silent		Drizzle	*Xirimiri*	WEATHER	DYNAMIC	COMMON
28-A-I-gulps1		Drink in gulps	*Zanga-zanga*	ACTION: INGESTION	DYNAMIC	COMMON
29-A-C-gossip		Gossip	*Zurrumurru*	ACTION: COMMUNICATION	DYNAMIC	COMMON
30-A-M-wade3		Walk in water	*Plisti-plasta*	ACTION: MOTION	DYNAMIC	COMMON

Continued

Continued

STIMULUS		GOAL	IDEOPHONE	SEMANTICS	TYPE	FUNCTION
31-A-BF-heartbreat3		Heart beating	*Punpada, taupada*	ACTION: BODY FUNCTION	DYNAMIC	ONLY
32-A-M-shuffle3		Shuffling	*Kirriz-karraz, terrel-terrel*	ACTION: MOTION	DYNAMIC	COMMON
33-T-leftovers		Leftovers	*Azur-mazurrak*	TRIFLE	STATIC	ONLY, RARE
34-A-H-smack4		Snack on face	*Zapla, zart, zapart*	ACTION: HITTING	DYNAMIC	COMMON
35-A-M-slid		Sliding	*Laprast*	ACTION: MOTION	DYNAMIC	COMMON
36-W-snow		Falling snow	*Fara-fara, mara-mara*	WEATHER	DYNAMIC	COMMON
37-A-M-spin		Windmill	*Firrindola, firrintaka*	ACTION: MOTION	DYNAMIC	COMMON

38-A-M-helter-skelter3		Run down helter-skelter	*Tarrapatan*	ACTION: MOTION	DYNAMIC	COMMON, RARE
39-A-BF-snore7		Snore	*Zurrunka*	ACTION: BODY FUNCTION	DYNAMIC	COMMON, ONLY
40-A-D-saw		Sawing	*Zirris-zarraz*	ACTION: DESTRUCTION	DYNAMIC	COMMON, RARE

Acknowledgements

This research has been funded by the Spanish Ministry of Science and Innovation (AEI/FEDER Funds: MOTIV PID2021-123302NB-I00), the Government of Aragon (Psylex H11-17R; MultiMetAR LMP143_21), and the Iberus Campus (ICON action group).

References

Akita, K. and Dingemanse, M. (2019). Ideophones (mimetics, expressives). In M. Aronoff (ed.), *Oxford Research Encyclopedia of Linguistics*. Oxford: Oxford University Press. doi:10.1093/acrefore/9780199384655.013.477

Akita, K. and Pardeshi, P. (eds) (2019). *Ideophones, Mimetics, and Expressives*. Amsterdam: John Benjamins.

Azkue, R. M. (1923–25). *Morfología Vasca*. Bilbao: Euskaltzaindia.

Camino, I. (2019). An overview of Basque dialects. *Linguistic Minorities in Europe Online* (LME). Available online at https://doi.org/10.1515/LME. Accessed 16 April 2023.

Childs, G. T. (1994). African ideophones. In L. Hinton, J. Nichols, and J. J. Ohala (eds), *Sound Symbolism*. Cambridge: Cambridge University Press, 178–206.

Diffloth, G. (1972). Notes on expressive meaning. *Papers from the Eighth Regional Meeting of the Chicago Linguistics Society* 8: 440–447.

Diffloth, G. (1976). Expressives in Semai. *Oceanic Linguistics Special Publications* 13: 249–264.

Dingemanse, M. (2012). Advances in the cross-linguistic study of ideophones. *Language and Linguistics Compass* 6(10): 654–672.

Dingemanse, M. (2018). Redrawing the margins of language: Lessons from research on ideophones. *Glossa: A Journal of General Linguistics* 3(1): 4. https://doi.org/10.5334/gjgl. 444

Dingemanse, M. (2022). Ideophones. In E. van Lier (ed.), *The Oxford Handbook of Word Classes*. Oxford: Oxford University Press, 466–476.

Doke, C. M. (1935). *Bantu Linguistic Terminology*. London: Longmans, Green, and Co.

Dryer, M. S. and Haspelmath, M. (eds) (2013). *WALS Online* (v2020.3) [Data set]. Zenodo. https://doi.org/10.5281/zenodo.7385533. Available online at https://wals.info. Accessed 16 April 2023.

Euskaltzaindia (1985–2011). *Euskal Gramatika: Lehen urratsak*. Bilbo: Euskaltzaindia.

García de Diego, V. (1968). *Diccionario de voces naturales*. Madrid: Aguilar.

Grammont, M. (1901). Onomatopées et mots expressifs. In *Trentenaire de la Société pour l'Étude des Langues Romanes*. Montpellier: Bureau des publications de la Société pour l'Étude des Langues Romances, 261–322.

Hamano, S. (1998). *The Sound Symbolic System of Japanese*. Tokyo: Kurosio Publishers.

Hinton, L., Nichols, J., and Ohala, J. (eds) (1994). *Sound Symbolism*. Cambridge: Cambridge University Press.

Hockett, C. F. (1958). *A Course in Modern Linguistics*. New York: The Macmillan Company.

Hualde, J. I. and Ortiz de Urbina, J. (eds) (2003). *A Grammar of Basque*. Berlin: Mouton de Gruyter.

Ibarretxe-Antuñano, I. (2006). *Hizkuntzaren bihotzean: Euskal onomatopeien hiztegia. Euskara-Ingelesera-Gaztelania*. Donastia-San Sebastian: Gaiak.

Ibarretxe-Antuñano, I. (2017). Basque ideophones from a typological perspective. *The Canadian Journal of Linguistics/Revue canadienne de linguistique* 62(2): 196–220.

Ibarretxe-Antuñano, I. (2019). Towards a semantic typological classification of motion ideophones: The motion semantic grid. In K. Akita and P. Pardeshi (eds), *Ideophones, Mimetics, and Expressives*. Amsterdam: John Benjamins, 137–166.

Ibarretxe-Antuñano, I. (2021). The domain of olfaction in Basque. In Ł. Jedrzejowski and P. Staniewski (eds), *The Linguistics of Olfaction. Typological and Diachronic Approaches to Synchronic Diversity*. Amsterdam: John Benjamins, 73–107.

Ibarretxe-Antuñano, I. (2023). Vindicating the role of ideophones as a typological feature of Basque. In J. P. Williams (ed.), *Expressives in the European Sphere*. Cambridge: Cambridge University Press, 313–334.

Ibarretxe-Antuñano, I. (in press). The segmentals and suprasegmentals of ideophones. In O. Fischer, K. Akita, and P. Perniss (eds), *Handbook on Iconicity in Language*. Oxford: Oxford University Press.

Iwasaki, N., Sells, P., and Akita, K. (eds) (2017). *The Grammar of Japanese Mimetics: Perspectives from Structure, Acquisition, and Translation*. London: Routledge.

Körtvélyessy, L. and Štekauer, P. (eds) (2024). *Onomatopoeia in the World's Languages*. Berlin: Mouton de Gruyter.

Mikone, E. (2001). Ideophones in the Balto-Finnic languages. In F. K. E. Voeltz and C. Kilian-Hatz (eds), *Ideophones*. Amsterdam: John Benjamins, 223–233.

Newmeyer, F. (1993). Iconicity and generative grammar. *Language* 68: 756–796.

Nodier, C. (1808). *Dictionnaire raisonné des onomatopées françaises*. Paris: Demonville.

Osada, T. and Badenoch, N. (2019). *A Dictionary of Mundari Expressives*. Tokyo: Research Institute for Language and Cultures of Asia and Africa, University of Foreign Studies.

Salaburu, P., Goenaga, P. and Sarasola, K. (eds) (2011). *Sareko Euskal Gramatika*. Available online at https://www.ehu.eus/seg. Accessed 16 April 2023.

Samarin, W. J. (1965). Perspective on African ideophones. *African Studies* 24(2): 117–121.

Santisteban, K. (2007). *Onomatopeia eta adierazpen hotsen hiztegia*. Bilbo: Gero.

Saussure, F. de (1916) [1959]. *Cours de linguistique générale*, ed. by Charles Bally, Albert Sechehaye, and Albert Riedlinger. Lausanne: Payot.

Schuchardt, H. (1925). *Das Baskische und die Sprachwissenschaft*. Vienna: Hölder-Pichler-Tempsky A.-G.

Urtel, H. (1919). *Zur baskischen Onomatopoesis*. Berlin: Reichsdruckerei.

Voeltz, F. K. E. and Kilian-Hatz, C. (eds) (2001). *Ideophones*. Amsterdam: John Benjamins

Williams, J. P. (ed.) (2013). *The Aesthetics of Grammar: Sound and Meaning in the Languages of Mainland Southeast Asia*. Cambridge: Cambridge University Press.

Williams, J. P. (ed.) (2023). *Expressives in the European Sphere*. Cambridge: Cambridge University Press.

Zamarripa, P. (1914) [1987]. *Manual del vascófilo*. Bilbao: Wilsen Editorial.

Zuazo, K. (2013). *The Dialects of Basque*. Reno: The Center for Basque Studies University of Nevada, Reno.

5

A multi-methods toolkit for documentary research on ideophones

Bonnie McLean and Mark Dingemanse

5.1 Introduction

Ideophones are lexicalized depictions, meaning that they employ an analogical mode of representation that invites and affords the construal of iconic mappings between form and meaning (Dingemanse 2012). For example, the Japanese ideophone *purupuru* depicts a jiggling movement, like that of a pudding. This meaning is not only conventional, but (to Japanese speakers at least) embodied by the sounds in the ideophone, from the softness of the /p/ to the quickness of the /r/. Since depictions are analogical, *purupuru* also implies the possibility of other ideophones, like *furufuru*, from which we can imagine an even gentler movement—the fluttering of feathers on a bird's wing—or *buruburu*, a stronger movement, like the vibrating of a drill. These simple examples demonstrate how ideophones begin to form dense and complex networks of meanings, which can be difficult to capture using traditional lexicographic methods (e.g. Akita 2016; Badenoch, Osada, et al. 2021; Nuckolls et al. 2017; de Schryver 2009). As an illustration, one study found that speakers of Japanese can identify ideophones from their dictionary definitions in only fifty percent of cases (Akita 2016). This is not, despite some claims, because ideophones do not have identifiable meanings (e.g. Bodomo 2006; Moshi 1993; Okpewho 1992), but rather because the kinds of meanings that ideophones possess are not easily reduced to ordinary descriptive language (Badenoch 2021; Diffloth 1972; Samarin 1967). It is a problem stemming from the distinct mode of representation ideophones employ, and here we argue that its solution also requires distinct methods—and a more diverse documentary toolkit.

The standard paraphrase, for instance, is often much more powerful when accompanied by a depiction. This was illustrated in the Japanese study by combining dictionary definitions of ideophones with pictures and short videos, after which participants were able to accurately identify the ideophone in as many as ninety percent of cases (Akita 2016). Digital media also provides opportunities for rethinking the traditional dictionary structure to better accommodate the unique organisation of ideophone lexicons, where meaning does not only reside in individual lexemes but emerges dynamically from wider ideophone networks (see

---

Bonnie McLean and Mark Dingemanse, *A multi-methods toolkit for documentary research on ideophones.*
In: *Capturing Expressivity.* Edited by: Jeffrey P. Williams, Oxford University Press. © Bonnie McLean and Mark Dingemanse (2025). DOI: 10.1093/oso/9780192858931.003.0005

Badenoch, Osada, et al. 2021 for some excellent examples of this in Mundari). In this chapter we synthesise effective techniques used to elicit ideophones and uncover their meanings, while simultaneously producing rich, polysemiotic representations of those meanings that can later feed into lexicographic projects. The techniques are chosen for the different viewpoints they offer, allowing us to explore the ideophone lexicon from both the emic and the etic perspectives. While each technique can stand on its own, there is a special advantage to combining them as together they offer cumulative insights and allow for methodological triangulation to bring the multifaceted semantics of ideophones into focus.

Figure 5.1 outlines the methods presented in the chapter, the analyses they afford, and the ways they can be combined to yield further insights. The first technique covered is MULTIMODAL CORPUS BUILDING. To use the other techniques, it is first necessary to be able to recognize and identify ideophones, and this knowledge is best gained through experience with ideophones in natural language use. We highlight specific speech styles to focus on, and discuss how to identify ideophones as lexicalized depictions. Emphasis is placed on the creation of *multimodal* rather than purely spoken or written corpora, as intonational and gestural cues are a vital resource for both the identification of ideophones and for determining their meanings and use.

Corpus data can then be complemented with data generated using more targeted elicitation techniques. STIMULUS-BASED ELICITATION is a particularly good pairing, as it allows researchers to target specific contrasts that may not appear as frequently in a corpus, but which can be used to investigate depictive conventions. It also offers a controlled way to collect comparable data on the use or non-use of ideophones across different semantic domains, and different languages and cultures, contributing to our understanding of the relative affordances and limitations of ideophones as spoken depictions (see e.g. Akita 2013; Dingemanse 2012; McLean 2021). Where stimulus-based elicitation can be thought of as a tool to map out the edges of the ideophone lexicon, techniques like FREE-LISTING are a way to fill in the middle—including by applying the studied depictive conventions. This also establishes networks of related ideophones, which can then be investigated collectively. SIMILARITY JUDGEMENT TASKS are one excellent way to investigate relationships between ideophones and the structure of the ideophone lexicon, this time using a bottom-up approach. While the top-down approach employed in (e.g.) stimulus-based elicitation is useful for comparative purposes, similarity judgement tasks offer an opportunity to investigate the lexicon on its own terms. Stimuli can be taken from data generated using stimulus-based elicitation and free listing, which ensures broad coverage of key domains, as well as opportunities to look at fine-grained relationships between connected ideophones in more detail.

The remaining techniques (sensory ratings, exemplar listing, folk definitions) tackle the question of ideophone meanings from different angles. SENSORY RATING TASKS provide a very broad picture of the sensory modalities involved in an

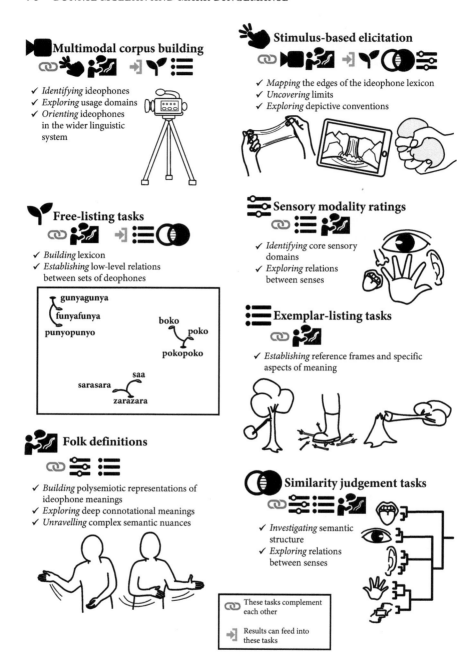

Figure 5.1 A multi-methods toolkit for documentary research on ideophones

ideophone's meaning from a quantitative, multisensory perspective. They can also inform the interpretation of results from other tasks, by providing a hint as to which aspects of meaning to focus on. EXEMPLAR LISTING is useful for establishing specific frames of reference, and for untangling relationships between similar ideophones. For this reason, it pairs well with free-listing data, as free-listing produces semantically close ideophones whose meanings can then be teased apart through a comparison of exemplars. Finally, FOLK DEFINITIONS round out the picture by bringing in an emic perspective on the contrasts most essential to ideophones in the language under study, as well as an opportunity to discuss deeper connotational meanings not touched on in other tasks (see e.g. Badenoch, Purti, and Choksi 2019; Choksi 2020a; Nuckolls 2010a, 2010b). Additionally, the relatively unstructured set-up in this task offers the flexibility to engage with a diversity of semiotic resources—gesture, drawings, stories, etc.—in explaining the meanings of ideophones.

At each step, the techniques provide results that can be used in the analysis and documentation of the ideophone lexicon, from semantic relations to polysemiotic illustrations. Moreover, the analytical insights from the free-listing, sensory rating, and similarity judgement tasks in particular, offer meaningful ways of structuring ideophone dictionaries that go beyond simple alphabetized lists of words, the inadequacy of which has long been noted (e.g. Samarin 1967).

We conclude the chapter with a discussion of ideophone lexicography, showcasing some of the most creative, pioneering examples of ideophone dictionaries today, as well as dreams for the dictionaries of tomorrow. Particular focus is given to *polysemiotic* representations of ideophone meanings—including different types of visual and aural media, gesture, metaphor, stories, and songs—and *dynamic* representations of lexical structure—achieved through tagged, networked lexical entries. From collecting ideophones, to determining their meanings, to representing them lexicographically, we hope that the toolkit presented in this chapter provides a useful guide for engaging with ideophones, those words that are 'such fun to use' (Welmers 1973) and so rewarding to study.

5.2 Collecting ideophones

Ideophones can be defined as 'marked words that depict sensory imagery'. If we wanted to strip this definition down to its most essential parts, we could say that ideophones are lexicalized depictions, as the markedness of ideophones and their connection to sensory imagery arises as a consequence of their depictive nature (for more discussion see Dingemanse 2012).

Looking for ideophones, then, is really about looking for lexicalized depictions. But what are depictions? The simplest way to think about depiction is as a mode of representation that involves *showing* rather than telling. Form–meaning relationships in depictive signs are built on analogical resemblance: aspects of form correspond to aspects of meaning, and small changes in form correspond to small changes in meaning (Taub 2001; Tufvesson 2011). For example, when Japanese speakers hear the ideophone *korokoro*, they imagine a light object rolling. If they hear *gorogoro*, they imagine a heavier object rolling. This is very different to the interpretation of ordinary words, in which small changes in form can correspond to an entirely different meaning (cf. Japanese *koshi* 'lower back' versus *goshi* 'etymology'), or to no meaning at all—a property known as lexical discreteness (Diffloth 1976).

The best place to look for depictions is natural language, which makes MULTIMODAL CORPUS BUILDING an important first step in establishing a class of ideophones in a language. Depictive signs, including ideophones, can be found both in the language of everyday conversation and at the highest levels of verbal art, but the common denominator is usually an attempt to communicate sensory experiences. In day-to-day use, ideophones are common in procedural discourse, particularly with tasks that engage the hands, body, and senses, such as cooking, healing, dancing, building, and crafting (e.g. Badenoch 2021; Hatton 2016; Mihas 2013; Muto 2003; Sakamoto et al. 2014; Tufvesson 2011; Yasui 2023). Ideophones also feature in verbal art, where they make narratives (e.g. Baba 2003; Badenoch, Choksi, et al. 2021; Lydall 2000; Noss 1970; Schaefer 2001), songs (Choksi 2020b; Ibarretxe-Antuñano 2017; Klassen 2000; Zide 1975), poems (Barrett, Webster, and Huumo 2014; Ibarretxe-Antuñano 2017; Kisku, Murmu, and Choksi 2020; Mphande 1992; Noss 1989; Nuckolls 2006; Webster 2008, 2017), and even jokes (Bermúdez 2020; Lydall 2000; Samarin 1969) and weather reports (Van Hoey 2018) more vivid and entertaining. Finally, ideophones feature in media, particularly comics (e.g. Gava 2018; Ibarretxe-Antuñano 2017; Pratha, Avunjian, and Cohn 2016), branding, and advertisements (Bahón-Arnaiz 2021; Ezejideaku and Ugwu 2010; Ibarretxe-Antuñano 2017; Medvediv and Dmytruk 2019), where they are used to engage and appeal to the senses. It hardly needs to be stated that a multimodal approach is ideal here, as researchers of ideophones have long noted that these are frequently accompanied by distinctive gestures and facial expressions which support their meanings (e.g. Diffloth 1972; Kita 1993; Klassen 2000; Kunene 2001; Dingemanse 2015a; Mihas 2013; Nuckolls 2020). Zlatev et al. (2023) provide a detailed account of their building of a multimodal corpus of speech, gesture, and depiction in recordings of Pitjantjatjara and Paamese sand-drawing performances. Although the study doesn't deal with ideophones specifically, it contains excellent methodological insights and strategies for working with and coding for polysemiosis in multimodal corpora, and as depictions the gestures and sand drawings are semiotically similar to ideophones (even though they occur in a different modality).

It is also a good idea to establish a collection of media (videos and pictures) of the things ideophones are used to depict, which can later become a resource for more targeted elicitation, or for the creation of dictionaries. This can be done alongside corpus building. See Section S1 of the online Supplementary Material for some examples.

When analysing corpora, there are three key strategies to look for which can indicate depictive speech. These are framing, foregrounding, and backgrounding (Akita 2021a). Examples of framing include the use of quotative particles, pauses, and isolated clauses to offset the depiction from the speech stream. Examples of foregrounding include the use of prominent intonation (distinctly high or low pitch), a marked voice quality (e.g. creaky voice, harsh voice, whisper), marked loudness (loud or quiet speech), marked speech rate (fast or slow), expressive morphology (e.g. lengthening, reduplication), and marked phonotactics to highlight the depiction. Examples of backgrounding include the use of low pitch, quiet speech, or fast speech to background the surrounding descriptive material and spotlight the depiction (for further discussion see Akita 2021a).

Pay attention to words that occur in these depictive constructions, and which look as if they might together form a coherent, open lexical class. Establishing such a class is usually (or most easily) done on morphophonological criteria. In many cases, it is even possible to identify a set number of morphophonological templates which ideophones employ (for examples see Abubakari 2017; Akita 2009; Diffloth 1976; Mihas 2012; Osada, Purti, and Badenoch 2020; Reiter 2012). Often, ideophones are phonotactically distinct from other native words. They might employ different syllable structures, or exhibit skewed phonotactic distributions. Feature harmony, particularly vowel harmony, is also common, while ideophones in tonal languages may show restricted tonal melodies (Dingemanse 2012).

These differences arise because ideophones use the phonemes of the language differently to how they are used in prosaic vocabulary (Diffloth 1979)—they use them for depictive purposes. For example, Japanese ideophones frequently employ voiced obstruents in the word-initial position, which is exceedingly rare among other native words (Akita 2009). This unusual distribution arises because voiced obstruents serve an important depictive function in the Japanese ideophone lexicon, where alternations between voiced and voiceless obstruents are used to represent semantic differences in intensity (as in the *korokoro* versus *gorogoro* example from earlier) (Hamano 1998; see also Tufvesson 2011 for similar examples in Semai).

Depictive conventions are another key thing to look for when identifying a class of ideophones. Alternations in consonant voicing, vowel quality, tone (where applicable), and nasality are commonly used with evaluative intent to represent differences in suprasensory properties such as size, intensity, and brightness (see Marks 1978: 52ff.). with evaluative intent. For example, vowel quality is used in Korean ideophones to indicate positive or negative evaluations of different colours, smells, and tastes, while the intensity and depth of the taste/smell/colour is depicted using Korean's three-way distinction between plain, tense, and aspirated stops (Rhee 2019; Rhee and Koo 2017).

Even more common are structural alternations such as lengthening and reduplication, or expressive morphology (Zwicky and Pullum 1987), which is commonly used to depict duration and aspect. When used depictively, these processes are often qualitatively and functionally different from their use in e.g. regular processes of inflection and derivation in other word classes. Specifically, they seem to offer more room for on-the-fly modification with analogical iconic interpretations. For example, while other uses of reduplication usually involve a set number of repetitions, depictive uses of reduplication in ideophones can involve varying numbers of repetitions, and even introduce pauses between repetitions, all with a very literal, iconic interpretation (e.g. Dingemanse 2015b; Osada, Purti, and Badenoch 2020).

Once you have uncovered depictive conventions operating in the ideophone system of a language, use of these depictive conventions is one of the best ways to identify particular forms as ideophones. It is also an excellent way to discover new ideophones. For example, for those who know how the Japanese ideophone system works, the existence of an ideophone like *korokoro* implies the possible existence of related ideophones like *gorogoro, kurukuru, guruguru, kirikiri, girigiri*, etc., all with related meanings.

The above methods for identifying ideophones are language-agnostic: they rely on the semiotics of depictive constructions and cross-linguistically attested properties of ideophonic lexical items to identify a lexical class of ideophones in a given language. Once such a class is identified, this will provide a view of relevant language-specific resources, for instance, particular grammatical categories or morphosyntactic devices (Akita 2017; Park 2020; Van Hoey 2023). Ideophones can constitute a distinct grammatical category in the language (e.g. Diffloth 1976; Doke 1935), but they can also straddle multiple categories (e.g. Abubakari 2017; Ameka 2001; Amy Pei-jung 2017; Newman 1968). Across languages, they are often associated with grammatical resources expressing properties and actions, such as adverbs, adjectives, converbs, and verbs, and existing grammatical descriptions may use such terms for ideophonic items.

5.2.1 Targeted techniques

Once you have an idea of how to identify ideophones in the language—using knowledge of their depictive conventions, morphophonological structures, and grammatical categories—it becomes possible to adopt more targeted approaches to collecting them. These should be seen as a supplement to rather than a substitute for corpus building, without which it is impossible to achieve a proper understanding of the broader functions and place of ideophones in a language. However, for internal investigations of the ideophone system, targeted experimental techniques can be very helpful. Here we discuss two such techniques—stimulus-based elicitation and free-listing tasks.

STIMULUS-BASED ELICITATION has its roots in the study of basic colour terms by Berlin and Kay (1969), where the naming of Munsell colour chips was used to identify abstract colour terms and compare their boundaries across languages. The purpose of the research was to identify universal constraints on the development of colour lexicons, although subsequent work has challenged the universality of the original claims (e.g. Haynie and Bowern 2016; Levinson 2000; Lucy 1997). Since Berlin and Kay, researchers have expanded the model to investigate the naming of stimuli in a wide variety of sensory domains (e.g. Majid et al. 2018). Stimulus-based elicitation has much to offer investigations of ideophones. Since ideophones depict sensory imagery, stimuli that target sensory experiences are particularly effective at eliciting them (Tufvesson 2007). And the depictive mode of representation which ideophones employ is expected to lead to certain constraints on their reference (Akita 2013; Dingemanse 2012; McLean 2021), which can be probed with stimulus-based elicitation tasks. Using stimuli also provides an opportunity to design contrasts into the task that can be used to explore depictive conventions.

However, the kinds of stimuli traditionally employed in these tasks are not necessarily the most appropriate for ideophones, and so applying this methodology to ideophones requires some rethinking. Figure 5.2 is a typical example of the type of

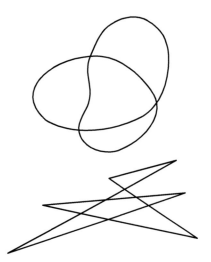

Figure 5.2 Unidimensional shape stimuli
Source: Köhler (1929)

stimuli used in these (comparative) studies.[1] The stimuli are designed to represent shapes, and so every other aspect of the stimuli—their size, colour, etc.—is kept constant. The shape of the stimuli then becomes the only thing participants can talk about. This design is very good for comparability, but it has some downsides when used with ideophones. One is that ideophones rarely encode single percepts. For example, there is an ideophone in Mundari that can be used for pointed things, *suisui*, but it's unlikely that a Mundari speaker would use it in response to the pointed shape in Figure 5.2, because it also encodes much more than that: it is used to talk about things like green rice shoots, and conveys a sense of health and vitality of something growing tall and well (Osada, Purti, and Badenoch 2019b). Rather than single percepts, the meanings of ideophones frequently encode *clusters* of sensations (e.g. Akita 2012; Badenoch 2021; Diffloth 1972; Nuckolls 2019; Samarin 1967), which are not necessarily evoked by abstract, unidimensional stimuli.

This is a well-known problem when imposing an etic perspective on language structure, to the neglect of the emic perspective (Pike 1967). On the other hand, without some kind of etic grid we lose the ability to make comparisons between languages (Dingemanse 2012). It is possible, however, to make space for both perspectives. One way is to standardize the structure of the elicitation task, but localize the stimuli (Tufvesson 2007).

Table S1 in the online Supplementary Material (https://osf.io/q8a6n/) presents a framework for how to structure a stimulus-based elicitation task to investigate the use (and non-use) of ideophones in key domains, while also exploring depictive conventions (semantic domains are based on previous work by Ibarretxe-Antuñano 2019; Van Hoey 2023). The domains are based on where we find *lexical gaps* in the ideophone systems of various languages. The distribution of these gaps across languages appears to be non-random, and driven by the depictive affordances of speech. This has led researchers to propose an *implicational hierarchy* for the semantic development of ideophone lexicons (Akita 2013; Dingemanse 2012; Kilian-Hatz 2001; McLean 2021): SOUND < MOVEMENT < FORM < TEXTURE < OTHER SENSORY PERCEPTIONS. The hierarchy predicts that languages possessing ideophones in one domain in the hierarchy will also possess ideophones in all domains *preceding* that domain. The last category in the hierarchy is deliberately vague, as the distribution of ideophones in these later domains is less predictable and is very likely influenced more by cultural preoccupations than depictive affordances (see discussion in McLean 2021). However, based on currently attested distributions, LIGHT, COLOUR, TASTE, SMELL, THERMOCEPTION, INTEROCEPTION, and EMOTION are suggested as relevant subcategories. Stimulus-based elicitation is an excellent means to test the predictions of the hierarchy in different languages, while also offering a starting point for exploring key corners of an ideophone lexicon.

---

[1] Taken from the classic malume-takete stimuli used in experimental research on sound symbolism (Köhler 1929).

It is also an excellent way to investigate depictive conventions, and added dimensionality is provided in Table S1 by contrasting suprasensory properties, particularly INTENSITY, QUALITY, DURATION, and EVALUATION (see Section S1 of the online Supplementary Materials for more details). Depictive language is particularly apt at encoding fine-grained, gradient distinctions in suprasensory properties. Eliciting contrasts in these suprasensory properties thus both encourages the use of ideophones, and also provides an opportunity to investigate depictive conventions and how these transfer between different sensory domains.

The stimuli chosen to represent these contrasts can then be decided on an individual basis, according to the goals of the particular study. For instance, comparative studies may wish to aim for a greater degree of standardization than studies of individual languages, where stimuli can be more localized. Our recommendation is to focus on ecologically relevant stimuli that evoke the rich, multisensory experiences of life. For example, Figure 5.3 presents some options for stimuli that may be better suited to elicit ideophones for curved and spiky shapes than the abstract unidimensional contrast of Figure 5.2. Further examples can be found in Section S1 of the online Supplementary Materials.

Figure 5.3 Multidimensional shape stimuli

The main caveat when using multidimensional stimuli is that it introduces greater room for uncertainty around which aspects of stimuli the elicited ideophones respond to (Samarin 1967). For this reason, the meanings of ideophones elicited during these tasks should never be taken for granted, but investigated in their own right at a later date. It is recommended to keep the tasks of collecting ideophones and investigating their meanings separate, as asking too many questions about the meanings of ideophones elicited using a stimulus kit not only slows down the task, but could also lead participants to use fewer ideophones in their responses if they feel the researcher is not able to understand them (see discussion in Diatka 2014: 32). Further guidance on the use of stimulus-based elicitation in linguistic fieldwork can be found in Majid (2012).

Stimulus-based elicitation is a good technique to map out the edges of the ideophone lexicon, and establish its limits. It is also very good for investigating depictive conventions. However, one limitation of stimulus-based elicitation is that it forces ideophones into particular sensory domains, when in reality the meanings of most ideophones straddle multiple domains (e.g. Badenoch 2021; Badenoch, Osada, et al. 2021; Nuckolls 2019). This is why in Figure 5.1 we recommend combining stimulus-based elicitation with sensory rating tasks (Section 5.3), as the sensory rating task allows for the exploration of multisensory aspects of ideophone meanings. For example, the core sensory domains used for stimulus-based elicitation (e.g. the domains in Table S1 in the Supplementary Materials) can also be used as the sensory domains on which these elicited ideophones are rated during sensory rating tasks, allowing researchers to explore the overlap between different domains and patterns of multisensoriality. Of course, a limitation of the domains proposed here is that they are informed by a Western model of the senses, based on divisions made in English. They may not necessarily form natural divisions in other languages, which is why it is also important to also investigate the emic perspective on the structure of the ideophone lexicon using techniques like similarity judgement tasks (Section 5.4) and folk definitions (Section 5.3), which centre the perspectives of ideophone users themselves, as suggested in Figure 5.1.

Another limitation of stimulus-based elicitation is that it is quite involved and time-consuming, which can be tiring for research participants. Stimulus-based elicitation is thus not a practical way to collect large numbers of ideophones. If this is the aim, then it is better to use less involved methods, like FREE-LISTING. There are two ways in which free-listing can be used as a technique to study ideophones. The first is to decide on a set of semantic domains (e.g. water sounds, animal movements, textures of food, etc.—see Table S1 for more ideas), and ask participants to list all the ideophones they can think of in each domain. A second way is to decide on a set of ideophones, and ask participants to list all the other ideophones that come to mind in relation to each of these ideophones. As Felix Ameka once said, 'ideophones are first and foremost a type of words' (Ameka 2001: 26), and speakers usually have a metalinguistic awareness of this that makes it possible to ask for 'more words of the same kind'. The technique can even be applied in a brute-force way to elicit examples of any kind of ideophone (regardless of semantic domain) (e.g. Murasugi and Akita 2021). However, as with all the methods presented here, the lexical status of elicited items should never be taken at face value. The ideophone class in any language can have fuzzy boundaries, and participants can include non-ideophonic words that show formal or semantic similarities to ideophones in their responses to these tasks. Morphophonological tests and semiotic analysis (as discussed in Section 5.2) can help to clarify the status of elicited words. Further analysis may also provide valuable evidence about folk conceptions of word classes and linguistic structures, and bring to light processes of language change that enable traffic between ideophonic and prosaic lexical strata.

Free-listing is not only a means of data collection. Although on the surface the technique appears very simple, the data produced in free-listing studies can be quantitatively analysed in ways that yield rich insights into the structure of different corners of the ideophone lexicon. Psychologists have long used free-listing data to study the organization of the mental lexicon (e.g. Deese 1965), which can then be visualized using techniques like multidimensional scaling (see Figure 5.4 for an example). Medin et al. (2010) illustrate the application of this technique to free-listing data on 'animals'. Several Japanese studies have also applied these techniques to data from stimulus-based elicitation, in the domains of food textures (Hanada 2020), surface textures (Doizaki, Watanabe, and Sakamoto 2017;

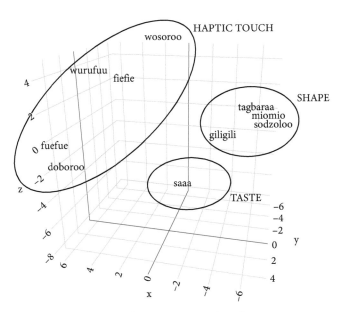

Figure 5.4 MDS plot showing relationships between Siwu ideophones

Sakamoto and Watanabe 2017), and surface appearance (Hanada 2016). However, these are all lab-based studies using very large stimulus kits, which may be difficult to replicate in a fieldwork setting. The MDS plot in Figure 5.4 was built using data from a similarity judgement task (see Section 5.4), and shows different sensory-based clusters of Siwu ideophones. As suggested in Figure 5.1, similarity judgement tasks make good follow-up studies to free-listing tasks, as the free-listing data can be used as stimuli for the similarity judgement task.

5.3 Determining the meanings of ideophones

One of the most challenging aspects of working with ideophones involves understanding and explaining their meanings. As an illustration, the authors of one Zulu dictionary found that entries for ideophones took an average of three times longer to compile than the entries for any other word class (de Schryver 2009). In this section, we introduce three types of data that can make unravelling the meanings of ideophones more manageable: sensory ratings, exemplars, and folk definitions.

SENSORY RATING TASKS, in which participants are asked to rate on a Likert scale how strongly they experience the meaning of different words through the various senses (e.g. by hearing, by seeing, by touching, by tasting, by smelling, etc.), are increasingly common in psycholinguistics, but have so far been underused in research on ideophones (though see Iida and Akita 2023; Yaguchi 2011 for some examples)—a key opportunity given the complex clusters of sensory information encoded in ideophones (see e.g. Diffloth 1972; Nuckolls 2019), and the burgeoning popularity of perceptual norming studies (e.g. Lynott et al. 2020). Early studies used the traditional five-senses model (e.g. Chen et al. 2019; Lynott and Connell 2009; Miklashevsky 2018; Morucci, Bottini, and Crepaldi 2019; Speed and Majid 2017), but recent approaches have introduced ratings of interoception (experienced 'by sensations inside the body') as well (Speed and Brybaert 2021). As we have already seen, interoceptive senses can also be relevant to the meanings of ideophones, and so a six-sense model is recommended for ideophones as well. As the visual domain is very broad, with subcomponents that do not appear to be equally treated in ideophone lexicons worldwide (McLean 2021), researchers applying this method to ideophones may also wish to further subdivide the visual domain into components like movement, form, light, and colour (see Table S1 in the online Supplementary Materials for examples).

Sensory ratings provide a means of representing the multisensory aspects of ideophone meanings. For example, the Japanese ideophone *ʤaraʤara* receives equivalently high ratings in the visual, auditory, and tactile modalities (with mean ratings of 4.56, 4.89, and 4.36 respectively) (Yaguchi 2011). It is used for things like bangles and keys and coins, and conveys a holistic impression of jangling

A MULTI-METHODS TOOLKIT FOR DOCUMENTARY RESEARCH   87

sounds, the hardness of the objects, and appearance of things all jumbled up. Sensory ratings can also be helpful when trying to understand connections between the variety of situations in which an ideophone is used, which can sometimes be confusing. For example, Badenoch (2021: 20) discusses the Santali ideophone *sɔ̄i-sɔ̄i*, which he found referred to such seemingly diverse situations as pre-boiling water, the darting forward of a snake as it strikes, and the flight of an arrow to its target. He eventually identified three core components of meaning linking these disparate uses: a *whiish* sound (of the small bubbles in the water, the snake moving across the ground, and the arrow moving through the air); a quick, straight movement (of the bubbles shooting to the surface, the snake shooting forward, or the arrow shooting through the air); and a sense of anticipation (of the water boiling, the snake biting, and the arrow hitting its target). Sensory ratings can facilitate such semantic investigations by providing a hint as to which *aspects* of the holistic sensory experiences depicted by ideophones are most central to their meanings, whether the sound, the image, or the emotions evoked in each situation.

The collection of these sensory scenes can also be formalized in EXEMPLAR LISTING TASKS. In an exemplar listing task, participants are provided with a list of ideophones and, for each ideophone, are asked to provide examples of things or situations to which the ideophone can refer (e.g. O'Meara, Kung, and Majid 2019; Ruts et al. 2004; Samarin 1970; Shepard 1999; Wnuk, Laophairoj, and Majid 2020; Wnuk and Majid 2014). As with the Santali example above, key elements of the ideophone's meaning can then be extracted from the variety of situations in which it is used. Exemplar listing data can also be helpful when dealing with sets of related ideophones as relevant aspects of meaning often become clear when items in the set are contrasted (Badenoch 2021; Samarin 1967). Again, Badenoch (2021) provides an illustration of this, in a comparison of Mundari ideophones for different textures of *dal*, a type of lentil curry:

lidapada—perfect dal, thick enough to scoop with roti (flatbread) without it falling off, beans are full and soft. Thick and stiff.

ladapada—dal that was *lidapada* but has been overcooked so the beans are starting to break down, there's less water, and it becomes too sticky. Thick and all in a mush.

ledepede—dal that is suitable for eating with rice; the shape of the beans is almost gone and it's more like a paste. Thin and slick.

lodopodo—dal that could have been *ledepede* but too much water was used in the cooking and it was cooked too long. Thin and sticky.

In considering the ideophones in relation to each other, key aspects of their meaning—such as the amount of water, the degree to which the beans are broken down, and the resulting stickiness— become apparent. It is therefore recommended when conducting an exemplar listing task to list ideophones with similar meanings together. This encourages the use of more informative exemplars that highlight differences between meanings. When items are presented in isolation, participants may simply provide an exemplar like 'dal' for *lidapada*, *ladapada*, *ledepede*, and *lodopodo*. By presenting these words together, exemplars are likely to be much more elaborate (e.g. 'dal for eating with roti'). For this reason, ideophones collected using the free listing method described in Section 5.2.1 make very good items on exemplar-listing tasks.

One limitation of the techniques discussed so far is that the analysis of meaning is largely through categories identified by the researcher. This neglects the emic perspective, which is why these tasks should be seen as supplements to rather than replacements for the core source of information about the meaning of ideophones—speakers themselves. FOLK DEFINITIONS provide perhaps the richest source of data on the meanings of ideophones. These are informal paraphrases explaining the meaning of a targeted word or group of words, collected in the language under study, and video-recorded to capture multimodal features such as gesture, facial expressions, and enactments that contribute to the explication (see Dingemanse 2015a for a complete guide). It may also be useful to provide participants with a pen and paper (or other drawing materials) that they can use to assist in their explications, or if discussing ideophones for which you have exemplars, to bring either the exemplars themselves or photographs or videos of these exemplars that the participants can refer to. For example, if the ideophones under study were elicited using stimuli, then it is good to use these stimuli when discussing them.

Many of the techniques speakers use to explain the meanings of ideophones— listing contexts of use, or referring to related ideophones as semantic anchoring points—overlap with the targeted techniques we have already discussed, providing some external validation for the usefulness of these methods. However, through folk definitions we have the opportunity to see the paths speakers take to make these links, which may not overlap with the paths taken by the analyst. The free setup employed in folk definitions, which contrasts with the highly structured nature of the other tasks, also provides an opportunity for speakers to engage with multiple semiotic resources—e.g. gesture, pictures, drawings, stories, metaphors—to explain the meanings of ideophones. These are often highly effective at communicating ideophone meanings, in ways that are hard to achieve through prosaic language alone.

For example, Nuckolls et al. (2017) provide some striking illustrations of how bodily and vocal performances can lead to better definitions of ideophone meanings. Using the example of the Pastaza Kichwa ideophone *polang*, the authors discuss how examining bodily performances accompanying this ideophone led to a 'light-bulb' moment that unified apparently disparate uses of the ideophone to refer to canoes gliding across the water, and animals floating upwards towards the surface. They noticed that in many of their video recordings participants seemed to 'become' the floating objects they were describing, particularly through their eye gaze. If the perspective of *polang* is from the object in the water, they realized, then "there is relatively little difference between gliding and floating upwards and gliding or floating across the surface of the water. Both involve movements that are done with relative ease, a minimum of effort, and an absence of thrashing" (Nuckolls et al. 2017: 166). This led them to propose the revised definition of *polang*: "Simulates a gliding movement *from underwater* to the surface or across water. Repetitions simulate bobbing movements" (Nuckolls et al. 2017: 166; emphasis is our own).

As another example of how multimodal representations can illuminate meaning where words fail, Dingemanse (2015a: 228) describes how the distinction between the Siwu ideophones *gìlìgìlì* and *minimini*—both of which have to do with roundness—became clear to him only after comparing the types of gestures that speakers used for them in folk definitions. He noticed that people consistently gestured *gìlìgìlì* by tracing circles in the air with their index finger, while for *minimini* they consistently moulded a sphere with both hands. From this it became clear that the difference between the two was a matter of dimension; *giligili* depicts a flat circular shape, while *minimini* depicts a sphere. Similarly, Badenoch et al. (2021) provide several examples of how gestures accompanying folk definitions of Mundari ideophones were helpful in extracting core features of their meanings.

As well as illuminating fine-grained semantic details, different performance strategies can more generally provide an indication of the kinds of sensory meanings an ideophone encodes. Sound ideophones, for instance, are less likely to be accompanied by gesture (Hatton 2016; Mihas 2013; Nuckolls 2020), but may be performed in qualitatively different voices, or even accompanied by vocal depictions (Akita 2021b; Badenoch, Choksi, et al. 2021). Ideophones relating to movement are most likely to occur with gestures depicting the type of movement, while eye gaze or tracing gestures may be used to indicate the path or direction of the movement (Kita 1997; Mihas 2013; Nuckolls 2020; Reiter 2012). Nuckolls (2020) conducted an in-depth analysis of gestures used with Pastaza Kichwa ideophones. She found that ideophones relating to shape frequently occurred with tracing and moulding gestures, or bounding gestures[2] to indicate an expanse of visual phenomena. Colour ideophones also frequently occurred with bounding gestures. Mihas (2013) found that ideophones depicting internal sensations are less likely to occur with gesture in general, but when they do occur with gesture this often involves deictic (pointing) gestures on the body indicating the origin of

---

[2] Bounding gestures are gestures involving the use of the fingers or hands to depict figurative distance or spatial extent. For an example, see the gestures with the Pastaza Quechua ideophone *shinki*, available at https://quechuarealwords.byu.edu/?ideophone=shinki (Nuckolls 2021).

the feeling. Anecdotally, Japanese ideophones for pain and emotions seem to frequently occur with distinctive facial expressions (some examples can be found in Akita 2019). Taste and smell ideophones are not as well investigated, but it appears that gesture may be rarer with these ideophones (Mihas 2013). A typology of vocal and bodily performances occurring with ideophones of different types is an important area for future research.

A final source of multimodal explications of ideophones which has not yet been explored, but which we believe has some potential, is games of charades.[3] These games are particularly suited to the study of ideophone meanings as they are highly performative, and require participants to home in on specific meanings, while distinguishing related meanings. Not only that, but they provide an excellent opportunity to collect data from a wider variety of participants than one might generally consult within a fieldwork setting. A real-life example involving Japanese ideophones, and available on YouTube, is provided in the online Supplementary Materials (Section S1). It is particularly informative to consider how the pantomimers alter their performances in response to incorrect guesses. For example, after the other participants incorrectly guess *puyopuyo* 'pudgy' for a gesture intended to represent the ideophone *boyon* 'blubbery', the pantomimer dramatically slows down and widens her gestures, at which point the other participants are then able to guess the ideophone correctly.

5.4 Representing ideophones lexicographically

Having collected all this information, the final challenge researchers of ideophones face is how to represent these words lexicographically. In this section, we discuss how the meanings of ideophones can be conveyed, what information might be included in ideophone entries in a dictionary, and how these dictionaries can be structured. The main conclusion is that ideophones require polysemiotic representations, adapted to their specific sensory properties. That is, different types of media and modes of representation are appropriate for different ideophones (see Akita 2016).

Lexical entries for ideophones can also benefit from a different structure to entries for other words. Some things to include are relevant sensory modalities, notes on cooccurring gestures or expressive pronunciations, phonosemantic mappings, references to related ideophones and the differences between them, and notes on collocational information and background frames.

---

[3] Pictionary could also be a good game to try if you want to collect visual representations of ideophone meanings, e.g. for use in lexicographic materials (see Section 5.4).

Finally, we discuss how ideophone dictionaries can be structured in a way that highlights the connections between different ideophones, the structure of the ideophone lexicon as a whole, and the depictive conventions operating in the wider ideophone system. This can be achieved through extensive use of tagging, and dynamic network visualizations that provide holistic representations of relations and structure in the ideophone lexicon.

5.4.1 Polysemiotic representations

Some of the most pioneering examples of ideophone dictionaries have exploited multiple modalities to represent ideophone meanings. Paper dictionaries, for example, have made heavy use of the visual modality; some examples are given in Figures 5.5, 5.6, and 5.7. Figure 5.5 is taken from Janis Nuckolls's seminal monograph *Sounds Like Life* (Nuckolls 1996), a third of which is devoted to a series of appendices describing, exemplifying, and illustrating the meanings of Pastaza Kichwa ideophones, often using elegant diagrams of hypothesized underlying sensory schemes. Depictive prosody is also captured through innovative typography in example sentences, shown in Figure 5.6. Here, the relative typographical height of ideophone tokens stands in analogical relation to the pitch at which it is pronounced.

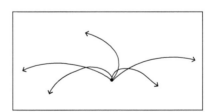

DEFINITION Describes expanded or random movement from or within a locus, by one or more entities or agents. Aspectually aorist, durative.

COMMENT *Sa* describes not a neat radial pattern, marked by symmetry and balance, but, rather, the disorderly order

Figure 5.5 Lexical entry for *sa*
Source: Nuckolls (1996: 145). Reproduced with permission.

16. Ña   apari-sha,   waska-ndi ña   sa $^{sa\ sa}$ ichari-shka
    then carry-COR   rope-both   now   sprinkle-PERF

"Then, carrying (the basket) with the rope, she sprinkled it *sa* $^{sa\ sa}$."

Figure 5.6 Example sentence for *sa*
Source: Nuckolls (1996: 147). Reproduced with permission.

noso noso [A][B]　　のそのそ

Describes moving slowly, clumsily. Often used to describe the movement of large people and animals. Lumbering

動きが鈍いさま。体が大きい人や動物の動きを表すことが多い。

Figure 5.7 Lexical entry for *nosonoso*
Source: taken from Gomi (1989) as below.

Figure 5.7 comes from another classic, Taro Gomi's (1989) *Illustrated Dictionary of Japanese Onomatopoeic Expressions*. Comparing the visual representations of ideophone meaning in Figure 5.5 and Figure 5.7 is itself a lesson in semantic typology. The illustrations for Pastaza Kichwa ideophones are very simple and underspecified compared to the illustrations for Japanese ideophones, which contain much more information—reflecting their highly specific frames (Akita 2012). For example, *nosonoso* does not refer to just any kind of slow, clumsy movement, but specifically evokes the lumbering of large people and animals. Pastaza Kichwa movement ideophones, on the other hand, take a much wider variety of referents (tokens of *sa*, for instance, find it referring to salt, logs, clothes, sea turtles, or even entire tribes of people; see Nuckolls 1996: 146). Pastaza Kichwa ideophones evoke very purely the type of movement, as Nuckolls's illustrations capture. Drawings of ideophone meanings are thus not only a tool to represent those meanings, but also a means of analysing them, especially when collected in large numbers from speakers themselves (e.g. through folk definitions, or games of pictionary).

The latest iteration in Nuckolls's documentation of Pastaza Kichwa ideophones is an online dictionary, called *Kichwa Realwords* (see Nuckolls et al. 2017; links to *Kichwa Realwords* and the other online dictionaries mentioned in this section are provided in the online Supplementary Material). Nuckolls actually refers to it as an 'anti-dictionary', because it defines Pastaza Kichwa ideophones not in terms of other words, but through video clips containing expressive gestures and vocalizations.

The effectiveness of multimedia representations of ideophone meanings (in comparison to verbal paraphrases) has been quantitatively investigated by Akita (2016), who found Japanese speakers were much better able to identify the intended ideophone when its dictionary definition was accompanied by an image or a video. Akita highlights the importance of adapting the choice of media to the sensory semantics of the ideophone. For example, photographs were better at representing ideophone meanings relating to texture, videos were best for movement, and cartoon (*manga*) drawings were best at representing emotions and inner sensations. Even then, the meanings of some ideophones were very challenging. For example, neither the dictionary definition nor the cartoon illustration used for the ideophone *gangan* '(e.g. one's head) pounding' provided the level of referential specificity needed to distinguish this ideophone from the related ideophone *zukizuki* '(e.g. one's head) throbbing'. Akita suggests that the addition of a metaphor referring to the clanging sound that *gangan* originally imitates may have helped participants to single out the intended ideophone in this instance.

A Multimedia Encyclopedia of Mundari Expressives (McLean and Purti 2018) is another resource that makes use of polysemiotic representations to convey the meanings of ideophones. It uses images, videos, stories, and songs. The stories and songs were particularly helpful in conveying the meanings of ideophones encoding emotion, by stimulating those emotions in the same way that the ideophones stimulate them for speakers of Mundari. For example, to explain the meaning of the ideophone *akul-bakul* 'so angry one cannot speak' Madhu Purti, masterful Mundari speaker and co-author of the *Dictionary of Mundari Expressives* (Osada,

Purti, and Badenoch 2019a), described a night when she was staying in a student dorm for women only, and one of the other women in the dorm brought a boy back to their (shared) room. She said the boy was her brother but everyone knew he was really her boyfriend; that night Madhu was really feeling *akul-bakul*. Recorded folk definitions (Section 5.3) are a useful source of these kinds of polysemiotic representations of ideophone meanings.

Table 5.1 summarizes strategies for representing ideophone meanings that make use of multiple semiotic resources, organized according to the relevant sensory domain. For smell and taste ideophones, as well as photographs of things exhibiting these smells and tastes, photographs of people's facial expressions when they experience these smells/tastes were also included. Further examples of ideophone dictionaries that make use of these different techniques are provided in Section S2 of the online Supplementary Materials.

Table 5.1 Strategies for representing ideophone meanings

Ideophone type	Techniques for representation
SOUND	• Expressive recordings of the ideophone (e.g. with distinctive voice qualities) • Expressive vocal renditions of the depicted sound • Videos of objects, people, or animals producing the depicted sounds • Sound effects
MOVEMENT	• Videos of things illustrating the movement (include the sounds produced) • Videos of gestures depicting the movement
SHAPE	• Videos of gestures depicting the shape • Photographs of things exhibiting the shape
COLOUR	• Photographs or videos of things exhibiting the colour (videos will be necessary for changing colours)
TEXTURE	• Photographs of things exhibiting the texture • Videos of things exhibiting the texture. The relevant tactile properties can be illustrated by manipulating the object, e.g. through poking, shaking, stretching, scratching, biting, or chewing (include the sounds produced) • Videos of gestures depicting the texture
TASTE	• Photographs of things possessing the taste • Photographs of facial expressions associated with the taste
SMELL	• Photographs of things possessing the smell • Photographs of facial expressions associated with the smell

Ideophone type	Techniques for representation
INTEROCEPTION	• Videos of gestures depicting the sensation and/or indicating the location of the sensation • Stories or short cartoons illustrating the sensation (including the situations which produce it) • Metaphors illustrating the sensation through something more tangible
EMOTION	• Stories or short cartoons illustrating the emotion (including the situations which produce it) • Songs conveying the same emotion • Metaphors illustrating the emotion through something more tangible

5.4.2 Detailed lexical entries

The same things that make the lexical entries of prosaic words informative—e.g. collocational information, semantic relations, and usage examples—also enrich the lexical entries of ideophones. In addition, there are certain features of ideophones that lexicographers may want to keep track of through lexical entries that are not necessarily as relevant to other word classes. For example, as the meanings of ideophones are so strongly tied to the senses, many ideophone dictionaries include information about sensory modalities in their lexical entries (Van Hoey and Thompson 2020). An example is shown in Figure 5.8, taken from *Kichwa Realwords*. Notice that the sensory domains are also hyperlinked. Linking to sensory domains supports the definitions in ideophone dictionaries by providing users with a point of access to these meanings through relevant senses. Sensory rating tasks, as discussed in Section 5.3, are an excellent source for this information.

The lexical entry in Figure 5.8 also has a section for paralinguistic information. In this case, it includes notes on how the initial bilabial in the ideophone *bhux* is strongly aspirated "to imitate an idea of a forceful burst out of water." Highlighting the connections between form and meaning in the lexical entries for ideophones can be very helpful, not only for understanding the meanings of individual ideophones, but also to provide a sense of depictive conventions operating across the wider lexicon as a whole, which can assist in the understanding of other ideophones as well. Stimulus-based elicitation, as discussed in Section 5.2.1, is a good technique for exploring these depictive conventions.

Phonosemantic mappings can even be cross-referenced across different entries. The online dictionary of Japanese ideophones, *Onomatopedia* (Imaginary Sound Creations 2018), achieves something similar to this through the use of semantic

BHUX

Pronunciation	[bux]
Related Ideophones	<u>polan</u>, <u>suni</u>, <u>tsupu</u>, <u>tupu</u>
Definition	An energetic bursting out of water by a freshwater dolphin
Sensory Modality	<u>MOVEMENT</u> > <u>Configurational</u> <u>MOVEMENT</u> > <u>Haptic</u> <u>MOVEMENT</u> <u>SOUND</u> <u>VISUAL</u>
Paralinguistic Description	Initial bilabial is strongly aspirated to imitate an idea of a forceful burst out of water. Final velar fricative is often expressively drawn out to imitate the duration of the movement of what is bursting out of water.

Figure 5.8 Lexical entry for *bhux*

Source: Nuckolls (2021). Reproduced with permission.

tags. All entries in the dictionary are tagged for semantic components, and users can click on a tag to see all the other entries in the dictionary sharing that tag. An example is shown in Figure 5.9. Being able to view ideophones with similar meanings together, and compare their formal features, allows users to gain intuitions about phonosemantic associations that lead to a deeper understanding of ideophone meanings. The reverse kind of searching would also be useful to implement, so that users could, for example, click on a tag to see all other ideophones with initial /k/, or all ideophones with medial /r/, along the lines of Hamano (1998). One of the hallmarks of true proficiency with ideophones is the ability to invent and interpret novel ideophones. Creating a dictionary of ideophones is therefore not only about creating a record of existing forms and meanings (which in iconic lexicons can go out of fashion relatively quickly, see e.g. Flaksman 2017), but perhaps even more importantly it is about conveying an understanding of *possible* forms and meanings, based on depictive conventions that are much longer-lasting.

Finally, many ideophones exhibit a kind of symbiotic relationship with paralinguistic features such as voice quality and gesture, which tap into and support core elements of the ideophone's meaning. As an illustration, in his survey of Bantu ideophones, William Samarin revealed that "some of the meanings I isolated were based almost exclusively on gestures," and that it was impossible to get speakers to use some of these ideophones without gesturing (Samarin 1971: 153). Ideophones depicting emotion often have a similar relationship with voice quality. While perhaps not impossible, it would at least involve a great deal of cognitive dissonance to produce the Japanese ideophone *wakuwaku* 'excited' using a deadpan intonation. In these cases, paralinguistic features like gesture and intonation can be considered as part and parcel of an ideophone's usage, in which case there should be a place for these in the lexical entry—just as there is a place for things like part of speech, or grammatical gender. Again, folk definitions (Section 5.3) are a useful source for this kind of information.

Figure 5.9 Searching for the tag 'curve'
Onomatopedia (Imaginary Sound Creations 2018)

5.4.3 Meaningfully structured interfaces

The final decision lexicographers make is how they want users to interact with their dictionary—ideally in ways that say something meaningful about the *operation* of the ideophone lexicon as a whole. We have already seen from *Onomatopedia* how tagging can be an effective way to uncover depictive conventions, and reveal connections between sets of related ideophones. But what if we want to zoom out to get a sense of relations in the wider lexicon as a whole?

SIMILARITY JUDGEMENT TASKS are one principled way to investigate the semantic structure of ideophone lexicons. They can be conducted in different ways. One approach—called pile sorting—is to present participants with ideophones on cards, and ask them to arrange the ideophones they feel belong together into groups (Dingemanse and Majid 2012). This is the fastest way, but it requires participants to be literate in the language under study. Another way is to present participants with triads of ideophones, and ask them to choose the odd one out each time (see Wnuk and Majid 2014 for an example). This does not require literacy, but it can take a lot longer as every possible combination of triads needs to be tested. To the best of our knowledge, these procedures have only been tested with ideophones in one language, Siwu (in Dingemanse and Majid 2012). The results revealed a lexicon structured primarily around fine-grained aspects of sensory perception, which is also how many lexicographers have independently chosen to structure ideophone dictionaries (*Onomatopedia* and *Kichwa Realwords*, for example, are both structured in this way). However, some interesting information which came out of this analysis was that ideophones relating to sound, sight, and touch, for example, were more closely connected than ideophones relating to taste, which formed an outgroup. Furthermore, shape ideophones were more closely grouped with ideophones for textures than they were with ideophones relating to aspects of surface appearance (particularly colour). This is also in line with how we think about relationships between the senses in ideophone lexicons cross-linguistically (McLean 2021).

Networks can be an effective way to visualize relationships between ideophones, and offer users a dynamic way to interact with ideophone lexicons and become familiar with their structure. We used the programming language R (R Core Team, 2022) together with the R packages *shiny* (Chang et al. 2020) and *visNetwork* (Almende, Thieurmel, and Robert 2019) to create some toy examples, the code for which is provided in the online Supplementary Materials. Figure 5.10 shows some of the top-level structure in the Siwu ideophone lexicon, based on the analysis in Dingemanse and Majid (2012).

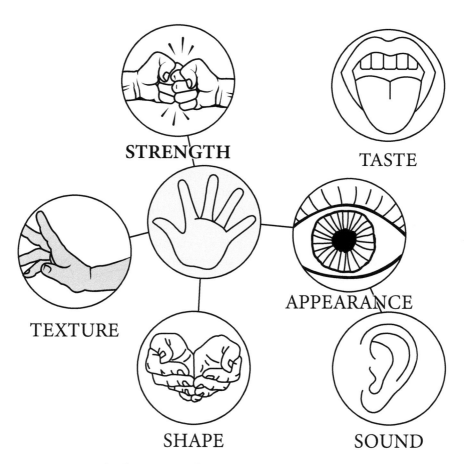

Figure 5.10 Top-level structure in the Siwu ideophone lexicon
Based on analysis in Dingemanse and Majid (2012)

Choosing a node leads to an expanded network of ideophones in each domain, as shown in Figure 5.11. The internal nodes in Figure 5.11 have been given abstract semantic labels following the analysis in Dingemanse and Majid (2012). Another possibility would be to use collocates of the daughter nodes from the prosaic lexicon. For example, the Japanese ideophones in Figure 5.9 could be grouped together under the verbal collocate *magaru* 'curve', which they all share. Double-clicking on a node allows users to expand or contract clusters of ideophones as they explore the lexicon. The visualization is available to explore at https://doi.org/10.5281/zenodo.14598830.

We created a second toy example of an interactive dictionary, this time using Japanese ideophones. In this example, users can hover over an ideophone to find a link to the lexical entry for that ideophone. We also show how multimedia (e.g. images and short videos) can be incorporated into the network visualization. The example with Japanese ideophones is available online at https://doi.org/10.5281/zenodo.14598876, and in the online supplementary material. The visualizations are derived from a file containing a list of nodes, and another file containing a list of connections between different nodes (or edges). These files are available in the online Supplementary Materials.

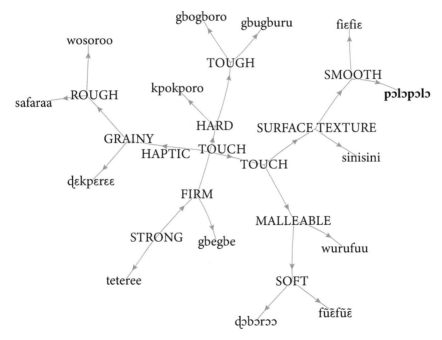

Figure 5.11 Network representation of Siwu ideophones
Based on analysis in Dingemanse and Majid (2012)

5.5 Conclusions, future directions

We began this chapter with the observation that traditional dictionaries frequently fall short of capturing the meanings of ideophones, and by now we hope to have covered some ways in which we can do better—starting from the very first stages of the investigation of ideophones in the language. While the focus of the chapter has been on documentation, in concluding we would like to highlight the theoretical insights that richer documentation can provide along the way.

We began by talking about multimodal corpora, tagged for markers of depictions. This was presented as a means of identifying and collecting ideophones, but such corpora are much more than simply a means to an end. They pave the way for a broader typology of depiction in language, including ideophones but also related phenomena, such as demonstrations, reported speech, iconic gestures, and the interactions between these, offering insights into the interplay between language-specificity and possible universality in depictive modes of communication (Ferrara and Hodge 2018).

We have emphasized the value of polysemiotic representations as an effective way to convey the meanings of ideophones. However, such representations can also be an object of study in themselves (Zlatev et al. 2023). We saw a glimpse of this when comparing the representation of Japanese versus Pastaza Kichwa ideophones through the medium of drawings, which led to insights into the encoding of meaning in the ideophone systems of each language. In analysing how meaning is transferred from one semiotic system to another, we have an opportunity to better understand the nature of these systems themselves.

Finally, we explored creative ways of presenting and interacting with ideophone dictionaries that better capture relational structure in the ideophone lexicon, and make visible underlying depictive conventions. The ephemeral nature of ideophones and the immense flexibility with which new forms and meanings are dynamically constructed in ideophone lexicons necessitated this. However, through this experience we have also seen how these dictionaries can be transformed from records of the ideophone system of a language, into tools for understanding it.

This raises the question: What other insights might we be missing not only in relation to ideophones, but also in other word classes, simply because existing tools were 'good enough'? Ideophones, by requiring the kind of multi-methods approach presented here, also teach us how we can do better at documentary linguistics in general, and we encourage readers to use these approaches not only where they must, but also wherever they can.

Supplementary Material

The supplementary material can be found online at https://osf.io/q8a6n/

Acknowledgements and Funding

MD acknowledges funding from Dutch Research Council grant NWO Vidi 016.vidi.185.205. The authors would also like to thank John Huisman for creating the illustrations in Figure 5.1. For the purpose of Open Access the authors have applied a CC BY public copyright licence to any Author Accepted Manuscript version arising from this submission.

References

Abubakari, Hasiyatu (2017). Ideophones in Kusaal. *Journal of West African Languages* 44(1): 45–57.

Akita, Kimi (2009). A Grammar of sound-symbolic words in Japanese: theoretical approaches to iconic and lexical properties of mimetics. PhD Dissertation, Kobe University.

Akita, Kimi (2012). Toward a frame-semantic definition of sound-symbolic words: a collocational analysis of Japanese mimetics. *Cognitive Linguistics* 23(1): 67–90.

Akita, Kimi (2013). The lexical iconicity hierarchy and its grammatical correlates. In Lars Elleström, Olga Fischer, and Christina Ljungberg (eds), *Iconic Investigations*. Amsterdam: John Benjamins Publishing Company, 331–349.

Akita, Kimi (2016). A multimedia encyclopedia of Japanese mimetics: a frame-semantic approach to 12 sound-symbolic words. In Kaori Kabata and Kiyoko Toratani (eds), *Cognitive-Functional Approaches to the Study of Japanese as a Second Language*. Berlin: De Gruyter Mouton, 139–168.

Akita, Kimi (2017). The linguistic integration of Japanese ideophones and its typological implications. *Canadian Journal of Linguistics/Revue canadienne de linguistique* 62(2): 1–21.

Akita, Kimi (2019). Mimetics, gaze, and facial expression in a multimodal corpus of Japanese. In Kimi Akita and Prashant Pardeshi (eds), *Ideophones, Mimetics and Expressives, Iconicity in Language and Literature*. Amsterdam and Philadelphia: John Benjamins Publishing Company, 229–246.

Akita, Kimi (2021a). A typology of depiction marking: the prosody of Japanese Ideophones and beyond. *Studies in Language* 45(4): 865–886.

Akita, Kimi (2021b). Phonation types matter in sound symbolism. *Cognitive Science* 45(5): e12982.

Almende, B. V., Thieurmel, Benoit, and Titouan, Robert (2019). *visNetwork: Network Visualization Using 'vis.Js' Library*. https://CRAN.R-project.org/package=visNetwork

Ameka, Felix K. (2001). Ideophones and the Nature of the Adjective Word Class in Ewe. *Typological Studies in Language* 44: 25–48.

Amy Pei-jung, Lee (2017). Ideophones, Interjections, and Sound Symbolism in Seediq. *Oceanic Linguistics* 56(1): 181–209.

Imaginary Sound Creations (2018). Onomatopedia. Available at https://web.archive.org/web/20221012233543/https://onomatopedia.jp/ Accessed 19 August 2024.

Baba, Junko (2003). Pragmatic function of Japanese mimetics in the spoken discourse of varying emotive intensity levels. *Journal of Pragmatics* 35(12): 1861–1889.

Badenoch, Nathan (2021). Sticky semantics: expressive meaning in Mundari. In Nathan Badenoch and Nishaant Choksi (eds), *Expressives in the South Asian Linguistic Area*. Leiden, Boston: Brill, 1–14.

Badenoch, Nathan, Choksi, Nishant, Osada, Toshiki, and Purti, Madhu (2021). Performance in elicitation: methodological considerations in the study of Mundari expressives. In Shailendra Mohan (ed.), *Advances in Munda Linguistics*. Cambridge: Cambridge Scholars Publishing, 131–141.

Badenoch, Nathan, Osada, Toshiki, Purti, Madhu, and Onishi, Masayuki (2021). Expressive lexicography: creating a dictionary of expressives in the South Asian linguistic area. *Indian Linguistics* 82: 25–40.

Badenoch, Nathan, Purti, Madhu, and Choksi, Nishaant (2019). Expressives as moral propositions in Mundari. *Indian Linguistics* 80(1–2): 1–17.

Bahón-Arnaiz, Cristina (2021). Knock, knock! the great success of ideophones in Korean journalism. *International Institute for Asian Studies Newsletter* 88: 8.

Barrett, Rusty, Webster, Anthony K., and Huumo, Tuomas (2014). Introduction: ideophones: between grammar and poetry. *Pragmatics and Society* 5(3): 335–340.

Berlin, Brent and Kay, Paul (1969). *Basic Color Terms: Their Universality and Evolution*. Berkeley, Los Angeles, and Oxford: University of California Press.

Bermúdez, Natalia (2020). Ideophone humor: the enregisterment of a stereotype and its inversion. *Journal of Linguistic Anthropology* 30(2): 258–272.

Bodomo, Adams (2006). The structure of ideophones in African and Asian languages: the case of Dagaare and Cantonese. In John Mugane, John P. Hutchison, and Dee A. Worman (eds), *Selected Proceedings of the 35th Annual Conference on African Linguistics: African Languages and Linguistics in Broad Perspectives*. Harvard: Harvard University Press, 203–213.

Chang, Winston et al. (2020). *Shiny: Web Application Framework for R*. Available at https://CRAN.R-project.org/package=shiny. Accessed 19 August 2024.

Chen, I-Hsuan et al. (2019). Mandarin Chinese modality exclusivity norms, edited by Zhiqiang Cai. *PLOS ONE* 14(2): e0211336.

Choksi, Nishaant (2020a). Expressives and the multimodal depiction of social types in Mundari. *Language in Society* 49(3): 379–398.

Choksi, Nishaant (2020b). Expressives in Hindi language film songs. In Nathan Badenoch and Nishaant Choksi (eds), *Expressives in the South Asian Linguistic Area*. Brill's Studies in South and Southwest Asian Languages. Leiden, Boston: Brill, 177–194.

Deese, James (1965). *The Structure of Associations in Language and Thought*. Baltimore: Johns Hopkins Press.

de Schryver, G. (2009). The lexicographic treatment of ideophones in Zulu. *Lexikos* 19: 34–54.

Diatka, Vojtěch (2014). Hindi ideophones. Master's thesis, Karlova University.

Diffloth, Gérard (1972). Notes on expressive meaning. *Chicago Linguistic Society* 8(44): 440–447.

Diffloth, Gérard (1976). Expressives in Semai. *Oceanic Linguistics Special Publications* 13 *Austroasiatic Studies* Part I: 249–264.

Diffloth, Gérard (1979). Expressive phonology and prosaic phonology in Mon-Khmer. In E. J. A. Henderson, Theraphan L. Thongkum, et al. (eds), *Studies in Tai and Mon-Khmer Phonetics and Phonology: In Honour of Eugenie J. A. Henderson*. Bangkok: Chulalongkorn University Press, 49–59.

Dingemanse, Mark (2012). Advances in the cross-linguistic study of ideophones. *Language and Linguistics Compass* 6(10): 654–672.

Dingemanse, Mark (2015a). Folk definitions in linguistic fieldwork. In James Essegbey, Brent Henderson, and Fiona McLaughlin (eds), *Language Documentation and Endangerment in Africa*. Amsterdam: John Benjamins, 215–238.

Dingemanse, Mark (2015b. Ideophones and reduplication: depiction, description, and the interpretation of repeated talk in discourse. *Studies in Language* 39(4): 946–970.

Dingemanse, Mark and Majid, Asifa (2012). The semantic structure of sensory vocabulary in an African language. In N. Miyake, D. Peebles, and R. P. Cooper (eds), *Proceedings of the 34th Annual Conference of the Cognitive Science Society*. Austin: Cognitive Science Society, 300–305.

Doizaki, Ryuichi, Watanabe, Junji, and Sakamoto, Maki (2017). Automatic estimation of multidimensional ratings from a single sound-symbolic word and word-based visualization of tactile perceptual space. *IEEE Transactions on Haptics* 10(2): 173–182.

Doke, Clement Martyn (1935). *Bantu Linguistic Terminology*. London: Longmans, Green and Co.

Ezejideaku, Emma and Ugwu, Esther (2010). The linguistics of newspaper advertising in Nigeria. *Language in India* 10(3): 1–17.

Ferrara, Lindsay and Hodge, Gabrielle (2018). Language as description, indication, and depiction. *Frontiers in Psychology* 9: 716.

Flaksman, Maria (2017). Iconic treadmill hypothesis. In Angelika Zirker, Matthias Bauer, Olga Fischer, and Christina Ljungberg (eds), *Dimensions of Iconicity*. Amsterdam: John Benjamins Publishing Company, 15–38.

Gava, Priscila Gerolde (2018). Translating sound into image: a comparison between American comic and Japanese manga onomatopoeia. *International Journal of the Image* 9(3): 1–21.

Hamano, Shoko (1998). *The Sound-Symbolic System of Japanese*. Stanford, CA and Tokyo: CSLI Publications and Kurosio.

Hanada, Mitsuhiko (2016). Using Japanese onomatopoeias to explore perceptual dimensions in visual material perception. *Perception* 45(5): 568–587.

Hanada, Mitsuhiko (2020). Food-texture dimensions expressed by Japanese onomatopoeic words. *Journal of Texture Studies* 51(3): 398–411.

Hatton, Sarah Ann (2016). The onomatopoeic ideophone-gesture relationship in Pastaza Quichua. Masters thesis, Brigham Young University.

Haynie, Hannah J. and Bowern, Claire (2016). Phylogenetic approach to the evolution of color term systems. *Proceedings of the National Academy of Sciences* 113(48): 13666–13671.

Ibarretxe-Antuñano, Iraide (2017). Basque ideophones from a typological perspective. *Canadian Journal of Linguistics/Revue canadienne de linguistique* 62(2): 196–220.

Ibarretxe-Antuñano, Iraide (2019). Towards a semantic typological classification of motion ideophones. In Kimi Akita and Prashant Pardeshi (eds), *Ideophones, Mimetics and Expressives, Iconicity in Language and Literature*. Amsterdam and Philadelphia: John Benjamins Publishing Company, 137–166.

Iida, Hinano and Akita, Kimi (2023). Perceptual strength norms for 510 Japanese Words, including ideophones: a comparative study with English. In Micah Goldwater, Florencia K. Anggoro, Brett K. Hayes, and Desmond C. Ong (eds), *Proceedings of the 45th Annual Conference of the Cognitive Science Society*, 2201–2207

Kilian-Hatz, Christa (2001). Universality and diversity: ideophones from Baka and Kxoe. In F. K. Erhard Voeltz and Christa Kilian-Hatz (eds), *Ideophones*. Amsterdam: John Benjamins, 155–163.

Kisku, Sarada Prasad, Murmu, Ganesh, and Choksi, Nishaant (2020). Expressives in the Santali poetry of Sadhu Ramchand Murmu. In Nathan Badenoch and Nishaant Choksi (eds), *Expressives in the South Asian Linguistic Area*. Leiden: Brill, 223–236.

Kita, Sotaro (1993). Language and thought interface: a study of spontaneous gestures and Japanese mimetics. PhD Dissertation, University of Chicago.

Kita, Sotaro (1997). Two-dimensional semantic analysis of Japanese mimetics. *Linguistics* 35: 379–415.

Klassen, Doreen Helen (2000). 'You can't have silence with your palms up': ideophones, gesture, and iconicity in Zimbabwean Shona women's ngano (storysong) performance. PhD dissertation, Indiana University.

Köhler, Wolfgang (1929). *Gestalt Psychology*. New York: Liveright.

Kunene, Daniel P. (2001). Speaking the act: the ideophone as a linguistic rebel. In Christa Kilian-Hatz and F. K. Erhard Voeltz (eds), *Ideophones*. Amsterdam and Philadelphia: John Benjamins Publishing Company, 183–191.

Levinson, Stephen C. (2000). Yélî Dnye and the theory of basic color terms. *Journal of Linguistic Anthropology* 10(1): 3–55.

Lucy, John A. (1997). The linguistics of color. In C. L. Hardin and Luisa Maffi (eds), *Color Categories in Thought and Language*. Cambridge: Cambridge University Press, 320–346.

Lydall, Jean (2000). Having fun with ideophones: a socio-linguistic look at ideophones in Hamar, Southern Ethiopia. In Richard Pankhurst et al. (eds), *Ethiopian Studies at the End of the Second Millenium*. Addis Ababa: Addis Ababa University, 886–891.

Lynott, Dermot et al. (2020). The Lancaster sensorimotor norms: multidimensional measures of perceptual and action strength for 40,000 English words. *Behavior Research Methods* 52: 1271–1291.

Lynott, Dermot and Connell, Louise (2009). Modality exclusivity norms for 423 object properties. *Behavior Research Methods* 41(2): 558–564.

Majid, Asifa (2012). A guide to stimulus-based elicitation for semantic categories. In Nicholas Thieberger (ed.), *The Oxford Handbook of Linguistic Fieldwork*. Oxford: Oxford University Press, 54–71.

Majid, Asifa (2018). Differential coding of perception in the world's languages. *Proceedings of the National Academy of Sciences* 115(45): 11369–11376.

Marks, Lawrence E. (1978). *The Unity of the Senses: Interrelations among the Modalities*. New York and London: Academic Press.

McLean, Bonnie and Purti, Madhu (2018). A Multimedia Encyclopedia of Mundari Expressives. Available at https://web.archive.org/web/20201020072056/https://sites.google.com/site/mundaexpressives/ Accessed 19 August 2024.

McLean, Bonnie (2021). Revising an implicational hierarchy for the meanings of ideophones, with special reference to Japonic. *Linguistic Typology* 25(3): 507–549.

Medin, Douglas et al. (2010). Naming the animals that come to mind: effects of culture and experience on category fluency. *Journal of Cognition and Culture* 10(1–2): 205–220.

Medvediv, Andrii and Dmytruk, Anna (2019). Peculiarities of conveying the structural and semantic specificity of Japanese onomatopoeia in translation of texts of advertising character. *Research Trends in Modern Linguistics and Literature* 2: 77–93.

Mihas, Elena (2012). Ideophones in Alto Perené (Arawak) from Eastern Peru. *Studies in Language*. 36(2): 300–344.

Mihas, Elena (2013). Composite ideophone-gesture utterances in the Ashéninka Perené 'Community of Practice', an Amazonian Arawak society from Central-Eastern Peru. *Gesture* 13(1): 28–62.

Miklashevsky, Alex (2018). Perceptual experience norms for 506 Russian nouns: modality rating, spatial localization, manipulability, imageability and other variables. *Journal of Psycholinguistic Research* 47(3): 641–661.

Morucci, Piermatteo, Bottini, Roberto, and Crepaldi, Davide (2019). Augmented modality exclusivity norms for concrete and abstract Italian property words. *Journal of Cognition* 2(1): 42.

Moshi, Lioba (1993). Ideophones in KiVunjo-Chaga. *Journal of Linguistic Anthropology* 3(2): 185–216.

Mphande, Lupenga (1992). Ideophones and African verse. *Research in African Literatures* 23(1): 117–129.

Murasugi, Keiko and Akita, Kimi (2021). Binomial adjectives in Japanese. *Nanzan Linguistics* 16: 67–80.

Muto, Ayak (2003). Azi-Kotoba-No Giongo/Gitaigo: Syoku-No Onomatope [Mimetics in taste expressions: onomatopoeia of the gourmet]. In Seto Kenichi (ed.), *Kotoba-Wa Azi-o Koeru: Oisii Hyoogen-No Tankyuu [Words Go beyond Tastes: Explorations of Tasty Expressions]*. Tokyo: Kaimeisha, 241–300.

Newman, Paul (1968). Ideophones from a syntactic point of view. *Journal of West African Languages* 5: 107–117.

Noss, Philip A. (1970). The performance of the Gbaya tale. *Research in African Literatures* 1(1): 41–49.

Noss, Philip A. (1989). The ideophone poems of Dogobadomo. *The Ancestors' Beads* (special issue of *Crosscurrent*) 23(4): 33–43.

Nuckolls, Janis B. (1996). *Sounds Like Life: Sound-Symbolic Grammar, Performance, and Cognition in Pastaza Quechua*. Oxford: Oxford University Press.

Nuckolls, Janis B. (2006). The neglected poetics of ideophony. In Catherine O'Neil, Mary Scoggin, and Kevin Tuite (eds), *Language, Culture, and the Individual*. Munich: Lincom Europa, 39–50.

Nuckolls, Janis B. (2010a). *Lessons from a Quechua Strongwoman: Ideophony, Dialogue and Perspective*. Tucson: University of Arizona Press.

Nuckolls, Janis B. (2010b). The sound-symbolic expression of animacy in Amazonian Ecuador. *Diversity* 2: 353–369.

Nuckolls, Janis B., Tod D. Swanson, Diana Shelton, Alexander Rice, and Sarah Hatton. (2017). Lexicography in-your-face: the active semantics of Pastaza Quichua ideophones. *Canadian Journal of Linguistics/Revue canadienne de linguistique* 62(2): 154–172.

Nuckolls, Janis B. (2019). The sensori-semantic clustering of ideophonic meaning in Pastaza Quichua. In Kimi Akita and Prashant Pardeshi (eds), *Ideophones, Mimetics and Expressives*. Iconicity in Language and Literature. Amsterdam and Philadelphia: John Benjamins Publishing Company, 167–198.

Nuckolls, Janis B. (2020). 'How do you even know what ideophones mean?': Gestures' contributions to ideophone semantics in Quichua. *Gesture* 19(2–3): 161–195.

Nuckolls, Janis B. (2021). Bhux. In Nuckolls, Janis B. et al. *Quechua Realwords: An audio-visual corpus of expressive Quechua ideophones*. Available at https://quechuarealwords.byu.edu/?ideophone=bhux Accessed 19 August 2024.

Okpewho, Isidore (1992). *African Oral Literature: Backgrounds, Character, and Continuity*. Bloomington: Indiana University Press.

O'Meara, Carolyn, Smythe Kung, Susan, and Majid, Asifa (2019). The challenge of olfactory ideophones: reconsidering ineffability from the Totonac-Tepehua perspective. *International Journal of American Linguistics* 85(2): 173–212.

Osada, Toshiki, Purti, Madhu, and Badenoch, Nathan (2019a). *A Dictionary of Mundari Expressives*. Tokyo: ILCAA.

Osada, Toshiki, Purti, Madhu, and Badenoch, Nathan (2019b). Suisui. In Toshiki Osada, Madhu Purti, and Nathan Badenoch (eds), *A Dictionary of Mundari Expressives*. Tokyo: ILCAA, 238.

Osada, Toshiki, Purti, Madhu, and Badenoch, Nathan (2020). Expanding the model of reduplication in Mundari expressives. In Nathan Badenoch and Nishaant Choksi (eds), *Expressives in the South Asian Linguistic Area*. Leiden: Brill, 78–99.

Park, Ji-Yeon (2020). Morphosyntactic integration of ideophones in Japanese and Korean: a corpus-based analysis of spoken and written discourse'. In Pamela Perniss, Olga Fischer, and Christina Ljungberg (eds), *Iconicity in Language and Literature*. Amsterdam: John Benjamins Publishing Company, 58–73.

Pike, Kenneth L. (1967). *Language in Relation to a Unified Theory of the Structure of Human Behavior*. The Hague: Mouton.

Pratha, Nimish K., Avunjian, Natalie, and Cohn, Neil (2016). Pow, punch, pika, and chu: the structure of sound effects in genres of American comics and Japanese manga. *Multimodal Communication* 5(2): 93–109.

R Core Team. (2022). *The R Project for Statistical Computing*. Vienna, Austria: R Foundation for Statistical Computing.

Reiter, Sabine (2012). Ideophones in Awetí. PhD Thesis, Christian-Albrechts Universität Kiel.

Rhee, Seongha (2019). Lexicalization patterns in color naming in Korean. In Ida Rafaelli, Daniela Katunar, and Barbara Kerovec (eds), *Lexicalization Patterns in Color Naming: A Cross-Linguistic Perspective*. Studies in Functional and Structural Linguistics. eds. Amsterdam: John Benjamins, 109–128.

Rhee, Seongha and Koo, Hyun Jung (2017). Multifaceted gustation: systematicity and productivity of taste terms in Korean. *Terminology. International Journal of Theoretical and Applied Issues in Specialized Communication* 23(1): 38–65.

Ruts, Wim et al. (2004). Dutch norm data for 13 semantic categories and 338 exemplars. *Behavior Research Methods, Instruments, and Computers* 36(3): 506–515.

Sakamoto, Maki, Ueda, Yuya, Doizaki, Ryuichi, and Shimizu, Yuichiro (2014). Communication support system between Japanese patients and foreign doctors using onomatopoeia to express pain symptoms. *Journal of Advanced Computational Intelligence and Intelligent Informatics* 18(6): 1020–1025.

Sakamoto, Maki and Watanabe, Junji (2017). Exploring tactile perceptual dimensions using materials associated with sensory vocabulary. *Frontiers in Psychology* 8: 569.

Samarin, William J. (1967). Determining the meaning of ideophones. *Journal of West African Languages* 4(2): 35–41.

Samarin, William J. (1969). The art of Gbeya insults. *International Journal of American Linguistics* 35(4): 323–329.

Samarin, William J. (1970). Field procedures in ideophone research. *Journal of African Languages* 9(1): 27–30.

Samarin, William J. (1971). Survey of Bantu ideophones. *African Language Studies* 12: 130–168.

Schaefer, Ronald P. (2001). Ideophonic adverbs and manner gaps in Emai. *Typological Studies in Language* 44: 339–354.

Shepard, Glenn Harvey (1999). Pharmacognosy and the senses in two Amazonian societies.' PhD dissertation, University of California.

Speed, Laura J. and Brybaert, Marc (2021). Dutch sensory modality norms. *Behavior Research Methods* 54(3): 1306–1318.

Speed, Laura J. and Majid, Asifa (2017). Dutch modality exclusivity norms: simulating perceptual modality in space. *Behavior Research Methods* 49(6): 2204–2218.

Taub, Sarah F. (2001). *Language from the Body: Iconicity and Metaphor in American Sign Language*. Cambridge: Cambridge University Press.

Tufvesson, Sylvia (2007). Expressives. In Asifa Majid (ed.), *Field Manual Volume 10*. Nijmegen: MPI for Psycholinguistics, 53–57.

Tufvesson, Sylvia (2011). Analogy-making in the Semai sensory world. *The Senses and Society* 6(1): 86–95.

Van Hoey, Thomas (2018). Does the thunder roll? Mandarin Chinese meteorological expressions and their iconicity. *Cognitive Semantics* 4(2): 230–259.

Van Hoey, Thomas (2023). ABB, a salient prototype of collocate–ideophone constructions in Mandarin Chinese. *Cognitive Linguistics* 34(1): 133–163.

Van Hoey, Thomas (2023). A semantic map for ideophones. In Fuyin Thomas Li (ed.), *Handbook of Cognitive Semantics Volume 2*. Leiden: Brill, 129–175.

Van Hoey, Thomas and Thompson, Arthur Lewis (2020). The Chinese ideophone database (CHIDEOD). *Cahiers de Linguistique Asie Orientale* 49(2): 136–167.

Webster, Anthony K. (2008). 'To give an imagination to the listeners': The neglected poetics of Navajo ideophony. *Semiotica* 2008(171): 343–365.

Webster, Anthony K. (2017). 'So it's got three meanings dil dil:' seductive ideophony and the sounds of Navajo poetry. *The Canadian Journal of Linguistics/La revue canadienne de linguistique* 62(2): 173–195.

Welmers, William E. (1973). *African Language Structures*. Berkeley: University of California Press.

Wnuk, Ewelina, Laophairoj, Rujiwan, and Majid, Asifa (2020). Smell terms are not rara: a semantic investigation of odor vocabulary in Thai. *Linguistics* 58(4): 937–966.

Wnuk, Ewelina and Majid, Asifa (2014). Revisiting the limits of language: the odor lexicon of Maniq. *Cognition* 131(1): 125–138.

Yaguchi, Yukiyasu (2011). Onomatope-o Mochiita Kyo-Kankaku-Teki-Hyogen-No Imi-Rikai-Kozo [The comprehension of synesthetic expressions with onomatopoeic words]. *The Japanese Journal of Cognitive Psychology* 8(2): 119–129.

Yasui, Eiko (2023). Japanese onomatopoeia in bodily demonstrations in a traditional dance instruction: a resource for synchronizing body movements. *Journal of Pragmatics* 207: 45–61.

Zide, Norman H. (1975). Twelve Jadur songs. *Journal of South Asian Literature* 11(1/2): 157–162.

Zlatev, Jordan et al. (2023). Analyzing polysemiosis: language, gesture, and depiction in two cultural practices with sand drawing. *Semiotica* 2023(253): 81–116.

Zwicky, Arnold M. and Pullum, Geoffrey K. (1987). Plain morphology and expressive morphology. In John Aske, Natasha Beery, Laura Michaelis, and Hana Filip (eds), *Proceedings of the Thirteenth Annual Meeting of the Berkeley Linguistics Society*. Berkeley: Berkeley Linguistics Society, 330–340.

6

Detecting and analysing expressives in a language corpus

Nicolau Dols and Pere Garau

6.1 Setting out the aims

As a first step for a research on expressives, extracting all units labelled as 'interjections', 'ideophones', 'onomatopoeias', from a text can help. The retrieved units are usually lexicalized and language-specific (Dingemanse 2012). This operation can be performed provided that such categories as those cited have been put to use during the processing of raw linguistic material. Other searches, such as those dealing with diagrammatic iconicity (Dingemanse 2011) can be executed by working on transcriptions, aiming at the detection of repetitive sequences of two or more elements, as for reduplication. However, for a certain amount of phenomena, phonetic cues are to be put into action (Sidhu and Pexman 2018; Masuda 2007). This is the case of unlexicalized items of imagic iconicity, as pitch, speed, or intensity, among other acoustic effects.

Working on corpora in connection with phonetic analysis can provide the tools to perform searches for phonetic cues over large amounts of phonetic material, pointing at those items requiring a particular attention by the researcher, and therefore ensuring efficiency (Boersma 2014). These particular tasks can be carried out by feeding a programme such as Praat (Boersma and Weenink 1992–2024) with pre-existing or specifically tailored scripts.

The fundamental aim of descriptive research on expressives is to gather as many of them as possible together with an explanation of the meaning they contribute to the whole of the speech act. It is not hard to see how this can be done if expressives are conceived as a close list of lexical items showing a close relation between form and meaning, i. e. with a high degree of iconicity. The need for tracking the traces of the core ingredient of expressiveness in areas of language other than lexicon has been long felt, as in Diffloth (1979) or Williams (2013). The fact is that iconicity is not an exclusive feature of certain words, but it can be found both in grammatical processes and figures of speech—reduplication, iteration, hyperbaton, parallelism—and in voice inflection. Iconicity can act via the deployment of systematic items and processes of the language as well as via the performance of more or less systematic behaviours during speech acts. In this sense, recognizing

Nicolau Dols and Pere Garau, *Detecting and analysing expressives in a language corpus*. In: *Capturing Expressivity.*
Edited by: Jeffrey P. Williams, Oxford University Press. © Nicolau Dols and Pere Garau (2025).
DOI: 10.1093/oso/9780192858931.003.0006

DETECTING AND ANALYSING EXPRESSIVES IN A LANGUAGE CORPUS 109

elements that can easily be transferred from orality to writing would be only half of the task; the rest of it deals with those other elements usually filtered out during the act of writing. Although gestures and proxemics have a word to say here, we shall concentrate on the detection of iconicity in lexical items, grammar processes, and changes in voice inflection.

We are aware of the grossness of the concept 'expressive' as understood here. We do not deal only with systematic or 'language' features, but also with 'casual' or speech features (just to state it in Saussurean terms), whereas emphatic pronunciation, for example, cannot be completely cast away on the basis of non-systematicity. On the contrary, the hypothesis is that those aspects of communication usually neglected contribute to the general meaning of speech acts. This is especially evident when receiver and decoding are taken into account in addition to the usual production models based on the encoding task of the sender.

We intend to analyse both levels of expression and to extract expressive elements from both a given text and its elocution, i.e. the way it is performed in a given speech act. When exploring the text two aspects should be given attention:

(a) The appearance of lexical items already listed in repertories as conventionally linked to iconicity (onomatopoeias, ideophones, phonaesthemes)
(b) The detection of any instance of recurrence especially audible, i.e. demi-syllables and larger units.

From the sound files, in turn, we expect variations intended to add at least an emotional bond to the meaning when not a more precise complement. For this reason sound variations should be noticed. In particular, variations in terms of

(a) Pitch or fundamental frequency (voice tone)
(b) Intensity (loudness)
(c) Speech rate (velocity as measured in words/time)

In a sense, these vocal elements alone can add information to the overall meaning of the utterance, and this fact independently justifies their detection. Further on, it can be hypothesized that systematic iconic items may receive a particular marking during their actual pronunciation. If this were to be the case, then these physical factors would be not only interesting by themselves, but also tokens of systematic iconicity.

Concentrating on iconicity items and phenomena customarily described in literature, the following categories are set:

Reduplicative ideophones (*nyam-nyam* MASTICATION)

Partial reduplication (reduplicative patterns with alternating vowels: *tris-tras* WALKING)

Syntactic reduplication (repetition of whole words or phrases: *per amunt, per amunt* 'up and up')

Morphological variation (repetition of the same stem eith different affixes: *criadum, criadam i criadim* 'servants' QUANTITY/DIVERSITY)

Interjections, exclamations, emphatic particles (*ai!* 'ouch!', *sí fa!* 'of course!')

Imitations, including non-linguistic items (*mmmm ...* HESITATION, *xiu-xiu* [ʃiwʃiw] FRYING OIL; WHISTLING; FIGHTING SCREAMS).

6.2 Method and tools

A parallel analysis is called for here, as both transcribed and spoken utterances will be under scope. To do so, the application of the program Praat for phonetic analysis, together with its complement TextGrids, will be thoroughly explained. The majority of the examples are taken from Dols (2023): a collection of twelve radio-broadcast folk tales matched with their transcriptions. In fact, those broadcasts can be understood as genuine examples of secondary orality (Ong 1982: 133), as they result from the radio-enacting folk stories collected at the turn of the twentieth century by the Majorcan lexicographer and folklorist Antoni M. Alcover (1862–1932). Dramatized readings by actors conducted by Alcover's disciple Francesc de B. Moll (1903–1991) in 1959 were recorded on tape and broadcast. Altogether the analysed corpus extends over five hours and thirteen minutes and consists of 63.000 words approximately.

A set of written texts and dramatized readings has been processed as explained in the following sections.

6.2.1 Preparing the corpus: matching sound and text

The corpus mentioned above has been annotated using Praat (Boersma and Weenink 2022). Praat is a well-known software package for linguistic research, mostly used in phonetics and speech analysis. It is open-source, freely available, and supported by the most common operating systems: Windows, Mac, and Linux. Praat uses an intuitive GUI (Graphical User Interface) to command most of the options available. Moreover, the true potential of Praat lies in scripting. Praat scripting, as scripting languages do, provides an efficiently automatized way to interact with the software. By means of this, the user is enabled to automatize actions and obtain results in a simple, swift, and safe way. Praat scripts are written in Praat's scripting interpreted language, based on C++ (the source language of Praat's coding). These scripts are executed line by line by an interpreter at runtime (Brinckmann 2014: 370). Praat scripting is commonly used to exploit corpus data created by annotation of oral files using TextGrids in Praat. This allows users to have at their fingertips almost all the resources needed to access data for their research in a single program, with no need for additional tools.[1]

---

[1] A speech corpus typically consists of a set of sound files, each of which is paired with an annotation file, and metadata information. Praat's strengths are in the acoustic analysis of the individual sounds,

First, audio files loaded in 'wav' format into the corpus have been automatically segmented using a boundary-insertion script modelled on 'mark_pauses' in Lennes (2017). By this means, segments deemed empty, i. e. those with a minimal duration of up to 0.2s and a maximum intensity of 46 dB, are delimited with boundaries placed with at a distance of 0.1 seconds from the following sound just to ensure a uniform time count (particularly relevant for speech-rate calculation). 'Silent' segments are labelled with a pause marker (<xxx>). The corpus contains 4,918 fragments, which have been transcribed using the orthographic records of the folk tales available in Grimalt and Guiscafrè's edition of Antoni Maria Alcover's *Rondaies mallorquines* (Majorcan folk tales) (Alcover 1996/2022), once corrected if necessary to match the actually recorded performances. The matching task has been developed in two steps to facilitate the annotation process. First, the plain text of every folk tale in its 'txt' file has been manually segmented by inserting a line break every time the script scanning the audio file placed a boundary. Then, a script based on 'label_from_text_file' in Lennes (2017) has been used to fill the transcription tier in the TextGrids: line after line, the script fills in the transcribed line in the corresponding interval, automatically avoiding intervals marked with <xxx> (see above), i. e. the silent segments. Finally, the correct synchronization of text and sound is ensured by careful examination of every record. The corpus files appear like the one produced in Figure 6.1, where the upper diagram corresponds to the sound's oscillogram, the central one to its spectrogram and F0 contour (the solid line), and the text in the bottom case to its orthographic transcription.

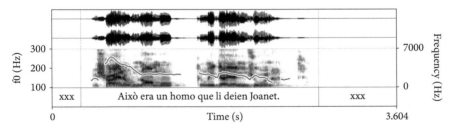

Figure 6.1 An example of an annotated segment

Note: image generated using a script by Ahn (2015). Data from authors' own corpus.

6.2.2 Corpus mining

According to our research aims, there are three relevant sets of values to be obtained from the corpus: pitch values, intensity values, and speech-rate values. Manual work for the gathering of those values would represent an enormous effort and, maybe, a less precise data set. The corpus implements two tools for data

in the annotation of these sounds, and in browsing multiple sound and annotation files across the corpus. Corpuswide acoustic analyses, leading to tables ready for statistical analysis, can be performed by scripting (Boersma 2014: 343).

112 NICOLAU DOLS AND PERE GARAU

collection: a Praat script, to collect all data referred to acoustic parameters; and a Python script to treat all the data, obtain speech-rate values, and mark the potential presence of expressives.

6.2.2.1 Acoustics

According to the hypothesized importance of pitch, intensity, and speech rate (see Section 6.1), a system is needed to compare all segments in the corpus in terms of the following factors: maximum pitch, minimum pitch, pitch differential (= maximum pitch—minimum pitch); maximum intensity, minimum intensity, intensity differential; segment duration, and number of words in every segment. All of the physical factors, primary and secondary, can be collected by running one script. In this chapter, the script 'collect_pitch_data_from_files' in Lennes (2017) has been adapted to the aforementioned purposes. In its original formulation the script scans 'the TextGrid files and the Sound files in a given folder, find sound-grid pairs that have the same name, open each pair, run through the TextGrid, collect data from labelled intervals and append the information to a simple tabulated text file (which you can later open in a statistical or spreadsheet program)' (Lennes 2017). The word count will be added later, when analysing text strings. The resulting Praat script used here (henceforth, PS) allows the user to get, for each labelled segment, all the acoustic data mentioned above.

The script iterates all through the files previously saved in the same folder and by pairs of 'wav' audio files and TextGrids each sharing a name. Every file pair is loaded to Praat. A Pitch object[2] and an Intensity object[3] are automatically created. For Pitch objects' creation the time step value is 0.1 s (like the value set when defining the segments; the time steps preceding and following a boundary are skipped by the analysis). After examining the pitch range, the minimum pitch is set to 75 Hz, and the maximum to 600 Hz. For Intensity objects operation values are set to 75 Hz for minimum pitch, 0.1s for time step; and no mean value has been calculated. Once these two objects are created, a scanning across the corpus starts, moving from segment to segment. If the segment contains the pause marker ('xxx'), the script avoids it. Only segments not marked with the pause marker are considered.

For each segment, starting and ending time points and duration values are saved. Also, the script gets maximum and minimum pitch of the segment and calculates, by subtraction, the pitch differential. The same procedure is applied to intensity values. In addition, PS saves the filename, segment number, and text label. The filename is saved in order to locate the segment within the corpus. The

---

[2] According to Praat's documentation, a Pitch object 'represents periodicity candidates as a function of time. It does not mind whether this periodicity refers to acoustics, perception, or vocal-cord vibration. It is sampled into a number of *frames* centred around equally spaced times.' (Boersma and Weenink 2022).

[3] 'An Intensity object represents an intensity contour at linearly spaced time points $t_i = t_1 + (i-1) dt$, with values in dB SPL, i.e. dB relative to $2 \cdot 10^{-5}$ Pascal, which is the normative auditory threshold for a 1000-Hz sine wave.' (Boersma and Weenink (1992-2024)).

DETECTING AND ANALYSING EXPRESSIVES IN A LANGUAGE CORPUS 113

segment number is stored to ensure access to the segment reference and position. The text label is conserved for further processing by means of a Python script.

Finally, the values are saved separated by semicolons in a 'csv' file, allowing further work with any statistical or data managing software. Temporary files are deleted. The result from the use of the PS is a single 'csv' file containing all values for pitch and intensity (maximum, minimum, and differential), duration, filename, segment number, and segment transcription. A complete overview of the process implemented by this script can be seen in Figure 6.2.

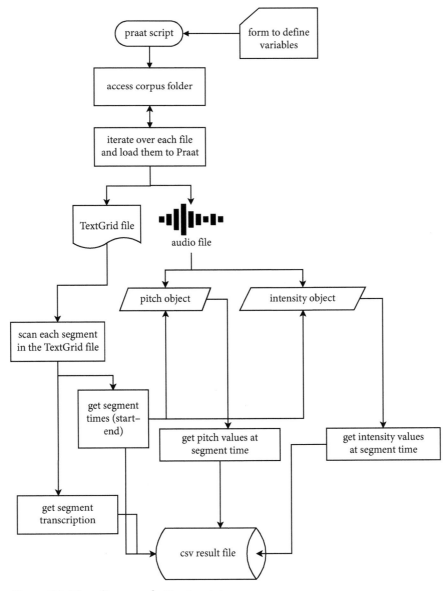

Figure 6.2 Flow diagram of a Praat script

As shown in Figure 6.2, the script has been fed with a Praat form (displayed by Praat's GUI, Figure 6.3) for the edition of variable values as the following: directory path to the corpus, sound file extension ('wav' files recommended), path to the resulting file, name of the TextGrid tier containing the speech segmentation and transcription (the corpus may include other tiers with supplementary information), time step, and minimum and maximum pitch.

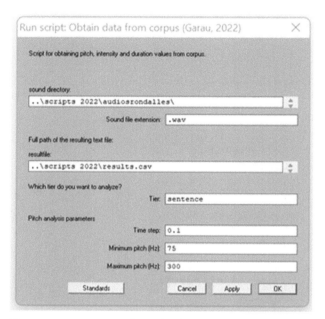

Figure 6.3 Praat script form for the edition of variable values

6.2.2.2 Text

Through the implementation of the PS, some of the elected values are covered. Additional work with a Python script is needed. Python is an interpreted language with a minimalist syntax, vastly applied in science and data managing.[4] One of the Python's functionalities is to compile codes from different users in a script. This function is performed by making use of libraries, coding collections defined by users or companies to supply useful tools for specific tasks and to avoid the creation of redundant tools. The Python script used here (henceforth, PyS) includes three popular Python libraries: *csv*, *re*, and *simplemma*, these three to be explained shortly.

PyS first reads the 'csv' data file generated by PS. From the PS data file, each segment transcription is saved as a variable for processing. By using the *re* library, the

---

[4] For a summary of Python functionalities related to science, view Oliphant (2007).

transcription is cleansed of all punctuation marks and all characters not matching with words. The *re* library allows Python users to access operations with regular expressions. Regular expressions (regex) are a commonly used type of finite state transducers[5] in language processing. Regex requires two types of information in order to proceed: an input (in our case a text variable) and a pattern (a string to match another string in the input variable). Further on, once a string has been found, the regex operation can edit it in case the found string meets the conditions stated in the expression. Another function of the regex expressions provides verification of a condition with a True / False check. In other words: '[t]hey are particularly useful for searching in texts, when we have a pattern to search for and a corpus of texts to search through. A regular expression search function will search through the corpus, returning all texts that match the pattern' (Jurafsky and Martin 2020: 3).

As explained, the first action applied in our PyS workflow is the modification of the text in a segment in order to avoid all signs not belonging to a word, such as punctuation marks, apostrophes, dashes, etc. This operation is carried out by regex number 1, available in (1). By operating the *re.sub()* function the program 'return[s] the string obtained by replacing the leftmost non-overlapping occurrences of *pattern* in *string* by the replacement *repl*. If the pattern isn't found, *string* is returned unchanged' (Van Rossum 2020). In addition, the function .*lower()* converts all letters to lower case. With this first action, text labels are cleansed and prepared for word counting in order to calculate speech-rate values. Example (1a) contains one instance of a raw text from a transcription and its output result after being processed with the *re.sub* function in (1b).

(1)   re.sub("[\.\[,:;\—-!\?¿'\'«»']", "", text).lower()
     a. —Una caseta, perquè aquella barraca li fa poquet, a sa dona!
        —Esperau una mica! Veiam el Bon Jesús què hi diu.
        'A small house, because that hut does not suit his wife!—Wait a
        little! Let's see what Jesus says'.
     b. una caseta perquè aquella barraca li fa poquet a sa dona
        esperau una mica veiam el bon jesús què hi diu

After cleansing the text transcription, word counting is performed by splitting the text string into an array and calculating its length. The number of words is used for speech rate, stated in words per second. To do so, the word number is divided by the segment's duration in seconds.

Once the analysis has been carried out and the values for each segment have been extracted, statistical procedures can be started to determine which segments are relevant in terms of pitch, intensity, and speech rate.

---

[5] Regular languages and relations may be encoded as finite state networks. Languages are represented by simple automata, relations by transducers. Any regular expression can be compiled into a network that represents the corresponding language or relation (Karttunen et al. 1996: 306, 307).

Regarding the text, individual examination can be guided by the previous detection of expressives as listed in a dictionary or in an ad hoc list. Also repetitive or quase-repetitive strings can be automatically detected. Although there is no conclusive evidence of statistical correlation in this field, a certain degree of interdependence can be expected, as Dols (2023) holds for the relation between pitch differential and expressives. Whichever the case may be in the domain of statistics, the processes explained so far allow swift access in the detection of acoustic and textual devices potentially adding meaning to the message. A careful examination of the highlighted items and sequences is needed, anyway.

The classification of expressives in our model follows the typology in Dols (2023). As mentioned in Section 6.1and repeated here for the sake of clarity, seven types of expressives have been explored in the text corpus cited: (R1) Reduplicative ideophones, (R2) Partial reduplication (reduplicative patterns with alternating vowels), (R3) Syntactic reduplication, (R4) Morphological variation, (I1) Interjections, exclamation, (I2) Imitation, and (A) Other types, emphasis. In (2) an example of each is given.

(2) R1 *Nyam-nyam* REPETITION (mastication)
      R2 *Tris-tras* CONTINUITY (walking)
      R3 *Demana qui demana* ('asks who asks') REPETITION (to ask)
      R4 *Camina caminaràs* CONTINUITY (walking)
      I1 *Ai!* INTERJECTION
      I2 *mmmm ...* HESITATION
      A *i ja ho crec que* ASSERTION ('I bet')

Instead of manually collecting all the expressives in the corpus, a section of them has been analysed to abstract their structure. Those abstract structures have been used to build regex patterns to search for similar cases in the whole corpus. Nevertheless, this method does not apply to lexical units, such as interjections (types I1 and I2), better handled by means of lexical searches. Regex expressions have a strong potential in text analysis, but they still need to incorporate more coding in particular cases, as will be shown for R2 and R4 types.

There are five types of expressives which can be detected with a single regex, with no need for extra code. They are R1, R3, I1, I2, and—partially—A. Expressives of the R1 type can be detected by regex, as shown in (3a). The regular expression is read as: 'find any word and check if the following one is a repetition of it'. As can be easily deduced, this regex is used to capture any word repetition, and, thus, it is useful to detect any possible R1-type expressive. This regular expression retrieves strings such as the ones collected in (4a). R3 expressives consist of a repetition of the same word or phrase. Typically, they are not two adjacent words, but they

DETECTING AND ANALYSING EXPRESSIVES IN A LANGUAGE CORPUS   117

appear separated by a function word. According to this, (3b) is read: 'find any word followed by a space and/or a different word (one or two), then check if the captured word is the same as the following one'. (4b) produces two examples retrieved by regex R3.

(3) a. (R1) '\b(\w+)(?:\W+\1\b)+'
     b. (R3) '\b(\w+)(\W(\w+)?(\s\w+\s?)?\s)+(\1\b)'

(4) c. (R1) *zas-zas, mèu-mèu, toc-toc, xiu-xiu, bitlo-bitlo ...*
     d. (R3) *per amunt, per amunt; cireres i cireres ...*

For I1 and I2 expressives a list of interjections, exclamations, emphatic words, onomatopoeias, and imitations is needed. These lists have been compiled by extracting the words of this category from Catalan dictionaries and grammars, particularly the following: *Diccionari de la llengua catalana* (DIEC), *Diccionari català-valencià-balear* (DCVB), *Catalan: A Comprehensive Grammar* (Wheeler, Yates, and Dols 1999), and *Diccionari d'onomatopeies i mots de creació expressiva* (Riera and Sanjaume 2011).

Special attention is required for types R2 and R4. R2 expressives consist of a sequence of two words differing from each other in one sound. Cases as *xino-xano, patim-patam*, or *nyic-nyac* belong to this type. They are often formed by an alteration of a syllable nucleus (a vowel) in the second member of the compound. To automatize the detection of R2 expressives, first all vowels in the text segment are replaced by the same symbol, by using regex (4). Then, regex (5) is activated to detect any sequence of two identical words. Since the vowels have been reduced to one symbol only, only consonantal characters can differ from one word to another. This is the way regex (5) detects identical word structures. Now, the script needs to differentiate between otherwise identical syllables containing the same vowel from those containing different vowels. This value is obtained by subtracting the number of already-found R1-type expressives from the number of identical items counted by (5). With this operation, the amount of identical words already detected is discarded from the final value of R2-type expressives.

(4) (R2) text_n = re.sub('[aàeèéiíoòóuú]', 'A', text)

(5) (R2) re.findall('\b(\w+)\s+\1\b', text_n)

Concerning the R4 type, more linguistic information is needed. These expressives are constructed on the basis of a stem repetition. This is to say that the same lexical stem receives different morphological affixes. To identify these constructions, analysis cannot rely on text-string identification. For this to be achieved, a lemmatization of the words is implemented. Lemmatization 'is the task of grouping together word forms that belong to the same inflectional morphological paradigm and assigning to each paradigm its corresponding canonical form called lemma'. (Gesmundo and Samardžic 2012: 368). In this way, comparing words in their canonical forms permits lexical identification, and, therefore, the finding of expressives of type R4. First, the text string is split into word units. Then words are lemmatized and lemmas are saved in a new text string conserving their original order. Lemmatization has been possible through applying the *simplemma* library, which 'provides a simple and multilingual approach to look for base forms or lemmata' (Barbaresi 2022), and supports forty-eight languages including Catalan. Finally, the same regex used to detect R1-type expressives (2a) is applied to the lemmatized text for searching duplicated structures. Also, as in the case of R2 in relation to R1, in order to avoid overlapping with R1 results, the R4 resulting value is subtracted from R1.

The last type of expressives (A) encompasses all the expressives not suitable for classification according to the types already explained. As an aid to their detection, a small dictionary has been built to spot stereotypical phrases used as emphasizers. The dictionary allows for searches in the transcribed text of fragments including items verbatim matching its entries. A loop is run in which each dictionary entry is searched all along the transcription. If the search succeeds, then the fragment is tagged. The dictionary can be manually expanded to include new entries for further identification. Examples of type A expressives can be found in (6).

(6)   (A) Què me'n direu; Esperau ...; Sobretot; Saps que ...; Estam; Te dic; I
      ja ho crec que; etc.
      [Literally, but widely used with a figurative emphatic sense in the
      original language:

      'What will you say to me; Wait ...; Above all; Guess what ...; We are; I
      tell you; And I know that; etc.']

Finally, all labels are saved to a 'csv' file, available for further exploitation with any statistical or data-managing software. The data file can be read and written to by using the *csv* library, a tool for managing 'csv' documents in Python. The resulting file is a compilation of the acoustic data extracted with PS and the result of the PyS labelling. Table 6.1 produces four examples of the program output, in a human-readable format that can be processed by any program for data analysis, such as Excel.

Table 6.1 Examples of the resulting data

File	Segment	Transcription	Max. pitch (Hz)	Min. pitch (Hz)	Pitch diff. (Hz)	Max. Intensity (dB)	Min. Intensity (dB)	Intensity diff. (dB)	Segment dur. (s)	Words	Speech rate	Expressives
En Joanet de sa Gerra	63	*En Joan ja estigué enfilat i per amunt per amunt.*[6]	18,037	12,839	51,97	84,66	30,97	53,69	3,74	11	2,94	R3
En Salom i es batle	188	*I l'hi dic davant davant.*[7]	26,827	16,043	10,784	86,41	35,37	51,04	1,70	5	2,95	R1
Es metge guinyot	611	*i tots es metges i tot es senyorum senyoram i senyorim*[8]	29,410	89,39	20,471	75,93	21,79	54,13	3,59	12	3,34	R2
Es tres mantells d'or	186	"Ah, Bernadet! Hmm*! Ja no és per aquí lo que tu cerques!"* No em sabríeu dir on para?*[9]	18,742	85,25	10,217	85,96	35,06	50,90	5,10	18	3,53	I1, I2

6.3 Concluding remarks and further research

A method has been presented to simplify working with expressives in a sound corpus. A battery of types is an independent theoretical need, and a condition for the practical analysis of expressives. Any careful examination of expressives should not disregard the importance of speech (acoustic) and textual elements, or already-known processes such as those dealing with repetitive patterns. There exist independent methods to work in both domains: scripts for acoustic analysis with Praat—TextGrids for acoustics, and regex devices for written texts. To find a connection between both fields is a challenge, but the tools are useful in any case for the exploration of any of them.

PS can be retrieved from Garau (2022a) and PyS from Garau (2022b). They are still only a first approximation to the code, as described here and experimentally implemented in the corpus observed. The application proved its ability to detect most of the fragments containing expressives. However, an optimization of the code is still required, as well as an improvement of the dictionary. Further work on the analysis of expressives is to be expected in order to allow for those improvements, and to acquire a robust mechanism for the automatic detection of expressives.

References

Ahn, B. (2015). draw-waveform-pitchtrack-spectrogram-overlaid.praat [Script for Praat]. Princeton University. http://byronahn.com/pub/draw-waveform-spectrogram-pitch track-overlaid.praat

Alcover, Antoni Maria (1996/2022). *Aplec de rondaies mallorquines d'en jordi d'es racó*, edited by Josep A. Grimalt and Jaume Guiscafrè. 9 volumes. Palma: Editorial Moll.

Barbaresi, A. (2022). Simplemma: a simple multilingual lemmatizer for Python [Computer software]. Berlin: Berlin-Brandenburg Academy of Sciences. Available at http://doi.org/10.5281/zenodo.4673264. Accessed 20 August 2024.

Boersma, Paul (2014). The use of Praat in corpus research. In Jacques Durand, Ulrike Gut, and Gjert Kristoffersen (eds), *The Oxford Handbook of Corpus Phonology*. Oxford: Oxford University Press, 343–360. https://doi.org/10.1093/oxfordhb/9780199571932.013.016

Boersma, Paul and Weenink, David (1992–2024). Praat: Doing Phonetics by Computer [Computer program]. Version 6.2.06, retrieved 23 January 2022 from www.praat.org.

Brinckmann, Caren (2014). Praat Scripting. In Jacques Durand, Ulrike Gut, and Gjert Kristoffersen (eds), *The Oxford Handbook of Corpus Phonology*. Oxford: Oxford University Press, 361–379. https://doi.org/10.1093/oxfordhb/9780199571932.013.012

Diffloth, G. (1979). Expressive phonology and prosaic phonology in Mon-Khmer. In Th. L. Thongkum et al. (eds), *Studies in Tai and Mon-Khmer Phonetics and Phonology in Honour of Eugénie J. A. Henderson*. Bangkok: Chulalongkorn University Press, 49–59.

---

[6] 'Suddenly Joan was climbing up and up'.
[7] 'And I say so just in front of him' [lit. 'And I say so in before before him'].
[8] 'And all the doctors and all the gentlemen-x, gentlemen-y, gentlemen-z' [x/y/z = collective affixes].
[9] 'Hey, Bernadet! Hum! What you are looking for is no longer here. Wouldn't you tell me where it is?.

Dingemanse, Mark (2011). Ezra Pound among the Mawu: ideophones and iconicity in Siwu. In Pascal Michelucci, Olga Fischer, and Christina Ljungberg (eds), *Semblance and Signification*. Amsterdam: John Benjamins, 39–54.

Dingemanse, Mark (2012). Advances in the cross-linguistic study of ideophones. *Language and Linguistics Compass* 6(10): 654–672.

Dingemanse, Mark and Akita, Kimi (2017). An inverse relation between expressiveness and grammatical integration: On the morphosyntactic typology of ideophones, with special reference to Japanese. *Journal of Linguistics*, 53(3), 501–532. http://www.doi.org/10.1017/S002222671600030X

Dols, Nicolau (2023). Analysing expressives in a spoken corpus of Majorcan Catalan. In J. P. Williams (Ed.), *Expressivity in European Languages* (pp. 269–292). chapter, Cambridge: Cambridge University Press.

Garau, Pere (2022a). expressives_praat.praat (v1.0) [Script for Praat]. *Zenodo*. Available at https://doi.org/10.5281/zenodo.7234113. Accessed 19 August 2024.

Garau, Pere (2022b). expressives_py.py (v1.0) [Python package]. *Zenodo*. Available at https://doi.org/10.5281/zenodo.7234119. Accessed 19 August 2024.

Gesmundo, Andrea and Samardžić, Tania (2012). Lemmatisation as a tagging task. In Haizhou Li, Chin-Yew Lin, Miles Osborne, Gary Geunbae Lee, Jong C. Park (eds), *Proceedings of the 50th Annual Meeting of the Association for Computational Linguistics*, 368–372. Available at https://aclanthology.org/P12-2072.pdf. Accessed 20 August 2024.

Jurafsky, Daniel and Martin, James H. (2020). *Speech and Language Processing. An Introduction to Natural Language Processing, Computational Linguistics, and Speech Recognition*. Third edition. New Jersey: Pearson Prentice Hall.

Karttunen, L., Chanod, J-P., Grefenstette, G., and Schille, A. (1996). Regular expressions for language engineering. *Natural Language Engineering* 2(4): 305–326. Available at https://doi.org/10.1017/S1351324997001563. Accessed 20 August 2024.

Lennes, Mietta (2017). *SpeCT - Speech Corpus Toolkit for Praat*. https://doi.org/10.5281/zenodo.375923

Masuda, Keiko (2007). The physical basis for phonological iconicity. In Elzbieta Tabakowska, Christina Ljungberg, and Olga Fischer (eds), *Insistent Images*. Philadelphia: John Benjamins, 57–72.

Oliphant, Travis E. (2007). Python for scientific computing. *Computing in Science and Engineering* 9(3): 10–20. Available at http://doi.org/10.1109/MCSE.2007.58. Accessed 20 August 2024.

Ong, Walter (1982). *Orality and Literacy: The Technologizing of the Word*. London: Methuen.

Riera, Manel and Sanjaume, Margarida (2011). *Diccionari d'onomatopeies i mots de creació expressiva*. Barcelona: Edicions 62.

Van Rossum, G. (2020). *The Python Library Reference*, release 3.10.8. Wilmington, DE: Python Software Foundation.

Sidhu, David M. and Pexman, Penny M. (2018) Five mechanisms of sound symbolic association. *Psychonomic Bulletin and Review* 25: 1619–1643.

Thompson, Arthur Lewis, & Do, Youngah (2019). Unconventional spoken iconicity follows a conventional structure: Evidence from demonstrations. *Speech Communication* 113: 36–46. https://doi.org/10.1016/j.specom.2019.08.002.

Wheeler, Max, Yates, Alan, & Dols, Nicolau (1999). *Catalan: A Comprehensive Grammar*. Rouledge.

Williams, Jeffrey P. (ed.) (2013). *The Aesthetics of Grammar: Sound and Meaning in the Languages of Mainland Southeast Asia*. Cambridge: Cambridge University Press.

7

Empathy and indirect methods for fieldwork with ideophones in Pastaza and Upper Napo Kichwa

Janis Nuckolls and Tod Swanson

7.1 Introduction

Ideophones are imitative words which use linguistic sounds, bodily gestures, intonation, and facial expressions to depict sensory perceptions, whether of sounds, movements, visual images, or internal bodily states. They may also communicate emotions, silence, and more abstract temporal concepts such as completiveness, instantaneousness, and repetitiveness. In this chapter we discuss what we have learned from field methods designed to record ideophones in eastern Amazonian Ecuador, among speakers of Upper Napo Kichwa (iso code: qvo) and Pastaza Kichwa (iso code: qvz), including those methods that have been less obviously successful. We argue that the special qualities of ideophones in Kichwa-speaking culture, and possibly in other cultures as well, require different approaches from traditional scientific and social scientific methods for data gathering. This is partly due to the nature of ideophones as a class of expressions and the ways in which they are articulated. The activity of performatively imitating and thus becoming another type of being, whether it is an earlier version of oneself or of one's actions, or of sensations emanating from another form of life, is fundamentally different from simply describing some state of affairs.

However, there are culturally specific uses of ideophones as well, and their cultural frameworks, combined with the unique qualities of ideophone semantics, have required skills and approaches that are not often acknowledged in linguistic descriptions and analyses of this class of expressions. In Kichwa discourse, for example, we encounter cultural beliefs about the possibility of animating the voices and actions of other species. In such instances, ideophones reveal detailed knowledge of these species, which is based on careful observations of their day-to-day habits.

An example of such detailed knowledge, which can be revealed within ideophonic depictions, emerged when Tod Swanson interviewed David during a walk in the forest. The purpose of the walk was not to elicit ideophones, but to learn

Janis Nuckolls and Tod Swanson, *Empathy and indirect methods for fieldwork with ideophones in Pastaza and Upper Napo Kichwa*. In: *Capturing Expressivity*. Edited by: Jeffrey P. Williams, Oxford University Press. © Janis Nuckolls and Tod Swanson (2025). DOI: 10.1093/oso/9780192858931.003.0007 about plants. They stopped when Swanson noticed a type of fruit growing on a small tree, which David stated was eaten by toucan birds. Toucans are highly valued for their stunning, colourful appearance. Their feathers adorn headdresses worn by men during festive dances. They are also a source of food, which makes their eating habits of great interest to all people, especially hunters.

The following example (Figure 7.1) presents David's meticulous depiction of a toucan's eating of this fruit. He imitates with four different ideophones, the microevents of this process. He uses the ideophone *tak*, a haptic ideophone, accompanied by his own touching of the fruit, to depict the way the bird initially grabs the fruit with its beak. He then continues with *tas*, a 'light' ideophone for a completive action, which he accompanies by pulling the fruit slightly away from its stem. This action of a 'mock' pulling of the fruit off of its stem is followed by repetitions of *kaw* to imitate the sound and movement of the bird's crunching of the fruit. The final ideophone, *ling*, an ideophone depictive of a boundary-crossing movement, is uttered simultaneously with his own gesture towards his mouth, to indicate the final gulping down of the fruit by the bird.[1]

Figure 7.1 A toucan's fruit

(1) kaj lulunda sikwaŋga upig aŋ; kajbi tag kaniɕa, tas ajsaɕa, kaw kaw kaw liŋ limpug aŋ.

'This fruit, the toucan is a drinker of; biting onto it *tag*, pulling it off *tas*, (chewing it) *kaw kaw kaw*, (and then) *ling*! it swallows it!'

---

[1] This example may be viewed at the following link, by scrolling down to video number 22: https://quechuarealwords.byu.edu/?ideophone=ling.

Although not explicitly expressed by the speaker, and difficult to prove empirically, it is not too much of a stretch to claim that such a detailed depiction is based in the speaker's empathy for what he is imitating. Aaltola (2013: 81) has defined empathy as 'an experienced insight into the experiences of others. When I empathize, I grasp (or rather I feel that I grasp) in an embodied, affective sense the mental states of another being—however, I do not need to feel those experiences as they originally occurred, nor do I simply intentionally produce detached flights of fancy or inference'. She argues, further, that empathy 'emerges as a bridge to the experiences of others, a clear insight—like a light suddenly illuminating a dark landscape—into what it is to be the other creature'.

The use of ideophones by Kichwa speakers, we argue, is often based on empathy for humans and non-humans, not only for their interior states, but for the minute details of their ways of being in the world. We are not aware of studies of the role of empathy in linguistic documentation, although studies arguing for the significance of empathy in discourse analysis and applied linguistics exist (Dörnyei 2007; Prior 2017). We have observed that the use of ideophones may be part of stances that are related to empathy, including emotional engagement and humour. All of these qualities, we argue, necessitate research methods that are distinct from some of the traditional methods of social scientific and linguistic research. Specifically, our own research methods have been heavily weighted towards indirect methodologies for gathering ideophones.

7.2 Our methodologies

Our methods have emerged from an interdisciplinary collaboration over a number of years, consisting of shared interactions with mutual Kichwa friends and of experiences within the Kichwa world. We are both linguists as well as anthropologists and have been trained to use a variety of techniques to study language and culture. One key method used for gathering and analysing all types of language data, whether phonemes, morphemes, or larger syntactic units, is comparison and contrast. The comparison and contrast method is essential for getting started with a linguistic analysis of a language's basic sound units. One such technique is assembling minimal pairs, which involves comparing words that are partially alike and partially different, to figure out which sounds of a language make a difference for meaning, thereby making it possible to map a language's phonological inventory.

Comparison and contrast is also necessary to determine the meanings of larger units. The presence vs absence of a morpheme in a noun or verb, for example, allows the linguist to ask a consultant targeted questions which can lead to inferences about that morpheme's functions and meanings. The nature of ideophones,

EMPATHY & INDIRECT METHODS FOR FIELDWORK   125

as used by Pastaza and Upper Napo speakers, however, requires that our fieldwork methods for gathering and documenting them have needed to be distinct from the more systematic ones used for analysing them as linguistic artefacts, once they are recorded. An example of an innovative technique for systematically analysing the role contributed by intonational factors to ideophones' iconically depictive meanings is found in the breaching experiments of Dingemanse (2011:179–183).

The need for different kinds of methods to gather ideophones, however, is driven by their special characteristics. This is more than an intuition. We were able to appreciate, in a unique way, such qualitative differences between ideophones and conventional descriptive words in an experimental setting during the summer of 2022. We conducted a neuroimaging experiment with Kichwa consultants, which involved the use of fNIRS technology to detect patterns of speakers' perceptions of ideophones compared with ordinary words.[2] We had seventeen speakers listen to a list of ten words to create a baseline recording of their perceptions, and then had them listen to a much larger sample of performatively articulated ideophones drawn from recordings we had made. A few speakers listened silently to the entire spectrum of recordings. A number of them, however, reacted to the baseline recordings by repeating each word out loud. When the ideophone recordings began, however, these same consultants listened silently rather than repeating the ideophones. We infer from this observation that speakers apprehended the ideophones as evoking something which didn't lend itself to a straightforwardly repeatable utterance. Examples of ideophones in use will help make the case for our claims about the need for indirect methods to study ideophones' evocative qualities.

One such example follows (Figure 7.2), of an interview during which empathy became foregrounded by the speaker, who was recounting a narrative which detailed the tragic death of her mother. The account began as a story about spirits called *supay*s, and Luisa Cadena recalled her father's telling of the experience of becoming aware that he was losing his wife, Luisa's mother. This experience was believed by her father to have been portended by the sounds of the *shalama* spirit,[3] which she depicts with repetitions of an ideophone. When questioned about the words accompanying the cry of the spirit, she explained that the cry was in effect expressing the sentiments of the words. The words were, in other words, her own translation of the spirit's cry.

---

[2] fNIRS stands for functional near-infrared spectroscopy, a method for detecting cortical responses to auditory stimuli by measuring oxygen levels in blood flow.

[3] This example may be heard at https://quechuarealwords.byu.edu/?ideophone=ii. The phrase 'oh woe is me' is communicated by the suffix *–pa*, which is used on the verb in this example. Comparing and contrasting examples of its use leads to the inference that speakers are using this suffix to evoke empathy in listeners, for themselves, and possibly as well as to evoke empathy for the referent, which in this instance is the speaker's dying wife.

Figure 7.2 A forest spirit's cry

(2) Wita awaiɕi iiii iii iiii iii; ɲuka warmimi waɲupan! Iiii iiiɕi wakara!

'Above the weeds, apparently, (it sounded) *iiii iii iiii iii* (saying) "My wife is dying, (oh woe is me)!" *iiii iii*, it was heard to have cried out.'

Besides the empathetic stance which often underlies their use, another key characteristic of ideophones is their tendency to communicate in ways that evoke memories, emotions, and realizations. Ideophones are particularly likely to evoke memories and the emotions of events from all kinds of life experiences. They may also evoke complex perspectives on these events, leading one to realizations about one's lived experiences (Nuckolls 2022). In the following example (Figure 7.3), featuring the ideophone *taras*, a sensory impression imitated by an ideophone condenses a memory which reveals the speaker's intricate knowledge of the forest and the interconnectedness of all activities, whether engaged in by humans or non-humans. This interconnected knowledge is illustrated by Luisa Cadena's recollections, related to me and my student in the summer of 2017, of trekking through the forest with her father when she was a very young child. She describes how she and her father perceived a rustling sound, which she imitated with *taras*:[4]

---

[4] This example may be viewed at the following link: https://quechuarealwords.byu.edu/?ideophone=taras (video 2).

Figure 7.3 A rustling sound

(3) tɕi paj taras̪ [pause] taras [pause] taras̪ [pause] runas iʎaɕka satɕai.

'And then [something goes] *taras* [pause] *taras* [pause] *taras* [pause] in a [part of the] forest where there are no people whatsoever.'

It is after hearing this sound that Luisa's father warns her, telling her that the spider monkeys he is hunting produce scat, which is a source of food for jaguars. The sound *taras*, therefore, might indicate that a jaguar is near by, moving about in the shrubbery. He warns her to stand by, watching her surroundings carefully, or they might end up becoming the jaguar's food.[5]

What is evoked by *taras*, then, is their awareness of the intricate interrelations of predation that are at play in this particular moment. The spider monkeys are feeding on the fruiting trees that surround the narrator and her father, who are attempting to hunt the spider monkeys for their own food. Then there is the possibility that a jaguar might be feeding on the spider monkeys' scat, or worse,

---

[5] The words she reports her father saying are:
ɲukata niwara jaja: Kuɕiʎu ismata, wira ismata mikuɕa purik man pumaga. rikuɕa ɕajangi! Mikwi tukuntɕima niwara ɲuka jaja!

'My father said to me: "Jaguars are eaters of spider monkey scat, which is full of fat. [So] stand by watchfully! [otherwise] We might also be eaten!" said my father.'

preparing to turn humans into its next meal. The evocation of these intricate interrelations also gives rise to distinctive emotions, namely, the narrator and her father's fear and their need to be in a state of high alert.

In contrast to the foregoing example, where a speaker's ideophonically rendered experience recalled feelings of tension and fear, the evocative qualities of ideophones may also lend themselves to intimate ease and relaxation, which can pave the way for humour in discourse to emerge. We are not claiming that ideophones are necessarily humorous in use, although they can be part of humorous moments in narratives and in interactions. In the following example, Tod Swanson interviews two sisters, Belgica and Eulodia, who are working in a garden. They are surrounding hot pepper plants with ashes to fertilize the soil.

One of the sisters, Belgica, has just explained to Swanson that one should sprinkle the ashes around the periphery of the plant's base, rather than close to it. She uses the ideophone *ki* for this sprinkling action.[6] In the following example (Figure 7.4) she reports what she has just said.

Figure 7.4 Sprinkling ashes

(4) Laɾowata kasna ki ki ki ki ki ki ki ki ki chuɾana aŋ niɾanimi, mana japakta ʎutaktaga, kasnaʎa.

'A little beside it like this *ki ki ki ki ki ki ki ki ki*, one is to put (them)', I said, 'not stuck together a lot, but just like this'.

Swanson then elicits a repetition of the ideophone *ki*, while she and her sister are still applying the ashes around the pepper plants, by asking Belgica to show with her hands exactly how the sprinkling with *ki* is done. After several instances of

[6] This video may be viewed at https://quechuarealwords.byu.edu/?ideophone=ki (video 3).

being asked to repeat *ki*, along with explanations of why she does this, he then asks her to show the specific way in which the hand enacts the sprinkling movement with *ki*. She obliges but then looks up at her sister, and they both laugh.[7]

This amused reaction is not an unusual, following a request for a Kichwa speaker to repeat an ideophone they have already articulated. Although they did not laugh while steeped in the performance of the ideophone in the original utterance, they might laugh when asked to re-create the ideophonic performance. We interpret this laughter as arising from a feeling of self-consciousness about re-creating part of a performative act while no longer being in a playfully performative frame. The laughter arises, we surmise, because of the request for a speaker to 'break frame' and enact a performance outside of its performative context (Goffman 1974).

It is obvious from this interaction, and from many others as well, that we are not inconspicuous observers, attempting to objectively document ideophones in use, while concealing our research interests in these expressions. We are biased fieldworkers whose personal relationships facilitate greater involvement with our speakers, their lives, and their ideophone usage. We are also biased insofar as we attempt to emulate the empathetic stance which often underlies Kichwa speakers' use of ideophones. As researchers we have tried to internalize an empathetic perspective from which we study ideophones, and interact with native speakers. In the next section, we explain how the interpersonal stances we adopt with our consultants have influenced how we select speakers to work with. We also delve into the ways in which our personal histories have influenced our research interests in ideophones, which have influenced our fieldwork practices.

7.3 Our relationships with Kichwa consultants

We have not attempted to use random sampling procedures or survey instruments to find consultants. Our relationships with Kichwa people are significant for us. We are not only researchers, we have long-standing, complex friendships, and kinship relations with a number of people. Our methods have emerged from an interdisciplinary collaboration over many years of experience with the Kichwa world, including shared interactions with mutual Kichwa friends.

We have chosen to work with people who we find relatable, and whose company we enjoy. With help from these relationships we have learned to joke like native speakers. Because of our long-standing relationships with our speakers, we have had ample opportunities to learn about their life histories and about how key life experiences have affected them.

One way in which knowledge of peoples' life histories matters concerns their language-speaking habits. Rather than attempting to survey people about their speaking habits and rely on their self-reports about such habits, we have relied on

---

[7] This video may be viewed at: https://quechuarealwords.byu.edu/?ideophone=ki (video 4).

our own observations to directly experience their speaking habits. Based on a pre-liminary, short-lived attempt to work with highland speakers of Kichwa, most of whom self-identified to some extent with European Spanish-speaking culture, and were reluctant to speak Kichwa with her, Nuckolls decided, early in her fieldwork, to try to work with people who lived in areas not dominated by this culture. She therefore spent her dissertation research time within eastern Amazonian Ecuador, where Kichwa speakers self-identified as Kichwa-dominant rather than Spanish-dominant. Although this necessitated conducting fieldwork in areas of Ecuador that were not accessible by road, and chartering flights to the military base and community of Montalvo, it was the only way to ensure that she would encounter people who were not only willing to speak Kichwa with her, but were also likely to use ideophones. Research on ideophones in African societies has determined that such use can be compromised within communities that are in contact with European colonial influences.

Although Kichwa over Spanish dominance was a given in this remote part of Ecuador, and continues to be relevant for most older speakers in the fifty- to eighty-year-old age ranges, it has become a complex issue more recently as we have expanded our research activities into more accessible areas, where Spanish language use is now established. The issue of dominance becomes especially complicated with some of our younger consultants in their thirties and forties, especially for those with at least some formal educational experience. For example, one such consultant, a gifted ceramic artist and eloquent narrator, is forty years old, and is comfortable speaking Kichwa, Shiwiar, and Spanish. She grew up in a very remote setting, but her father facilitated formal education for his children by bringing a Spanish-speaking teacher from the nearest military base to his tiny community.

Their first attempt failed because the teacher could not adjust to their ways of life in such a remote place. The second attempt succeeded, and our con-sultant and her siblings enjoyed their experiences learning Spanish and liter-acy skills from the teacher, who stayed to teach them for a number of years. This speaker's father also, at some point in her childhood, took another wife, a Shiwiar-speaking woman, which exposed her to this language on a regular basis through interactions with members of her extended family. She credits her time spent playing with Shiwiar children her age for helping her develop flu-ency in this language as well. It would in fact be difficult to decide whether this consultant feels more aligned with Kichwa or Shiwiar, especially as she is now in a relationship with a Shiwiar man who does not speak Kichwa. What is significant about this speaker is that she has learned to speak Spanish, but Spanish-speaking cultural norms have not inhibited her ideophone use. More-over, Swanson has observed that some Kichwa-dominant speakers of his family will occasionally switch into Spanish, but will insert ideophones into their Spanish utterances.

The matter of language dominance, language use, and ideophone use can also become complicated for our older speakers, some of whom have entrenched prejudices about certain languages. One such speaker, a woman in her seventies, was raised in a Kichwa family but, while a very young child, spent substantial amounts of time interacting with Shiwiar speakers, with the result that she became fluent in this language as well. Yet she recounts that whenever she spoke this language, which was viewed as a low-status language by her older sisters, she was scolded and told not to speak it. She continues to be able to speak Shiwiar, but most of her language interactions are with her Kichwa-dominant sisters. Because of such entrenched attitudes and prejudices held by Kichwa speakers, especially older people who are closer to memories of traumatic events linked to inter-tribal warfare between different groups, it would be difficult to gather useful information about peoples' speaking habits based on the kinds of self-reports which tend to be used in structured surveys.

7.4 Personal histories informing methodologies

Because our distinctive histories and academic formations are relevant to the various methods we have developed, we will briefly review each separately. Nuckolls's interest in ideophones began while studying Kichwa as an undergraduate at the University of Wisconsin. Her fascination with the brief mention of these words in a pedagogical grammar of Highland Ecuadorian Kichwa catalysed an academic focus which has consistently informed her research into various aspects of their structures, including their phonology, morphology, syntax, semantics, discourse properties, cultural semantics, and co-occurring gestures. This fascination is related to an earlier, pre-university interest, while attending two different art schools, in the aesthetics of visual media, especially experimental, non-representational film-making by artists such as Stan Brakhage and Jordan Belson. Struck by the imagic, analogical potential of a form of expression embedded within the very different structures of conventionally descriptive language, she set out to try to understand the nature of ideophones as a linguist. In attempting to understand ideophones from a linguistic perspective, Nuckolls originally considered her goals to be focused on understanding the ways in which ideophones as expressions are principled in their structures. Her goals have evolved, however to understand not only their principled structures, but also to grasp how they expand the margins of what has traditionally been considered 'linguistic' (Dingemanse 2018). To this end, she has been able to delve into their performative intonation (Nuckolls 1996) and their gestural properties (Nuckolls 2021) while working with Luisa Cadena and other members of her extended family for over thirty years.

Luisa Cadena became a key consultant for Nuckolls, not only for her language expertise, but for her friendship at a critical juncture in Nuckolls's dissertation fieldwork. After approximately twelve months of working in the remote community of Puka Yaku and the small town of Puyo, Nuckolls was experiencing a psychological low point, having spent significant amounts of time in Puka Yaku without yet attaining much in the way of functional speaking abilities. Also contributing to her psychological unease were the many unanswered questions about what ideophones meant and how they were used.

Her methods in that early phase consisted of gathering and noting examples of ideophones overheard by speakers in daily conversations taking place in natural settings. These settings consisted of families gathered together for work-related tasks such as weeding, gardening, and cooking food, as well as larger social gatherings consisting of groups of people sitting together in their homes. The gathering and noting of ideophones was sometimes audio-recorded, but often was simply written into a small notebook during this initial phase of fieldwork, which lasted for about one year. Ideophones were identified by their performative elaboration. If a lexical item was foregrounded in any way, whether by louder or softer pronunciation, expressive lengthening, or a pitch that was noticeably distinct from its surrounding speech, especially a high rising pitch, it was written down. Additional attributes considered relevant for identifying a word as an ideophone included word-final stress, expressive repetition, and a pause following a word's pronunciation.

When her speaking abilities improved, she was able to directly question people about their ideophone usage. For example, when she asked the question: *Imata tak kimirina?* 'What does it mean to lean on something *tak?*', the response from a man was to take his blowgun and lean it against one of the support poles of his house so that only the tip touched the support pole. However, he also clearly illustrated the meaning of the ideophone *tak* by pronouncing it at the exact moment when the tip of the blowgun touched the support pole. Such eloquent demonstrations of ideophone meanings were not easy to elicit, however.

After this initial phase of noting and gathering ideophones she encountered Luisa Cadena, one day, while waiting for a flight out of the military base at Montalvo. This was a critical development in her fieldwork because she had made numerous observations and taken many notes about ideophones, but was having difficulties understanding their semantics and functions in the larger scheme of Kichwa grammar. She was struck immediately by Sra Cadena's friendliness and obvious love of storytelling, which seemed to engage all around her. After their flight landed, she approached Cadena with a request for help with Nuckolls's learning of Kichwa. Sra Cadena readily agreed and they began to work together in Puyo almost every afternoon for several hours of interviews, for about five months.

EMPATHY & INDIRECT METHODS FOR FIELDWORK   133

This arrangement also worked well for Sra Cadena, who had recently had abdominal surgery and was unable to do her usual work of washing clothes to supplement her income. Being able to work with Sra Cadena was a pivotal, breakthrough experience for Nuckolls who, for the first time in her fieldwork, began to experience the Kichwa language as a flow of ideas. Although the 'interviews' were designed to elicit, they often unfolded as conversations, with many back-and-forth exchanges between Nuckolls and Cadena. The interviews were structured, following the advice of her dissertation supervisor Paul Friedrich, who suggested making a list of 200 Kichwa verbs. The goal was to attempt to test how acceptable each verb would be with each ideophone that she had observed in actually occurring discourse.

In one sense the interviews were not at all successful. Luisa Cadena did not find the structure of these questions to be interesting, possibly because many ideophone/verb combinations which were hypothetically paired did not work and had to be rejected. Yet, in the process of rejecting suggested combinations, Sra Cadena offered narratives, which included many of her own ideophone/verb combinations. Nuckolls continued with this line of questioning, and was able to record narratives, songs, and conversations, which resulted in over 800 pages of transcriptions by means of this indirect methodology. These transcribed recordings contained many examples of ideophones, which formed the basis of her dissertation.

In addition to the questions about possible ideophone/verb collocations, Nuckolls also began a line of questioning about Kichwa verbs themselves. The goal was to try to grasp the semantics of approximately 200 different verbs to see which, if any, ideophones they would spontaneously call up for Sra Cadena. These 'verb portrait' interviews resulted in many more narratives, conversations, and some songs. The result of asking about one such verb, *astana* 'to load' is presented in (5). This elicitation evoked one sense of the ideophone *polang*, which is the depiction of the way something floats and moves across the surface of water, either by gliding along smoothly, or by intermittently bobbing.[8] The interview emerged as follows:

(5) a.   Imata 'astana'?

       'What does *astana* mean?'   Nuckolls

   b.   ɲaupa kanoawaŋ ɾik aɾanchi Piwi yakuma, ɲukanchi tambugama.

       'At an earlier time we used to go by canoe to *Piwi* pond,
       as far as our shelter.'   Cadena

---

[8] Audiovisually recorded examples of this ideophone in use can be viewed at https://quechuarealwords.byu.edu/?ideophone=polan

c. tɕajma puriŋgaw, ɲukanchi astak aranchi aswata

puɲunata; tɕigunawaŋ polaŋŋŋ rik aranchi
'In order to travel there, we would load *aswa*, and bedding;
and with those things we would (go) *polann*
(gliding across the water).' Cadena

d. tɕi-manda, Piwi jakuma paktanchi. Palandata pitinchi, sarata
pitinchi

'Then we arrive at *Piwi* pond. We cut plaintains, we cut corn.' Cadena

e. aɕaŋgama, aɕaŋgama tɕuranchi; yandata tsalinchi

'In baskets, in baskets, we put them; (then) we split wood.' Cadena

f. tɕita ɕuk waŋguta tsalinchi. Tukwita kanoama astanchi

'We split a bundle of it; (and) we load everything into the canoe.' Cadena

g. tɕi maŋ 'astana'.

'That's what loading is.' Cadena

As is obvious from the foregoing example, the ideophone *polan* was indirectly elicited within the context of a short narrative about the meaning of the verb *astana* 'to load'. This verb, however, is only tangentially related to this particular ideophone. People load things into canoes which float down the river in a *polan*-like way, i.e. with buoyancy. There are a variety of entities whose manner of floating may be depicted with *polan*, however, and there are other verbs with which *polan* can occur.

Despite the indirectness of this method of elicitation, it has proven extremely helpful for understanding some of the natural contexts where ideophones occur. This method of not focusing on ideophones themselves, but allowing them to emerge from narratives, has also helped to unravel the complex meanings of the ideophone *polan*, meanings which have not yet been attested in any other ideophone-rich language.[9] To hear ideophones in their contexts would not have been possible with the kinds of forced-choice questions which had originally been formulated. And these 'interviews' formed the basis for a working relationship and a close friendship, which continues to flourish.

---

[9] The claim for *polan*'s uniqueness is based on searching published materials on ideophones, and posing an informal query to an online discussion forum, the Linguistic Typology Group. There may be semantic analogues of *polan* somewhere in the world. As of the present moment, however, they are not attested.

Swanson, who grew up in Ecuador, has ties with Kichwa speakers going all the way back to his childhood. His relationship with the Kichwa language and people began when his parents moved to the Pastaza valley in 1961. As a child his parents entrusted him to the care of a Kichwa man named Agustin Tapuy, who regularly took him hunting and fishing in the forest. During the sixties and early seventies he also accompanied his father on visits to clinics in Shuar communities and spent significant time in Arajuno and on the Curaray River. He later married a Kichwa woman, Josefina Andi, from the Napo valley.

From early childhood Swanson was impressed with the rhetorical magic of Kichwa stories about the forest. These were stories of encounters that were humorous, beautiful, and terrifying. Interest in these stories precedes his academic career and is in part what led him there. On graduating from high school in Ecuador, Swanson pursued an undergraduate degree in Linguistics at the University of Minnesota, hoping that this discipline would help him make sense of his fascination with Kichwa narratives. However he found the focus on generative grammar, which was dominant at that time, to be an inadequate tool for the task. He therefore went on to pursue a PhD in comparative religion, specializing in Kichwa traditions, at the University of Chicago.

There he was influenced by William James's *Varieties of Religious Experience*, which motivated him to record various genres of Kichwa narrative experiences and to reflect on how their distinctiveness problematized monotheistic paradigms. While continental philosophers from Kant to Rudolph Otto, Paul Tillich, and Mircea Eliade argued for a universal religious experience of the ineffable and ultimate (the subjective experience of the ultimacy of a monotheistic god), Swanson sought to capture the unique and personal emotional qualities of Kichwa social relations to nature, relations which are often framed as 'animistic' by sociocultural anthropologists working in Amazonian Ecuador.

These were not experiences of the eternal but rather of empathy for the vulnerability, the passing joys and sufferings of nature, associated with the finitude of changing multilateral relations, an emotion Kichwa speakers refer to as *llakichina*. Because these narratives express empathetic connection with the experiences of others, including other species at the outer limits of communicability, Swanson was especially interested in how the Kichwa language evoked things difficult to convey in conventional concepts. These concerns then led to his interests in the use of ideophones, gestures, and the analogies between the human and the non-human which were presupposed by such usages.

To capture expressions of Kichwa animistic experience, Swanson first sought to record the kinds of narratives that had made an impression on him in childhood. To do this he sought out people he already knew were good narrators and with whom he had a long personal relationship. Because he was attempting to recapture narratives of an earlier time he also sought to film people who naturally spoke and thought more like the older people he remembered from his childhood.

136 JANIS NUCKOLLS AND TOD SWANSON

This meant learning from people whose ways of speaking were less influenced by Spanish grammar, the media, and formal schooling.

In learning how to draw out the interviewee, so as to capture moving narratives, Swanson sought to emulate the interviewing style of journalists, rather than that of social science researchers. This required abandoning standard social-scientific methods such as: attempting to maintain neutrality, using standardized questions across interviews, avoiding leading questions, or trying to get a representative sample. Instead, he tried to put interviewees at ease, so that they felt comfortable to laugh, cry, or wonder. He asked leading questions designed to draw out the unique perspectives, histories, and interests of each narrator. Much of Swanson's academic career has been an attempt to capture these moments audiovisually, so that they can be used to represent the literary powers of Kichwa art and storytelling for English-speaking readers. Although his methods did not deliberately seek to elicit ideophones, they indirectly produced a diverse corpus of expressive narratives that are particularly rich in ideophones. This is most likely because he intentionally sought recordings of performances with heightened emotional impact, rather than random Kichwa speech.

Swanson's ethnographic videos have been incalculably valuable as resources for Quechua Real Words, an audiovisual dictionary of ideophones which have been extracted from these and many other videos, and posted on this site in very short clips. At the same time, each clip is linked to its longer narrative so that viewers can see how the ideophone functions within its larger context. This extraction process has been a very collaborative enterprise which has been aided by undergraduate and graduate students with Kichwa language expertise. Students have worked on the site, not only by culling ideophones from narratives, but also as transcribers of the Kichwa utterances for specific ideophones, and occasionally as videographers.[10]

Because we worked together at the Andes and Amazon Field School over multiple summers, we have often thought about the functions of ideophones together and have often had joint conversations about them with the narrators. These

---

[10] We are grateful to the following students, who have been the most actively involved with the Quechua Real Words site in varying capacities: Alexander Rice made the GIF image on the site's home page, and has audiovisually recorded a number of the ideophones on the site. Diana Sun conceived an original template, which was used to construct the site with WordPress. Sarah Hatton made an early archive of videos for YouTube, in which a number of ideophones have been found. Sidney Jensen Ludlow isolated many ideophone clips from videos, which appear on the site. Many of the Kichwa utterances, including the ideophones on the site, have been phonetically transcribed by Barrett Hamp. Auna Nygaard has participated in a number of interviews which she has uploaded to our YouTube channel, Quechua Research Group, and has also added ideophones to the QRW site. Charles Alger has been going through the QRW site, transcribing and translating many of the entries. Valuable contributions to Quechua Real Words have also been made by graduate and undergraduate students from a variety of universities, including Santiago Swanson, Christina Collicott, Lisa Warren Carney, and Kelsey Bergeson, all of whom have helped with audiovisual recordings of our interviews with Kichwa speakers. Austin Howard has contributed several high-quality recordings and has isolated a number of ideophones which have been added to the site.

conversations have led to new narratives, continued recording, and many conversations. Throughout these exchanges, Swanson has often been more interested in the role of the ideophones in the larger literary context while Nuckolls has focused on trying to understand their semantics and pragmatics, and attempting to analyse how they work with specific verbs and gestures. Nevertheless, we have shared a broad interest in the animistic narratives and in the lives and emotions of our common narrator friends, collaboratively seeking to understand what they were talking about and how the ideophones functioned to get their message across.

Filming can of course be intrusive in intimate conversation. For this reason we often don't film from the start. Instead we approach this kind of documentation much as people do when they want to capture memorable moments with their friends on social media. When a close friend says something funny or moving it is now common to whip out a cell phone and say something like 'Wait! Say that again!' (so that it can be shared on Facebook, Instagram, or Snapchat). Just as friends will usually oblige and retell the story or joke with a similar degree of expressivity to the original, so too do our Kichwa consultants, as happened with the examples of ideophones in examples (1) and (3). Since we are audiovisually documenting performances we usually choose the background and lighting carefully. If an ideophone or series of ideophones occurs within a casual conversation, as happened in example (1), with the toucan bird's fruit, we may also do additional takes of the ideophone, by saying something like'Wow! What was that like again? Can you say that again?'

Our consultants usually have no trouble re-involving themselves in the performance of an ideophone, although subsequent re-performances will often vary somewhat from the originals. An exception to this practice of re-eliciting happens when speakers are engaged in telling a narrative. Such tellings are not usually interrupted. If an unfamiliar ideophone occurs during the telling, however, we will query the speaker about it when the performance is finished. If a re-performance results in interestingly different variations, either involving differences in gestures, intonation, or metacommentary by the speaker, we post these different versions on that ideophone's page in the Quechua Real Words site, in order to present the ranges of performative possibilities.

7.5 Indirect and direct methodologies

Although we have found that indirect methodologies have been overwhelmingly more successful than direct ones for documenting ideophones, there have been occasional 'success stories' with direct elicitation as well. This occurred with the ideophone *hyaw*, which is possibly one of the most interesting ideophones we have ever observed. It was first discovered by Swanson while interviewing our consultant Eulodia about the way she had painted a design on her face. This design evoked a memory of encountering a *pundzhana palo* or 'agouti snake', which is a type of pit viper. She became aware of this pit viper because of the sounds it was making, which she imitated with repetitions of *hyaw*.

This ideophone illustrates something that was unexpected for us. Despite widespread assumptions about the 'simplicity' of onomatopoeic words, which we define as ideophones that exclusively imitate sound, their semantics can be complex. Eulodia's example illustrates this complexity with the following example (Figure 7.5). This ideophone is semantically unusual because the snake is not simply reported to be making a sound. Onomatopoeic *hjaw* has a double perspective embedded within it. Its meaning was explained by Eulodia, as an imitation of the sound made by a snake who is said to be imitating the sound of a rodent, in order to lure rodents to himself, so that the snake can then pounce on them for his next meal. Example (6) illustrates Eulodia's depiction of this sound *hyaw*, which she then explains is the sound of a type of rodent called a *pundzhana*:[11]

Figure 7.5 An agouti snake's sound

(6) ɲa hʲaw hʲaw hʲaw hʲaw nira pundʐana ɕina

   'Then it (a snake) said *hyaw hyaw hyaw hyaw* (sounding) like an agouti.'

In order to determine how widespread Eulodia's understanding of this ideophone is, and how other speakers might interpret its use, Swanson asked a Napo Kichwa speaker, Daniel, about it. Daniel not only verified its existence, he performatively imitated the same ideophone (Figure 7.6), *hyaw*, used by Eulodia. He then

---

[11] Examples of this onomatopoeic word can be heard at: https://quechuarealwords.byu.edu/?ideophone=hyaw (videos 1 and 2).

explained that hunters who are attempting to find agoutis for their own food will imitate these rodents' sounds, not by using *hyaw*, but by imitating their own perceptions of the actual sounds of an agouti, which he produced with a series of high-pitched whistles, using his hand to create the airflow for a stronger sound.[12]

Figure 7.6 An agouti snake's whistle

(7) ɲukanchi kaj satɕaj satɕa puriɕa, sikugunaɾa na kaʎaɾi ɾukuguna uɕanuɕka pajguna sikuɾa kayatɕinga hʲaw hʲaw hʲaw hʲaw niɕka, siku tɕibi mas ɕu sikugunas pajwapuɾa mantɕi niɕa shamunuɕka mas iɕki o kinsa, karanpuɾamanda shamunuɕka. Kasnami niɕka silbanga ɾawni (whistles)

'So when we are walking in the forest, well the old ones, being able, they would attract agoutis by calling (how they sound) going *hyaw hyaw hyaw hyaw*; and the agoutis thinking "that's one of our kind" would come. So like how they called (them), I'm going to whistle (whistles).'

Although this particular example from Daniel was directly elicited, it was only possible to ask directly about this ideophone after learning of its existence by indirectly asking about an entirely different matter, namely, the question about

---

[12] The whistles, and Daniel's explanation, can be heard at: https://quechuarealwords.byu.edu/?ideophone=hyaw (video 3).

Eulodia's face-painting design. It was this question which triggered her memory from a time when she, as a fourteen-year-old girl, went out into the forest to look for oriole hatchlings to take home and raise as pets. And it was while searching for the hatchlings that she heard the snake calling out, which she imitated with *hyaw*. It would not have occurred to either of us that there might be an ideophone for a snake imitating a rodent in order to attract the rodent to itself. Moreover, the direct questioning of Daniel by Swanson resulted in other interesting realizations, such as the fact that human hunters seem to learn some of their hunting techniques from other animals, and that speakers are aware of how different an ideophonically rendered sound is, is from one's perception of that sound.

Another insight that becomes apparent through indirectly gathering ideophone data, is that their meanings, which are evident in different contexts of use, are probably impossible for speakers to exhaustively enumerate. The implications of this have been recognized by Tsujimura (2016). She has argued that even the most conventionalized ideophones, which are called 'mimetics' in Japanese, are underspecified by design, indeterminately flexible, and capable of infinite polysemous extensions. Such flexibility, according to Tsujimura, is one of the characteristics which make Japanese ideophones distinctive from the prosaic (i.e. non-ideophonic) lexicon.

An example which shows how impossible it may be to conceive of every possible use of a Kichwa ideophone became apparent very recently when Nuckolls was interviewing our consultant Belgica about her knowledge of childbirth procedures. This occurred during an advanced Kichwa class while asking our speaker about her knowledge of these practices. To contextualize this enquiry, the day before, we had visited a clinic operated by Kichwa midwives who had given us a demonstration of their traditional birthing techniques. Belgica was also present during this demonstration and when asked about it during class the next day, added her own perspectives and advice to what we had heard.

She explained, for example, that breathing with one's mouth closed rather than open was important during labour because open-mouth breathing would delay the baby's emergence. It was the ideophone she used to depict the consequences of breathing with the mouth open, however, that was surprising (Figure 7.7). She used two ideophones, *an* to depict an open mouth, which was not a surprising usage, but then used the ideophone *polan*, to depict the way a baby would rise up in the womb, rather than drop down:[13]

---

[13] This example of *an* (video 3) occurs at: https://quechuarealwords.byu.edu/?ideophone=ang.
Examples of *polan*, including example (5c) (video 13) may be viewed at: https://quechuarealwords.byu.edu/?ideophone=polan.

Figure 7.7 A baby rising up

(8) tɕigaŋ ɕimita aŋ paskakpi wawami polaŋma ɕajaɾiŋga nig ag aɾa tɕasna tukuɕa mana wajɾa ɕina ʎukɕiŋgatɕu wawa nig an. polaŋma ɕajaɾiŋga niɾa tɕi

'And so with that, if one opens one's mouth *ang* (while breathing), the baby will rise up *polan*, they say, and becoming like that, the baby will not come out quickly, they say; it will rise up *polan*.'

Her use of *polan* was surprising because our definition of one of the senses of this ideophone, based on our understanding of its use, was that it always involved something rising upwards from under water and becoming visible on the water's surface. The following definition, was, until we heard this particular usage, our characterization of this ideophone's semantics:

1. Depicts the way something rises from under water and is suddenly evident as it breaks through to the water's surface. It may focus on the duration of the upward-thrusting movement, or its momentary, punctual occurrence.

A second sense for this ideophone's use is also attested. This is the sense used in example (5c), where the speaker depicted a canoe floating across the water's surface:

2. May depict the way something floats and moves across the surface of water, either by gliding along smoothly, or by intermittently bobbing.

Our definition for sense 1, however, has now been amended as follows. The novel sense is underlined below:

1. Depicts the way something rises from under water and is suddenly evident as it breaks through to the water's surface. It may focus on the duration of the upward-thrusting movement, or its momentary, punctual occurrence. *May also depict the rising up of a baby inside a watery womb during labour.*

The extension of sense 1 to depict a process of rising up inside the body was a complete surprise to us. As usages go, it is definitely an outlier, since every other documented example of this ideophone involves movements within bodies of water such as rivers and lakes. Yet this example illustrates clearly how richly polysemous ideophones can be, making the task of defining their senses a real challenge. It is no wonder that one scholar has stated: 'Ideophones are a lexicographer's worst nightmare' (De Schryver 2009: 38).

We offer some closing observations on recent attempts to do fieldwork investigations on ideophones with an extended family who have had little experience with linguists, with ethnographic and linguistic interview questions, or with members of mainstream societies generally. During the summer of 2022 we had the opportunity to travel to a remote part of Amazonian Ecuador, along the Curaray River, which is home for Wao Tedero people. Their language is not well-studied by linguists and their remote location, which necessitates lengthy day long canoe travel, has not made it convenient for anyone to work with them in their traditional forest setting.

Although Swanson had established relationships with certain members of this community, our attempts to do even the most preliminary investigations of ideophones faced unexpected challenges. For example, we found ourselves in the forest one day with a woman in her fifties or sixties, who was knowledgeable about plant medicines. When we came across a *Piperaceae* plant which Swanson had heard was used by Wao as love medicine, our consultant told us that it was also used to attract fish, and began to show us how to put it on the leaf of a hook with the bait, which would then be thrown into the water. Nuckolls immediately wondered how the sound of something falling into water would be ideophonically depicted. As we walked to the riverbank, she asked our consultant, who could speak some Kichwa, how this would sound, and told her that in Kichwa it would sound *tsupu*. Our friend put her finger to her lips as a sign of keeping silent and kept on imitating how one should tiptoe while walking and fish silently. When we arrived at the river, Swanson threw a big stick into the water, and tried again to ask her for an ideophone. She responded by saying that any fish hearing that sound would swim away, and she'd have to go further downriver to fish. She added further that her elders taught her to fish silently.

Another difficulty arose when we asked a man about the same age as our fishing companion about the sound made by a howler monkey. Our consultant began to imitate, in a very detailed way, the pathos-filled cry of such a monkey, which he had once shot with a poison dart from a blowgun. His performance was so deeply imitative, and also enacted with such elaborate gestures and facial expressions, that it would have been extremely difficult to reduce it to an orthographic form. We suspect that a conventionalized ideophone for this sound exists, but that it would most likely be found in a traditional narrative context. It was clear to both of us that direct elicitation was difficult, and that we would have to achieve more proficiency in this language in order to gain access to some of the traditional stories, which would undoubtedly yield ideophones we could document.

7.6 Conclusions

With this chapter we have reflected back over our careers to articulate retrospectively what we have learned from our successes and failures at eliciting ideophones. If it is a coherent method it is one that has emerged gradually over time, both by trying out methods from our academic training, and also by trial and error, and love for the subject matter. The very nature of ideophones, as well as the ways in which they are used culturally by Kichwa speakers to evoke empathetic experiences, has led us to indirect elicitation far more often than direct elicitation. We also recognize that we have been fortunate in being able to develop long-term friendships with our Kichwa consultants, which has facilitated more humanistic-based research methods and formats for enquiry. Although we have enjoyed certain advantages from these long-term relationships, we are convinced that even fieldwork on ideophones which is limited by short-term involvements can be enhanced by the use of indirect methods. Some of these include: interviewing while involved in tasks which speakers find engaging and enjoyable, asking about subject matter which speakers find interesting, moving, or humorous, and allowing ideophones to emerge from conversations before attempting to ask targeted questions about their use. Once ideophones are found, more systematic methods for analysing their structures, their discourse patterns, and their semantics can be used.

References

Aaltola, Elisa (2013). Empathy, intersubjectivity, and animal ethics. *Journal of Environmental Philosophy* 10(2): 20–35.

de Schryver, Gilles-Maurice (2009). The lexicographic treatment of ideophones in Zulu, *Lexicos* 19: 34–54. https://doi.org/10.5788/19-0-429

Dingemanse, Mark (2011). The meaning and use of ideophones in Siwu. PhD thesis, Radboud University. [Max Planck Institute for Psycholinguistics Series, Volume 64.]

Dingemanse, Mark (2018). Redrawing the margins of language: Lessons from research on ideophones. *Glossa: A Journal of General Linguistics* 3(1): 1–30, https://doi.org/10.5334/gjgl.444

Dörnyei, Zoltan (2007). *Research Methods in Applied Linguistics: Quantitative, Qualitative, and Mixed Methodologies*. New York: Oxford University Press.

Goffman, Erving (1974). *Frame Analysis: An Essay on the Organization of Experience*. Cambridge, MA: Harvard University Press.

Nuckolls, Janis B. (1996). *Sounds Like Life: Sound-Symbolic Grammar, Performance, and Cognition in Pastaza Quechua*. New York: Oxford University Press.

Nuckolls, Janis B. (2021). How do you even know what ideophones mean?': Gestures' contributions to ideophone semantics in Pastaza Quichua. *Gesture* 19(2/3): 161–197.

Nuckolls, Janis B. (2022). The mindful animism of ideophony in Pastaza and Upper Napo Kichwa. *Ethos: Journal of the Society for Psychological Anthropology*. Published online 31 August 2022. https://doi.org/10.1111/etho.12356

Prior, Matthew T. (2017). Accomplishing 'rapport' in qualitative research interviews: Empathic moments in interaction. *Applied Linguistics Review* 9(4). DOI 10.1515/applirev-2017-0029

Tsujimura, Natsuko (2016). How flexible should the grammar of mimetics be? A view from Japanese poetry. In Noriko Iwasaki, Peter Sells, and Kimi Akita (eds), *The Grammar of Japanese Mimetics: Perspectives from Structure, Acquisition and Translation*. Abingdon: Routledge, 103–128. https://doi.org/10.4324/9781315646695

8

Documenting stealth lexicon

Field methods to collect the use of ideophones in Yucatec Maya

Olivier Le Guen and Rodrigo Petatillo Chan

8.1 Introduction

While ideophones have been by now quite well-documented in many languages, the existence of these words in certain parts of the world remains a debated question. In Mayan languages, for instance, several studies have been conducted (Maffi 1990; England 2006; Vázquez-Álvarez, Juan Jesús 1971–2011; Pérez González 2012; Martínez Guerrero 2013), but their label and the very definition of what constitutes an ideophones are still under discussion. For Yucatec Maya, Le Guen (2012) is the first to have proposed the existence of ideophones in this language, carefully examining their status as parts of speech and their morphological formation. Amazingly, even when ideophones are widely used in Yucatec Maya everyday speech, especially in Quintana Roo, previous researchers did not notice their presence, often confusing them with onomatopoeias (that only describe sounds). Although ideophones in Yucatec Maya are salient in the language, their use is complex and they can be easily missed if one does not pay enough attention. Because of this pragmatic stealth, documenting ideophones in this language can be challenging.

Previous research on ideophones have already pointed out this fact and one main characteristic of ideophones is that their expressive dimension is intrinsically present along with the propositional truth they carry (Anttila 1977; Dingemanse 2011, 2017). Because they encode and pragmatically entail involvement and emotive responses from the speaker as well as the speaker's stance on the narrated event, ideophones are often more depictive than descriptive (Dingemanse 2017). As a result, many speakers, and most of the modern linguistic tradition, consider them 'not real words', as childish language, or as having a peripheral linguistic status. For field linguists, such views imply that documenting ideophones is a hard task, theoretically as well as practically (often elicitation out of the blue is nearly impossible).

Olivier Le Guen and Rodrigo Petatillo Chan, *Documenting stealth lexicon*. In: *Capturing Expressivity*. Edited by: Jeffrey P. Williams, Oxford University Press. © Olivier Le Guen and Rodrigo Petatillo Chan (2025).
DOI: 10.1093/oso/9780192858931.003.0008

In everyday speech, especially in relaxed interactions, humans tend to favour the use of multimodality, iconicity, and voice effects. For this reason, ideophones are very practical multidimensional parts of speech, as they allow the collapse of several modalities in a unique, often syntactically isolated, word. As Dingemanse points out, ideophones are performative in nature and, unsurprisingly, often introduced by quotatives or verbs such as "do" or "say" (Dingemanse 2013: 114). Also commonly mentioned in the literature is the use of voice effect and gesture along with the verbal ideophone. Several studies have not only mentioned the presence of gesture but also systematically document some instances of multimodal production (Nuckolls 1995, 2000, 2020; Kita 1997; Dingemanse 2013; Mihas 2013). This multimodal dimension increases the difficulty of documenting ideophones.

This chapter aims at describing what ideophones are in Yucatec Maya, how they are used, and what fieldwork methodologies have been used so far to describe them. First, we will describe what ideophones in Yucatec Maya are and how they are constructed based on existing roots. We will discuss their iconic and multimodal character, as well as their everyday use, and how they can be considered 'stealth words' in this language. Finally, given what we have previously discussed, we will consider what methodologies are best-suited for collecting ideophones in Yucatec Maya.

8.2 Ideophones in Yucatec Maya

Ideophones in Yucatec Maya describe events in a multimodal way, encompassing three main features: sound, movement, and suddenness. The production of these words often involves a change of voicing (breathy voice), a louder pronunciation with respect to the sentential context (depending on the level of involvement of the speaker), and usually they are more phonologically isolated in the sentence. At the morphological level, roots derive ideophones according to three types of derivation, presented in more detail below: vowel alteration, suffixation, and derivation templates. Because ideophones are derivations in Yucatec Maya, they encompass two layers of meanings, one provided by the meaning of the root and the other by the meaning of the derivation. Finally, at the syntactic level, ideophones precede either a verb with an aspect, a quotative, or a pause (usually at the end of an utterance).

In Yucatec Maya, ideophones primarily describe events in terms of contact, movement, and velocity, blending visual and auditory dimensions while suggesting the idea of suddenness. These dimensions, especially visual and auditory, can be seen as displayed along a continuum and, according to the meaning of the root it derives, the ideophone can lean more towards a visual or an auditory representation. In order to illustrate how an ideophone can describe a more acoustic or visual event, consider the following example (1),[1] the story of how an old man got hit on the head with a baseball.

(1) Hit by a baseball
    le   ka'   t-u-síin   le   boolah-o',   **TUP'**[Figure 8.1a]
    DET CONJ TR.CP-3A-stretch DET ball-TD IDEO.hit

    t-u-táanho'olah   **kíihli'im**[Figure 8.1b] ka' bin-ih,   kíim-ih
    PREP-3A-forehead IDEO.shake   CONJ go-B3SG die-B3SG

    tumeet   e nohoch máak-o'
    CP-A3-do-CP-B3SG DET great person-TD

'When the (pitcher) threw the ball, *tup'* on his forehead, *kíihli'im* he went, the old man just passed away (= was knocked out)'
(2015_06_24_1541_Utsibalil_San_Juan5)

Figure 8.1 Gestures used with ideophones in a multimodal performance

In his recounting of the event, the speaker produces two ideophones to describe how an old man was hit by a baseball and fell, unconscious. Although both ideophones are accompanied by a gesture, the first is more deictic, as the ideophone focuses on the sound of the event, while the second is more iconic and descriptive, displaying some visual components encoded in the ideophone.

The scene the speaker recounts is highly emotional and exacerbates the unexpectedness of the event. An old man was watching a baseball match and suddenly got hit on the head by a ball and got knocked out. As we mentioned, the first ideophone insists on the sound of the ball hitting the old man's head, while the second describes more the way he fell on the ground. The gestures that accompany both ideophones (see Figure 8.1a,b) visually specify the manner in which the verbal

---

[1] The figure displays the gesture produced by the speaker, usually at the phase known as the 'stroke'. The production of the gesture is referenced in the examples: the part of the text underlined specifies the duration of the gesture that accompanies the speech and in brackets is the specific figure referenced.

expressions should be understood by the listeners (Kendon 2004). In the first part of the scene, the ball hits the old man's forehead and what is foregrounded is the unexpected impact and sound of the hit. The ideophone used is based on the root *tup'* "to hit" and its phonological realization relies on iconicity (see section 8.7): the ideophone uses a short vowel, mimicking the sound of a swift impact. The gesture is iconic (showing the quick hit on the head) but also deictic, displaying the trajectory of the ball hitting the forehead (see Figure 8.1a). The second part of the scene is more complex and it is reflected by the morphological derivation of the ideophone, as well as the gesture produced by the speaker. The ideophone is based on the root *kil* "shake, thunder", derived as *kíihli'im*, using the typical template for falling events. The use of the derivational template suggests the image of the old man falling, and, with the root *kil*, the speaker aims at rendering the impact of the body as if it made the earth shake, also alluding to the idea that the old man did not even try to catch his fall. To make this point even clearer, the speaker gesturally takes the perspective of the character in his story, extending both arms on each side and pretending to be falling backwards (see Figure 8.1b). This second ideophone and its accompanied performance are clearly located at the more visual end of the continuum.

8.3 Ideophones are derivations of existing roots

In many languages, ideophones form a separate class of words, sometimes even using specific phonemes not present in the standard lexicon (Dingemanse 2011). In Yucatec Maya, however, ideophones are based on CVC roots, as is most of the lexicon in this language. Root instantiation or derivation is highly productive in Yucatec Maya (Lois and Vapnarsky 2006; Le Guen 2015). Le Guen (2012) proposes three main forms in which ideophones can be derived: 1) by modifying the value of the vowel, 2) by using suffixes, and 3) through derivation, using specific templates. Each form carries a specific meaning (short vowel for a short event, specific template for falling or contact event, a suffix for internal repetition, etc.) that add to the meaning of the root. More precisely, the root carries a conceptual or notional meaning (the idea of explosion, for instance) and the derivation will render this concept into a concrete event, that is, making explicit the manner in which the event is occurring. Consider, for instance, the following example in (2):

(2) Exploding chips

> **wáahk'a'ach**   kih   u-wáak'-al   e   saabrita-o'
> IDPH.explode   QTV   3A-explode-NOM   DET   chips-TD
>
> '*wáahk'a'ach* says the explosion of the (package of) chips [when opened under pressure]'

In this example, the same root, *wak'*, is used as an ideophone as well as a noun (note that *wak'* can also be used as a verb). While the second use is unproblematic, and just means 'its explosion', the derivation into an ideophone with template C₁v́vhC₂v'v-*ch* adds the meaning of contact between entities. Both meanings collapsed suggest the idea of resistance and explosion. Additionally, the production of the ideophone stands out syntactically and prosodically in order to describe the sound of the event, a fact highlighted by the use of the quotative.

The three main types of derivations proposed in Le Guen (2012), themselves divided in particular forms with specific meanings, are summarized in Figure 8.2. Let's consider each of them, with some examples.

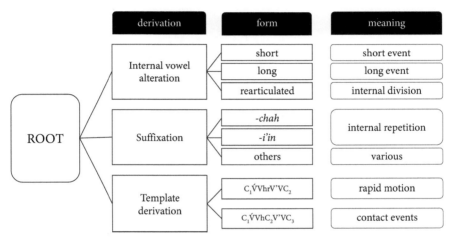

Figure 8.2 Schematization of the possible derivations of a CVC root in an ideophone in Yucatec Maya

8.4 Vowel derivation

In Yucatec Maya, the value of the vowel for CVC roots is flexible, and it is even used for a variety of grammatical purposes (marking voices for instance). When ideophones derive CvC roots, the value of the vowel becomes iconic. A short vowel represents a short or rapid event, a long vowel (usually phonetically lengthened) describes a lasting event, and a rearticulated internal vowel is particularly suited for retelling an event with a two-part sound or double click.

Consider the following example, in (3), that uses a short vowel with the root *ch'aj* 'drip' in order to describe how one puts a watery remedy into his/her eye. The speaker uses a character perspective (introduced in the speech with a manner deictic), as if he was dripping a drop of the remedy into his right eye (see Figure 8.3).

(3) Short vowel for rapid event—Drop in the eye

k-a-mach'-k-e'	k-a-ch'a-ik	t-aw-ich	beya'
HAB-A.2-grasp-TR.IC-TD	HAB-A.2-take-TR.IC-TD	PREP-A.2-eye	MAN.

ch'aj [Figure 8.3]. (.) chen ka'a-p'e goota
IDEO.drip   only two-CLAS drop

'You grasp (the wet cloth), you take it to your eye like so "*chaj!*" (.) only 2 drops (is enough).'(2023-02-02_1802_69479-DC)

Figure 8.3 The speaker uses character perspective to represent how the remedy should be put in one's eye

DOCUMENTING STEALTH LEXICON   151

A long vowel suggests a lasting event. While long vowels do exist in Yucatec Maya, in expressive use, they are generally also phonologically lengthened as an iconic process (to mimic the length of the event). For instance, to describe how an egg is fried in a pan with hot oil, the speaker uses the root *ts'aj* 'to fry' but lengthens the vowel to imitate the sound of the egg sizzling, see example (4).

(4)   Long vowel for lasting event—Frying egg

Bey   tun-teehe   le   he'-o',   k-u-bin   te
MAN PRG.3A-crack-NOM   DET   egg-TD   HAB-3A   go PREP   oil-TD

áaseyte-o' **tsaa:::::h.**   ki'
IDEO.fry   QOT

'As the egg is cracked, it goes into the (burning) oil and says: "*tsaa:::::h!*"'

Rearticulated vowels (i.e. a vowel with an internal glottal stop), are iconic too and represent events with an internal division, that is, a two-part sound. Consider, for instance, example (5), on how a woman describes how easy it is to frighten animals in the forest. The ideophone she uses is *so'oh*, derived from the root soh 'to pile up'. It refers to the sound made by someone stepping on dry leaves, which makes not just one noise, but rather multiple cracks.

(5)   Rearticulated vowel for two-part event—stepping on dry leaves

wáa   yaan   tu'ux   ken   a-wu'uy   **so'oh**
COND   ASEG   where   SUB   A2-listen   IDEO.pile up.

k-u-p'u'h-ul   ba'al   bin=e'
HAB-frighten-PAS-ICP   thing   EVID=TOP

tumeen   (l)e   aalak'=o'   yaan   up'u'uhul=e'   yaan   u-bin
because   DET   domesticated-TD   ASEG   A3-frighten=TOP   ASEG   A3-go

'If you were to listen and "*so'oh!*", they get frightened, so they say, because the animals will be frightened (and) they'll go.'
(2021-09-29_Susana1)

8.5 Suffixation

Ideophones in Yucatec Maya can be formed using a specific suffix with a determined meaning to a CVC root. Such ideophones are morphologically harder to identify and a syntactic context is needed. Le Guen (2012) describes two suffixes used in Quintana Roo, *-i'in* and *-chaj* with the meaning of internal repetition. Note that a few others from different regions have been collected, but not examined for meaning yet. In example (6), the ideophone is based on the root *nich'* 'to bite', using the suffix *-i'in*. The idea suggested here is that the itching is like several little bites (like the ones of an ant).

(6) Suus seating in Carrillo

kul-ukbal-en   Kaariyo,   **níich'i'in**   **níich'i'in**   kih   bey-a'
seat-POS-1B   Carrillo   IDPH.bite   IDPH.bite   QTV   MAN-TD

pero   m-in-la'ach-ik   tumen   su'ulak-en
but   NEG-1A-scratch-TR   because   ashamed/shy-1B

'I was seated in Carrillo, "**níich'i'in níich'i'in**" it says like this, but I didn't scratch it because I was ashamed/shy.' (note_SCC_01.09.08)

8.6 Templates

The final, and probably most marked form of transforming a root into an ideophone in Yucatec Maya, is with the use of what Le Guen (2012) calls a 'template'. The root is derived and not only is the vowel altered, but some phonemes are inserted within the CVC structure. In some cases, a last consonant can even be added, carrying its own meaning. So far, two main templates have been identified with specific meanings. The first is $C_1\acute{v}vhrv'vC_2$ and the second is $C_1\acute{v}vhC_2v'vC_3$. The latter has a third consonant that triggers a specific meaning to the template.

Template 1 or $C_1\acute{v}vhrv'vC_2$ carries the meaning of a rapid motion. The extension of the root into a longer word (especially with the infixation of the /hr/ phoneme) allows for more iconicity and onomatopoeic effects. In the following example (7), the root *buts'* 'to swallow through a tight channel' is derived with Template 1. The ideophone puts emphasis on the motion of an aliment being ingested and running through the oesophagus with some effort.

(7) swallowing bits

búuhru'uts'   ka'   t-u-luk'-aj
IDEO.swallow   CONJ   CP.TR-swallow-TR.CP

'"búuhru'uts'" he swallowed it.'

Template 2 or $C_1\acute{v}vhC_2v'vC_3$ typically describe forms of contacts. This template is used to describe events that involve some kind of interaction between objects (frequently a figure and ground). What is distinctive about Template 2 is that a specific meaning is attached to the last consonant ($-C_3$). In order to better exemplify how this template functions, let's consider a single root, but derived into each sub-template. The root considered is *hup'*, which means 'to insert a figure into a tight ground'. So far, three sub-templates have been identified, each having a precise implication: $C_1\acute{v}vhC_2v'v$-**ch** indicates an impact between the figure and the ground (as in 8a), $C_1\acute{v}vhC_2v'v$-**n** refers to a fall of the figure on the ground (as in 8b), and, finally, $C_1\acute{v}vhC_2v'v$-**ts'** signifies a movement of the figure into or near the ground (as in 8c). We see that each instance slightly differs in meaning and reflects the semantics of the root combined with the one of the templates.

(8) Sub-templates 2 $C_1\acute{v}vhC_2v'vC_3$ used with the same root *hup'* 'figure inserted into a tight ground'

    (a) *húuhp'u'uch*   'movement of someone entering his hand into water, person stepping in the mud'

    (b) *húuhp'u'un*   'a thick piece of wood entering someone's foot stepping on it'

    (c) *húuhp'u'uts'*   'a plug entering a socket, piece of wood entering a hole just fitted to its size'

In order to further exemplify Template 2, consider example (9), in which a man explains how he was asked to kill a cow swiftly. The person who tried before him was doing a poor job, making the animal suffer without being able to properly slaughter it. He explains how he stabbed the cow in the neck and she fell down. The way she fell is verbally codified by the ideophone and visually displayed by the gesture. The ideophone suggests the idea of the cow falling, lying down on the ground, and the gesture displays how the front legs were spread out (Figure 8.4).

(9) Stabbing cow

háak-máan-en	t-u-tséel-il-a'		yéet	uy-ich táanil	ka'
slip-move-1B	PREP-3A-side-FOC-TD		CONJ	3A-face-forward	CONJ

t-in-PAAT-EH	beyo'	**móohcho'on**[Figure 8.4]	ka'	j	bin-i'
CP.TR-1A-leave-SBJ	MAN	IDEO.lie.down	CONJ	CP.IT	go-CP.IT

'I slipped her on her side with her face forward, and I put it like that and she went: móohcho'on' (2028-08-07_1818-58:19)

Figure 8.4 The speaker uses character perspective to represent how the cow felt on the ground

8.7 Iconicity

In expressive morphology, iconicity is a productive process that underlines the resemblance between the form and the meaning of a linguistic sign. While use of iconicity is common in expressive language, not all ideophones in Mayan languages rely on this process, and notably, Pérez González (2012) shows how ideophones in Tseltal are anti-iconic.

Ideophones in Yucatec Maya make use of iconicity, modifying the word and its phonological production so that it resembles or suggests the event it describes. Several processes are commonly used.

The first is iteration, which consists in repeating the word as many times as an event is unfolding. However, the number of repetitions may only suggest multiple events, and does not have to exactly coincide with them. While two repetitions tend to reflect that the event or action generally happens only twice, three start a series and this is very much fitted to imply multiple repetitions (i.e. three or more). For this reason, it is fairly common for speakers to pronounce an ideophone

DOCUMENTING STEALTH LEXICON 155

three times but to suggest a repeated action (for instance **boh boh boh** *kumáan up'up'uchk e hoonaho'* '**boh boh boh** he goes knocking on the door').

As we have mentioned already, the very formation of ideophones (as words) in Yucatec Maya is also subject to iconicity: vowel length can be reduced, rearticulated, or lengthened to mimic the action described. As also mentioned, phonetic modifications of ideophones are common: vowel lengthening, voice and pitch effects are regularly used by speakers to foreground the word in the sentence (see example (13) and Figure 8.8). Templates also carry some iconicity in themselves, especially for longer words and with the insertion of a voiceless fricative /h/ and sometimes a flap /r/.

Interestingly, iconicity is also bound to the semantics of the ideophonic derivation. All the templates but one allow for 'tail reduplication', that is the possible reduplicating of the last -VC of the ideophone. Consider for instance examples (10a,b), both derivations of the root *ha'at'* 'to scratch an uneven surface'. Traditional wooden houses in Quintana Roo are made of big pieces of wood tied together vertically. Scraping the uneven surface of the wood with a stick will usually be described as *háarha'at'*. Another event, possibly easier to imagine for the reader, is to scrape a computer keyboard with a pen. In (10a) the ideophone describes the event as short, while in (10b) the person does not stop scraping the wall. The idea of duration is provided by the repetition of the last syllable of the ideophone -*at'* over and over.

(10) *ha'at'* in template 2 and with tail reduplication

    (a) *háarha'at'*   scraping a traditional wooden house wall with a stick

    (b) *háarha'at'at'at'at'at'a*   scraping a traditional wooden house wall with a stick for a long time

The template $C_1\acute{v}vhC_2v'v$-**n** used to describe falling events does not allow for tail reduplication, probably because the fall of an object is considered a finite event.

8.8 Multimodality

As pointed out by many authors, ideophones are semantically multimodal words. Probably because of this feature, they are often accompanied by co-speech gestures (Kunene 2001; Dingemanse 2011; Mihas 2013; Nuckolls 2020) (see Le Guen 2012 for Yucatec Maya). Thought, speech, and gestures have been shown to be closely linked (McNeill 1992; Cooperrider 2017), therefore if we want to analyse ideophones in their context of production and as a part of a performance by the speaker, we must pay attention to the multimodal aspect of language, specifically to co-speech gestures. However, considering gestures in the analysis can be complex: what is the proper unit of analysis? What kind of gestures to look at? etc.

While our focus is on ideophones, the unit of analysis needs to be greater than just one word. One main reasonable unit of analysis is the utterance, for two main reasons. The first is that, because ideophones in Yucatec Maya can have a similar form to other parts of speech, they can sometimes only be identified syntactically. Therefore, it is helpful to know how they are introduced in the sentence and if they constitute predicates on their own. As we will discuss later on, it is also crucial to consider, when possible, the whole conversation.

The second reason has to do with multimodality. Especially in everyday and informal interactions, speakers tend to formulate their utterances using what Enfield regards as 'composite utterances', that is, the semiotic composition of speech and gesture (Kendon 2004; Enfield 2009). When taking into account multimodal productions, it is important to underline that gestures are not always produced exactly in synchrony with their verbal counterparts and it is not uncommon for gestures to be performed before or after the word they accompany (see Cooperrider 2017).

The type of gesture is also to be taken into account in the analysis. As pointed out by Mihas (2013) and Nuckolls (2020), there seems to exist a correlation between the increasing complexity of ideophones and their accompanying gestures. Example (1) (see also Figure 8.1) provided some evidence for this claim: the more auditory ideophones were accompanied by a deictic gesture while the more imagistic ideophones with the use of character perspective.

In order to consider the combination gesture-ideophone, let's consider the next three examples in (11), (12), and (13).

In example (11), a woman is telling how the sound of an owl is regarded as an omen to humans, generally linked to the death of someone. According to the informant, the pitch of the owl's hoot can mean that either a man or a woman is going to die. Additionally, when it flies away, the owl makes a sound described here with the ideophone *che'eh che'eh che'eh*, based on the root *cheh* which refers to the 'movement and sound of pieces being shaken' (like a marimba or a rattlesnake tail, for instance). Note that the root is used as a verb in the next sentence (*u-cheh-i'in-k* 'it shakes it'). What the ideophone refers to in this utterance is the sounds of the owl leaving flying away with the nails of the person who is going to die. Because this ideophone expresses more a sound than an image, the accompanying gesture is relatively simple, with only the same stroke repeated three times (Figure 8.5). The hand, half closed and moving downwards, represents the owl shaking the nails of the dying person.

In example (12), we see that the verb *hots'* 'to extract a large figure from the ground' (like a molar extracted from the mouth, for instance) is used in the first sentence and it is the same root that derives the ideophone *hóohts'o'on* at the end of the description. The gesture (presented in Figure 8.6) is an iconic gesture that describes the action explained in the verbal expression *ka' t-u-kóol-ah* 'and he pulled it'. After a slight pause, the ideophone is produced. What is interesting in this example is that the gesture shows the action performed by the characters in the story and then compacted in one multimodal word, the ideophone *hóohts'o'on*.

DOCUMENTING STEALTH LEXICON 157

(11) Owl *chikúul*

wáa xiich'	ky-a'a-k=eh	xii'	k-u-kumih,
COND xiich'	HAB.A3-say-IC.	TR=top	man,

pero	wáa	xook'e'	ch'uup kunkumih,
HAB-A3-die-ICP. but	COND xook'=	TOP FEMALE	SBK.A3-die-ICP

pero	le	ken	ts'o'ohke',	tun-bin-e'	che'eh[Figure 8.5a]
CONJ	DET	SBJ	finish=TOP	PROG.A3-go-TOP	IDEO.shake

che'eh[Figure 8.5b]	che'eh[Figure 8.5c]	k-aw-u'uy-k
IDEO.shake	IDEO.shake	HAB-A2-hear-TR.IC.

u-cheh-i'in-k	e	ba'al-oh,	y-a'al-a'al-e'
A3-shake-PART-TR.IC	DET	thing-TD,	A3-say-PAS=TOP

le	te'	uy-íik'ach	tun	bin	e	aanima-o'
DET	DEIC.	A3-nail.	CONJ	EVID	DET	dead-TD

'If the owl says *xiich'* (it means) a man dies, but if it says *xooch'* (it means) a woman will die. Then, when it goes: "*che'eh che'eh che'eh*", you hear it shakes it, they say that the nails of the dying that are leaving.' (2021-10-03_Antonia1)

Figure 8.5 Gesture accompanying the ideophone *che'eh* 'shake'

In this story, a man is facing various challenges and, along his journey, he is helped by various animals. In this point in the story, he comes across a jaguar. The jaguar asks the man to take off one of its claws that will help him later, in case he gets too tired. So, the jaguar extends his paw for the man to extract its claw. This is the scene that the narrator is representing in Figure 8.6. His right hand represents the paw of the jaguar while his left hand embodies the hand of the character extracting the claw from the animal's paw. The ideophone used afterwards summarized the event, visually describing the claw (the Figure) firmly anchored in the paw (the Ground) being extracted as a sudden and unique event (using the template generally employed for a falling event) and, auditorily, reproducing the sound of the claw being pulled off the foot. Compared with the previous example in (11), the scene described is more complex, involving an interaction between two characters. Not only is the ideophone richer semantically, but the gesture performed is also more depictive, taking the perspective of two characters at the same time and describing an entire event (the removing of the claw).

(12) Removing the claw

    'he'l-a'!   hots'-eh'   k-y-a'al-a'   bin   ti'
    PRES-TD   extract-SUBJ.TR   HAB-3A-say-PAS   EVID   PREP

    ka'   t-u-mach-ah   ka'   t-u-kóol-ah[Figure 8.6]   (.)   **hóohts'o'on!**
    CONJ   CP.TR-3A-grasp-CP.TR   CONJ   CP.TR-3A-pull-CP.TR   IDEO.extract

'"Here it is! Remove it [the claw]" it was said to him, so they say, so he grasped it and he pulled it, *hóohts'o'on.*'
(2009-07-05_1910-narr-baalche-DC_9:39)

Figure 8.6 'and he pulled it, *hóohts'o'on*'

DOCUMENTING STEALTH LEXICON 159

While gestures combined with speech are generally what we consider multimodality, voice effect and phonological salience should not be ignored. As Nuckolls points out, ideophones' pronunciation may be louder, softer, higher-pitched, lower-pitched, pronounced more slowly, or more quickly, than their surrounding discourse (Nuckolls 1995). Such effect is part of the syntactic and pragmatic aloofness of ideophones (Dingemanse 2011), making them more salient in the discourse and more performance-like.

Consider the following example (13), where a man is retelling what happened when he went hunting. As he was waiting up in a tree at nightfall, he saw two deer who managed to pass by and get away, climbing a fence and escaping though the sheep's enclosure. In order to describe the deer's fall in the sheep's enclosure, he uses the ideophone *ts'óohpo'om*, based on the root *ts'op* 'to perforate, to puncture', used with template 2 for falling events. The gesture that accompanies the ideophone (see Figure 8.7) is produced with two flat hands opening at the sides, displaying how the ground (probably made of dry leaves) opened under the weight of the deer as they hit the ground.

(13) Hunting narrative

ti'	k-u=ki'=náak-l		yikna	e	ba'al-o'	bey	yáanal
PREP	HAB-3A-tasty-climb.up-PAS		LOC	DET	thing-TD	MAN	under

yaan	**ts'óohpo'om**!	Che' u-bin	tu'ux	k-u k'áax-a
EXIST	IDEO.make a hole in	rapid A.3-go	where	HAB-A3-tie-PAS

boreego-e'
sheep-TOP

'There, they easily climbed into the thing [fence] (and) because it's under (the tree I'm in) "*ts'óohpo'om*" they went in a hurry where the sheep are enclosed' (2008-07-31_1821-Narration_Hunt-EMM)

Figure 8.7 The speaker showing how the deer fell into the sheep's enclosure

Phonologically, the production of the ideophone is also salient compared to the rest of the sentence. Figure 8.8 shows a spectrogram of the last sentence. Clearly, the ideophone is phonologically salient, pronounced more loudly than the rest of the sentence. The ideophone production ranges from 440Hz (54.2dB) (at the beginning) and goes as high as 2864Hz (78.3dB). In comparison the rest of the sentence oscillates between 750Hz (52.7dB) and 2155Hz (71.2dB).

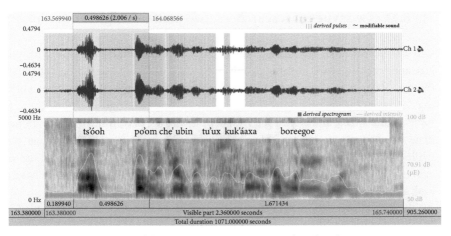

Figure 8.8 Spectrogram of the sentence encompassing the ideophone

8.9 Data gathering and methodologies

Given what we have exposed above, in order to understand and document the complexity of ideophone production, specific methodologies should be employed. In this section, we will detail some of the methods we used and the types of data they allow researchers to gather. We will also discuss our own status as researchers in the community and how it can affect the process of data collection. We must, however, first discuss the specific status of ideophones in Yucatec Maya, specifically the fact that they are elusive words.

8.10 Stealth words

In some languages ideophones are obligatory words in the speakers' lexicon, as they constitute the only way to express concepts or events such as emotion, textures, or certain common actions (Voeltz and Kilian-Hatz 2001; Dingemanse 2011; Tufvesson 2011; Mihas 2013). This is not the case in Yucatec Maya. While Yucatec Maya has a great resource of expressive words (see Le Guen 2015), not all have the same status or use in everyday language. Some expressive words are more lexicalized than others. The grade of lexicalization also usually corresponds to the integration to formal speech. Because ideophones are highly expressive and syntactically and pragmatically isolated, they dwell on the edge of the lexicon. Furthermore, they are used in highly informal interactions, making them very hard to document and record.

8.11 Two types of researchers, two methodologies, one aim

Our current research on Yucatec Maya ideophones is conducted in the same village and basically with the same people but by two different researchers. The first, Olivier Le Guen, is a French researcher fluent in the language, who has been working for twenty years among the Mayas. The second, Rodrigo Petatillo Chan, is native to the village and is working with people who are his kin and even his immediate family. Rodrigo is doing his PhD working on his own native language. So, while both approaches have a similar goal, describing the formation and use of expressive lexicon, the way research is conducted is slightly different. Let's have a look at how each researcher deals with the same issue.

Olivier's approach. In 2011, I started working as a postdoc at the Max Planck Institute for Psycholinguistics in the Netherlands, in the Culture and Cognition Group run by Stephen Levinson. I assisted on a workshop in ideophones. While listening to the various presentations I was wondering if such words existed in Yucatec Maya. Although I was already fluent in the language and had been for several years, I had my doubts as to whether such words existed in Maya. On my next fieldwork trip I started listening more closely and had prepared some stimuli (see section 8.15). What a surprise it was to acknowledge that these words were almost everywhere in daily interactions! Although it hurt my pride as a fluent speaker, I also realized that none of my colleagues noticed these words, usually confused with simple onomatopoeias. Also, I quickly realized that for speakers themselves, these words were not considered 'true words', often discarded as just 'something you say'. At first, I would just manage to recognize one instance of an ideophone, but could not quite work it out, and I would ask people to repeat their sentence. They would, but leaving out the ideophone ... Through the months I spent in the field I was able to 'educate' or 'socialize' my collaborators to have a metalinguistic awareness of these words and after some time some friends would come to me and say 'Olíibye, I have one for you, you'll like it', and start explaining it to me. After returning to the Netherlands and figuring out how ideophones worked, I was able to have a more constructive method of elicitation. Because ideophones in Yucatec Maya are derivational, I could sometimes make one up and ask if people would be able to apply it to a situation. I also designed a set of auditory stimuli to ask people what ideophone would describe best these sounds. As a foreign learner of the language, I could 'play dumb' (a very useful tool for an ethnographer, at least at the beginning) and ask silly questions regarding how to say things. Because I work on gesture and multimodal interactions, my usual way of collecting data relies heavily on video recording everyday interactions. However, and although my collaborators and friends are now used to this, they would start using more ideophones while the camera was turned off. When I would start recording, they would usually slightly modify their way of talking and avoid using many ideophones. So I had to start annotating them in a small booklet I always carry around with me. For

DOCUMENTING STEALTH LEXICON   163

this reason, my corpus is mainly constituted of written notes and a more reduced number of actual uses on video.

Rodrigo's approach. As a new researcher, I had to put myself in the role of a 'local researcher'. As a member of the community, I have to present myself as a 'student' (*xoknáal*). Members of the community know that as a student I will do recording, ask questions, and conduct interviews. This task, however, was made easy, as several foreign researchers had also conducted similar work for many years in my community. What differs for me, however, is that I have to try to have an external (researcher's) point of view, meaning being able to observe everything that happens around me and to detect in everyday/familiar events, phenomena that can be interesting for the various issues I am investigating. This technique is usually what foreign researchers treat as participant observation, although in my case it means stepping out of my role as a member of the community and starting to have a more external look at things. The second technique I am using is closer to other more common strategies used by linguists, that is eliciting data, prompting speakers to produce multimodal expressive constructions by presenting them with of small audio or video clips.

Common ground. Both approaches, long participant observation and elicitation, are taken as complementary. In Olivier's case it implied learning the language, gaining people's trust to be included as an (honorary at least) member of the community. In Rodrigo's case, it means stepping somehow outside the community in order to become a local researcher and gaining people's trust to respond to a different kind of interactions.

8.12 Ideophones in the wild

As we already mentioned, ideophones in Yucatec Maya (and many other languages), occur in very informal interactions, which make them very hard to collect and even more complex to elicit. Pragmatically, ideophones are very close to swear words (i.e. not insults directed at people but words that punctuate discourse). Ideophones, like swear words, only tend to be used in friendly, secured, and relaxed interactional contexts (see Voeltz and Kilian-Hatz 2001). Like swear words too, ideophones are used to express emotional content or attitude towards a situation or a discourse. Finally, and maybe because of this emotional reaction, like swear words, when there is a request for them to be repeated, or in other initiated repairs, ideophones are often taken out of a sentence. Interestingly, at a more psycholinguistic level, ideophones are not completely conscious, in that people seem to not always be aware they have used one. What is fascinating, however, and in contact with expletives, for instance, is that ideophones' meaning is quite precise and carries some propositional content. Ideophones are not only pragmatic words, but they convey a specific description of an event or a situation. In this sense, ideophones can be considered 'stealth words', on the edge of the formal lexicon. As such, the use of ideophones implies creativity and a great mastery of the language; therefore, it is not surprising to see them disappearing from the vocabulary of more bilingual (Spanish-Maya) speakers.

As expressive lexicon, ideophones are often employed to describe a very specific situation. This means that it is sometimes hard for collaborators to come up with a description of an ideophone or to imagine a particular situation where an ideophone can be used. It is not uncommon that, when asked if such or such an ideophone exists, people would answer negatively, but would use it later on when a specific and appropriate context comes up.

8.13 Narratives

Narratives are one of linguists' favourite supports, as they form a compact, often stand-alone, piece of language production. They are indeed a good source of linguistic examples and expert narrators often make use of expressivity, multimodality, and ideophones. Ideophone production is, however, scarcer in narrative than in informal conversations. One advantage of narratives is that they are easier to video-record, as the narrator is usually is seated, allowing for a stable and good-quality recording.

Two types of narratives where ideophones are commonly used are mythic stories and personal experiences. Usually, narratives are recounted to the researcher who, while being fluent in the language, remains mostly a passive interlocutor, compared to participants in informal dialogues. Additionally, because narratives are stories, with a specific timeline and prepacked knowledge, it may be harder for speakers to show more emotionality than when retelling personal events in an informal context. For this reason also, the use of expressive recourses, ideophones in particular, rests on the speaker's expertise and ability to make the story more vivid.

8.14 Corpus building of natural conversations

Because deophone use is not predictable and occurs in extremely informal contexts, it is usually necessary to record long interactions, in trusted environments, in order to collect some spontaneous occurrences. For this reason, we relied on the use of the conversational-analysis model (Sacks, Schegloff, and Jefferson 1974; Duranti and Goodwin 1997; Vázquez Carranza 2019) and the ethnography of communication/speech (Gumperz and Hymes 1972).

Conversational analysis's main aim it to analyse naturally occurring interactions. Although historically and owing to technical limitations, CA began with an emphasis on verbal interactions (especially with the analysis of phone calls), lately more and more researchers incorporated multimodality in their collected data. While silences, hesitations, and other verbal clues were considered, the inclusion of face-to-face data allows consideration of other non-verbal interactions like gesture, eye-gaze, facial expressions, etc. This new and augmented approach has been labelled 'multimodal ethnography' (Kendon 1997; Haviland 2000: 201; Goodwin 2006; Sicoli 2020). As Sicoli puts it, this process involves an 'analysis of the semiotic processes that build connections in resonances between participants' talk, body movements, and actions with objects represented in the video corpus' (Sicoli 2020: 25). Sicoli (2020) takes language as 'a multimodal ecology' that incorporates not only speech in isolation, but also the context, gestures, gaze, wink, silence, etc. and endless resources used by speakers for communication.

Naturalistic data collected using the methodology of CA allows for a more contextualized analysis of ideophone use as well as an examination of the multimodal production that generally accompanies it. However, because natural data occur in non-controlled environments, the quality of the data is not always perfect and elicitations comes a good complementary tool.

Methodologically, what multimodal ethnography implies is the use of one or several video cameras, good microphones, and willing participants. Of course, filming people without their consent is out of the question, so cameras are always visible and people are aware they are being recorded. Such commitment from the part of the participants involves a lot of trust towards the researcher, but also some socialization. The first few times people are being filmed (and generally in the first few minutes of a recording) they are shy, talk about the camera, the researcher, etc. Usually, after a few times (or a few minutes), people get back to their everyday talk, forgetting the camera is even there. What is necessary, however, is to record for long periods of time. This means a lot of 'garbage' (i.e. unusable or not directly interesting data). While this method is demanding, especially in field conditions, it is also highly rewarding.

Consider, for instance, this example of a natural conversation between three adult men that lasted one hour and twenty-one minutes. In a total of 2,137 utterances, only fourteen ideophones were uttered. Interestingly, twelve of the fourteen ideophones occurred in a fifteen-minute period (between minute 57 and 1 hour 13 minutes). Having the whole conversation also allows us to examine when and why people decide to use ideophones. During most of the interaction, the men are talking about house-building and their recent experiences in the field of construction. However, when they come to discuss how one of the men was asked to kill a cow (see example (9) and Figure 8.4), the discussion becomes livelier and more theatrical and this is when seven different ideophones are used (some are repeated several times).

8.15 Elicitations using stimuli

Although ideophones are hard to elicit out of the blue, it is, however, not impossible using appropriate stimuli. Various sets of audio stimuli were used, some made by colleagues at the MPI. However, the most productive was one made by O. Le Guen, who recorded various real events (frictions, chock between objects, various types of falling objects) directly on the field, using local objects. Additionally, using modern technology, the pitch and order of certain recordings were modified. Although ideophones in Yucatec Maya describe, in their great majority, visual events, the fact that participants only listened to a sound gave them the opportunity to imagine what event produced each sound. Interestingly, many participants did describe similar scenes and sometimes the actual event that produced the sound. Auditory stimuli turned out to be very a useful tool not only to elicit ideophones but also to compare participants' responses.

We are currently working on a set of visual stimuli. However, based on the few results from the pilot study, this project might be more difficult because visual stimuli seem to restrict greatly the participant's experience and creativity to recreate an event. As Nuckolls (2020) points out, many ideophones are primarily visual semantically and exhibit a strong propensity for (bounding) gesture. While sound can trigger an associated event, visual information seems to generate more descriptive comments. This means that ideophones are creative in nature and are a way to vividly but mentally represent the world to an interlocutor.

8.16 Conclusion

As we have covered in this chapter, ideophones in Yucatec Maya are semantically multimodal words and also part of a performance by the speaker that involves the production of gesture and voice effects. In contrast with other languages, ideophones in Yucatec Maya are not obligatory words for speakers and, in some regions of the Yucatec peninsula, they are not in use any more. Additionally, speakers only used them in very emotional and relaxed situations. Such characteristics make them stealth words, particularly difficult to document.

In our own research we used complementary methodologies that have both benefits and limitations. Narratives are practical because they approximate a stand-alone discourse. However, while they provide easy materials for the researcher, the use of ideophones in Yucatec Maya narrations depends on the narrative talent and linguistic abilities of the speaker. Natural conversations turn out to be one of the best supports in gathering naturalistic data, in this case ideophones, in their full context of production. However, video-recording conversations requires a great commitment on the participants' part as well as the researcher's. Data can be messy and demand a long time to properly process. Finally, the use of stimuli is very productive and provides comparative data. Nonetheless, the creation of such material can be challenging and the data lack context of production. A combination of data gathered with each methodology can help provide a better understand of the Yucatec Maya stealth lexicon, its formation and use in this language.

References

Anttila, Raimo (1977). Toward a semiotic analysis of expressive vocabulary. *semiosis* 5: 27–40.

Cooperrider, K. (2017). Foreground gesture, background gesture. *Gesture* 16(2):176–202. Available at https://doi.org/10.1075/gest.16.2.02coo. Accessed 22 August 2024.

Dingemanse, M. (2011). *The Meaning and Use of Ideophones in Siwu.* Nijmegen: Max Planck Institute for Psycholinguistics.

Dingemanse, M. (2013). Ideophones and gesture in everyday speech. *Gesture* 13(2):143–165. Available at https://doi.org/10.1075/gest.13.2.02din. Accessed 22 August 2024.

Dingemanse, M. (2017). Expressiveness and system integration: on the typology of ideophones, with special reference to Siwu. *STUF—Language Typology and Universals* 70(2): 363–385. Available at https://doi.org/10.1515/stuf-2017-0018. Accessed 22 August 2024.

Duranti, A. and Goodwin, C. (1997). *Rethinking Context, Language as an Interactive Phenomenon.* Cambridge: Cambridge University Press.

Enfield, N. J. (2009). *The Anatomy of Meaning Speech, Gesture, and Composite Utterances.* Cambridge: Cambridge University Press.

England, N. C. (2006). El papel de palabras afectivas en la narración en Mam (Maya). In Z. Estrada Fernández, R. María. Ortiz Ciscomani, and M. del C. Morúa (eds), *VIII Encuentro Internacional de Lingüística en el Noroeste: memorias.* Hermosillo: Editorial UniSon (Serie Lingüística (Hermosillo, Mexico)), 157–171. Available at http://books.google.com/books?id=BN0uAAAAYAAJ. Accessed 13 February 2023.

Goodwin, M. (2006). Talk and practical epistemology—Jack Sidnell. *Journal of the Royal Anthropological Institute* 12(4): 993–994. Available at https://doi.org/10.1111/j.1467-9655.2006.00372_33.x. Accessed 22 August 2024.

Gumperz, J. J. and Hymes, D. (1972). *Directions in Sociolinguistics: The Ethnography of Communication.* New York: Holt, Rinehart and Winston.

Haviland, J. B. (2000). Pointing, gesture spaces, and mental maps. In D. McNeill (ed.), *Language and Gesture.* Cambridge: Cambridge University Press, 13–46.

Kendon, A. (1997). Gesture. *Annual Review of Anthropology* 26(1): 109–128.

Kendon, A. (2004). *Gesture: Visible Action as Utterance.* Cambridge: Cambridge University Press.

Kita, S. (1997). Two-dimensional semantic analysis of Japanese mimetics. *Linguistics* 35(2): 379–416.

Kunene, D. P. (2001). Speaking the act. The ideophone as a linguistic rebel. In F. K. E. Voeltz and C. Kilian-Hatz (eds), *Ideophones*. Amsterdam/Philadelphia: John Benjamins, 183–191.

Le Guen, O. (2012). Ideophones in Yucatec Maya. In *CILLA V*, 6–8 October 2011, Austin, TX.

Le Guen, O. (2015). Expressive morphology in Yucatec Maya. In J.-L. Léonard and A. Khim (eds), *Patterns in Mesoamerican Morphology*. Paris: Michel Houdiard Editeur (Colloques), 178–211.

Lois, X. and Vapnarsky, V. (2006). Root indeterminacy and polyvalence in Yukatekan Mayan languages. In X. Lois and V. Vapnarsky (eds), *Lexical Categories and Root Classes in Amerindian Languages*. Bern: Peter Lang, 69–116.

Maffi, L. (1990). Tzeltal Maya affect verbs: psychological salience and expressive functions of language. In D. J. Costa (ed.), *Proceedings of the Sixteenth Annual Meeting of the Berkeley Linguistics Society: Special Session on General Topics in American Indian Linguistics.* Berkeley: Berkeley Linguistic Society, 61–72.

Martínez Guerrero, F. (2013). *Chante' wa xjul b'esniye'. Los animales y sus señales entre los tojolabales de saltillo, las margaritas, chiapas.* Master's thesis. UNAM. Available at www.academia.edu/38601843/Chante_wa_xjul_besniye_Los_animales_y_sus_se%C3%B1ales_entre_los_tojolabales_de_Saltillo_Las_Margaritas_Chiapas. Accessed 13 February 2023.

McNeill, D. (1992). *Hand and Mind*. Chicago: University of Chicago Press.

Mihas, E. (2013). Composite ideophone-gesture utterances in the Ashéninka Perené 'community of practice', an Amazonian Arawak society from Central-Eastern Peru. *Gesture* 13. Available at https://doi.org/10.1075/gest.13.1.02mih. Accessed 22 August 2024.

Nuckolls, Janis B. (1995). Quechua texts of perception. *Semiotica* 103(1–2): 145–170. Available at https://doi.org/10.1515/semi.1995.103.1-2.145. Accessed 22 August 2024.

Nuckolls, Janis B. (2000). Spoken in the spirit of gesture: Translating sound symbolism in a Pastaza Quechua narrative. In J. Sherzer and K. Sammons (eds), *Translating Native Latin American Verbal Art*. Washington DC: Smithsonian Press, 233–251.

Nuckolls, Janis B. (2020). 'How do you even know what ideophones mean?': Gestures' contributions to ideophone semantics in Quichua, *Gesture* 19(2–3): 161–195. Available at https://doi.org/10.1075/gest.20005.nuc. Accessed 22 August 2024.

Pérez González, J. (2012). *Predicados expresivos e ideófonos en tseltal.* Master's thesis, CIESAS.

Sacks, H., Schegloff, E. A., and Jefferson, G. (1974). A simplest systematics for the organization of turn-taking for conversation. *Language* 50(4): 696–735.

Sicoli, M. (2020). *Saying and Doing in Zapotec: Multimodality, Resonance, and the Language of Joint Actions.* London and New York: Bloomsbury Academic. Available at: https://doi.org/10.5040/9781350142190. Accessed 22 August 2024.

Tufvesson, S. (2011). Analogy making in the Semai sensory world. *The Senses & Society* [Preprint].

Vázquez-Álvarez, J. J. 1971- (2011) *A grammar of Chol, a Mayan language.* PhD thesis, University of Texas at Austin. Available at https://repositories.lib.utexas.edu/handle/2152/ETD-UT-2011-08-4293 Accessed 13 February 2023.

Vázquez Carranza, A. (2019). *Análisis conversacional: Estudio de la acción social.* Guadalajara: Universidad de Guadalajara.

Voeltz, F. K. E. and Kilian-Hatz, C. (2001) *Ideophones.* Amsterdam/Philadelphia: John Benjamins.

9

Studying Japanese mimetics

Kimi Akita

9.1 Introduction

Japanese is somewhat special as a language rich in expressive lexemes, which are known as 'mimetics' (*giongo/gitaigo*) or 'ideophones.' As with Korean, this language has an exceptionally long history of research on expressivity that is often based on native speaker linguists' introspection, dictionaries, large corpora, and neatly designed experiments. The enormous body of literature on Japanese mimetics consists of at least a few thousand papers and books and more than 20 dictionaries devoted to them, with the largest one (Ono 2007) containing approximately 4,500 items (Akita 2005–2010).

Thanks to this special situation, Japanese has made several key contributions to expressivity research. Mester and Itô (1989) demonstrated the significance of mimetics in theoretical phonology. Kita's (1997) two-dimensional semantic analysis of Japanese mimetics, inspired by Diffloth (1972), was later developed into the now widely accepted semiotic distinction between 'depiction' (illustrated by expressive words) and 'description' (illustrated by prosaic words) (Dingemanse 2015). Hamano's (1998) comprehensive description of the sound-symbolic system of Japanese mimetics has been viewed as a model case of linguistic phonosemantics. Imai et al. (2008) pioneered the experimental explorations in the role of iconicity in children's lexical acquisition. Developing previous insights (Kakehi 1986; Dingemanse 2017), Dingemanse and Akita's (2017) study using a multimodal corpus of Japanese quantitatively showed the correlation between mimetic syntax and expressivity, which has since been replicated in many languages (Akita and Dingemanse 2019; for more contributions from Japanese mimetic research, see Akita 2019a).

This chapter describes the representative methods of collecting and analysing mimetics adopted in Japanese linguistics and discusses important findings from a general, cross-linguistic perspective. Section 9.2 introduces the basic formal and functional properties of Japanese mimetics. Section 9.3 focuses on major dictionaries of Japanese mimetics and research examples using them. Section 9.4 deals with primarily quantitative reports from corpus-based studies. Section 9.5 summarises notable experiments to elicit mimetics from native Japanese speakers. Section 9.6 concludes this chapter by discussing possible future direction.

Kimi Akita, *Studying Japanese mimetics*. In: *Capturing Expressivity*. Edited by: Jeffrey P. Williams, Oxford University Press. © Kimi Akita (2025). DOI: 10.1093/oso/9780192858931.003.0009

9.2 Japanese mimetics

Japanese mimetics fit Dingemanse's (2019: 16) cross-linguistic definition of expressive lexemes as 'member[s] of an open lexical class of marked words that depict sensory imagery'. They imitate various types of sensory information, both auditory and non-auditory, and due to this imitative mode of signification, they typically have characteristic morphology and phonology. They are conventionalised lexical items, but native speakers can readily make new items, too.

Japanese has several morphological types of mimetics, which can be summarised in terms of root length (monomoraic or bimoraic) and template type (reduplicated, suffixed, CVCCVri, etc.), as in (1). As the percentage indicates, the three templates together account for nearly 80% of the 1,620 entries in Kakehi et al. (1996).[1]

(1)	Monomoraic root ((C)V)	Bimoraic root ((C)VCV)
a. Reduplicated (35.25%)	*ponpon* 'popping repeatedly', *poipoi* 'throwing away many things', *zaazaa* 'pouring down', *nyaanyaa* 'meowing repeatedly'	*pokipoki* 'snapping repeatedly', *huwahuwa* 'floating lightly', *karikari* 'crunching repeatedly', *nikoniko* 'smiling broadly continuously', *ukauka* 'careless'
b. Suffixed (33.77%)	*poQ/pon* 'popping once', *poiQ* 'throwing away one thing', *zaQ* 'quick, rough'	*pokiQ/pokin/pokiri* 'snapping once', *huwaQ/huwan/huwari* 'floating up lightly', *kariQ* 'crunching once', *nikoQ/nikori* 'smiling once', *ukaQ* 'careless'
c. CVCCVri (8.09%)	n/a	*pokkiri* 'completely snapped', *hunwari* 'fluffy', *nikkori* 'smiling broadly', *ukkari* 'careless'

As illustrated in (2), Japanese mimetics are typically used as (part of) adverbs, verbs, and adjectives (Sells 2017).

(2) a. Buta-ga   buu-to   nai-ta.   (adverbial)
     pig-NOM   MIM-QUOT   cry-PST

     'A pig cried "oink".'

---

[1] The abbreviations used in this chapter are as follows: COP = copula, DAT = dative, GER = gerundive, MIM = mimetic, NOM = nominative, PST = past, Q = glottal stop (or the first half of a geminate cluster when followed by a quotative marker, as in *poQ-to* /potːo/), QUOT = quotative, TOP = topic.

b. Haruko-wa   tuyu-ni   unzari-si-te   i-ta.   (verbal)
   H-TOP   rainy.season-DAT   MIM-do-GER   be-PST

'Haruko was tired of the rainy season.'

c. Heya-wa   gutyagutya-dat-ta.   (adjectival)
   room-TOP   MIM-COP-PST

'The room was messy.'

The vast majority of Japanese linguists are native speakers of the language, a situation that is shared by few expressive-rich languages in Africa, South Asia and Southeast Asia, and the Americas. Japanese linguists' introspection has revealed that onomatopoeic (i.e., sound-imitating) mimetics (termed 'phonomimes' or *giongo*) prefer adverbial realisation, often followed by a quotative marker, whereas mimetics for inner feelings (termed 'psychomimes' or *gijōgo*) prefer verbal realisation, typically combined with the verb 'do'. The rest of the mimetic lexicon (termed 'phenomimes' or *gitaigo*) consists of diverse semantic and syntactic types of items, and reduplicated ones can often appear as adjectives with the help of a copula (Akita 2009).

As can be seen from the above examples, Japanese mimetics cover a wide range of sensory meanings, from sound to movement, texture, and interoception. However, unlike in languages such as Ewe (Ameka 2001), Korean (Sohn 1994), and Mundari (Badenoch and Osada 2019), we cannot find any single mimetic that unambiguously represents colour, taste, or smell. In addition to these sensory mimetics, Japanese has a class of mimetic or mimetic-like words that are sometimes called 'quasi-mimetics' or 'demimeticised words' (Akita 2009, 2017a; see also Tamori and Schourup 1999). As shown in (3), quasi-mimetics have the same morphological shapes as the prototypical mimetics illustrated in (1) but are by far more frequent owing to their abstract, prosaic-like meanings.

(3) a. Frequency/timing:

   tyoityoi 'often', *tyokutyoku* 'often', *zuQ-to* 'all the time', *yaQ-to* 'finally', *dondon* 'one after another', *dandan* 'gradually'

   b. Degree:

   kikkari 'exactly', *sukkari* 'completely', *mekkiri* 'remarkably', *guQ-to* 'much', *kiQ-to* 'for sure', *sikkari* 'properly'

   c. Quantity:

   un-to 'a lot', *tappuri* 'plentifully', *tyobiQ-to* 'a little bit', *tyoppiri* 'a little bit'

Assuming that mimetics constitute a prototype category with a fuzzy boundary (Childs 1994; Akita 2009), the existence of these non-prototypical mimetics is no

172 KIMI AKITA

surprise, and one may (correctly) argue that they do not deserve a special label (Lovestrand 2022). Nevertheless, it is worth noting that quasi-mimetics are also found in other expressive-rich languages such as Korean (Park 2019) and they sometimes exhibit different behaviours from prototypical mimetics, as shown in Section 9.4. The existence of quasi-mimetic items makes it difficult to determine whether a word is mimetic or not and, consequently, how many conventional mimetics a language has. Japanese researchers typically use dictionaries to make this judgement.

9.3 Dictionaries

Numerous mimetics are registered as 'adverbs' in standard dictionaries of Japanese. In addition, various dictionaries are devoted to mimetics and provide detailed semantic descriptions, example sentences, and illustrations (Asano 1978; Atoda and Hoshino 1995; Hida and Asada 2002). Some mimetic dictionaries are published in English (Gomi 1989 [2004]; Chang 1990; Kakehi et al. 1996) and Chinese (Guo 2019). Two Japanese-written dictionaries are worth special attention. One is Yamaguchi (2003 [2015]), who provides historical descriptions and actual text examples for each mimetic. The other is Ono (2007), the largest mimetic dictionary, which contains many obsolete and dialectal mimetics. As for dialectal mimetics, the National Institute for Japanese Language and Linguistics (NINJAL) compiled a booklet of Tohoku (northeast) Japanese mimetics (Takeda 2012) for doctors and nurses from other regions of Japan who had communication problems with local patients just after the Great East Japan Earthquake in 2011. For example, *zerazera* is a local mimetic meaning 'getting phlegm in one's throat', which is not understandable without any context to non-Tohoku Japanese speakers.

These dictionaries have helped Japanese linguists to identify several structural patterns of conventional mimetics, including the productivity of the major mimetic templates presented in (1) (Akita 2009). Another notable achievement is Hamano's (1998) phonosemantic descriptions of mimetics. She used approximately 1,450 entries in Asano (1978) to discuss the distribution of phonemes in mimetics and their semantic associations. She demonstrated that monomoraic mimetic roots are more iconic than bimoraic mimetic roots, which are more linguistically constrained. According to Hamano, the consonantal symbolism of the bimoraic root of *pakaQ* 'split wide open' would be analysed as follows: C_1 /p/ = the taut surface of a light object (tactile information); C_2 /k/ = opening (kinetic information). On the other hand, /p/ in the monomoraic-based mimetic *pan* 'with a small bang' simultaneously imitates the tactile and kinetic properties of the banging object.

Some mimetic dictionaries classify mimetics semantically. Asano (1978) employs a three-way classification of mimetics into phonomimes, phenomimes, and psychomimes. Kakehi et al. (1996) use three semantic labels: 'S' for sound, 'M' for manner, and 'Fig' for figurative. According to these labels, the mimetic *pin* has all three types of meanings: 'cracking; snapping; flicking' (S), 'stretched tight; coming to realise or understand something' (M), 'one's nerves or atmosphere strained or tense' (Fig) (Kakehi et al. 1996: 938–940). Chang (1990) and Ono (2007) provide more fine-grained semantic classes, such as laughter and water movement. These semantic classifications are often useful when we want to know whether there are any semantic tendencies in particular forms of mimetics (recall the semantics-syntax correlation illustrated in (2)) and how mimetics extend their meanings (e.g. *bokoboko* 'burbling' → 'having many large holes') (Akita 2013). However, it should be noted that these dictionaries often fail to include unconventional or new meanings of mimetics, such as the 'getting one's work done efficiently' meaning of *sakuQ* 'crunching' (Kakehi et al. 1996: 1062–1063). Furthermore, these semantic classifications are not accurate enough to reflect the multisensory nature of mimetic meaning (Nuckolls 2019). For example, *zaazaa* 'pouring down' can simultaneously depict the sound and the manner of pouring rain, but the dictionaries treat this mimetic as sound-imitative (e.g. Kakehi et al. 1996: 1280–1281).

The full-scale investigations into the entire expressive lexicon sketched here are not possible in languages whose expressives are yet to be fully documented. Despite their usefulness, however, mimetic dictionaries only contain conventional items and do not allow us to discuss one-shot and ephemeral forms. This is a crucial limitation, given the extremely high creativity of expressive lexemes in general (Dingemanse 2019; Park 2019: Chapter 6). Moreover, mimetic dictionaries only provide limited information about how and how often mimetics are used. We can overcome these limitations by using corpora and experiments, which are the topics of the next two sections.

9.4 Corpora

In the past decade, primarily thanks to NINJAL's intensive projects, various large corpora of spoken and written Japanese have become available free of charge. Many of them are searchable on an online interface called Chunagon (https://chunagon.ninjal.ac.jp/).[2] It is also common for researchers to make their own corpora for their specific research purposes. These technical advancements have led to some important, especially quantitative, discoveries about mimetics. Section 9.4.1 discusses key findings about the phonological, syntactic, and semantic properties of mimetics. Section 9.4.2 focuses on synchronic and diachronic

---

[2] The detailed information of each corpus is available on the following website: https://clrd.ninjal.ac.jp/en/ (23 September 2022).

174 KIMI AKITA

variations of mimetic uses. Section 9.4.3 picks up recent findings about the multimodal characteristics of mimetic utterances. Section 9.4.4 provides a few cautionary notes on corpus-based approaches to expressive lexemes.

9.4.1 Phonology, syntax, and semantics

Novels and other literary works have long constituted one of the major data sources for researchers of Japanese mimetics (Yamaguchi 2002; Kawase 2005, 2006). Literary works not only are a fertile source of conventional uses of conventional mimetics but also allow writers to create new mimetics and use conventional mimetics in an innovative way. For example, the novelist and poet Kenji Miyazawa has attracted much attention from linguists and literary scholars with his creative and even mysterious uses of mimetics (Tamori 2010). Nasu (2004) examined how creative literary mimetics may be, with special reference to the phoneme distribution of mimetics in manga. He found that even innovative mimetics prefer unmarked phonological patterns in Japanese, such as /u/ following /z/ (e.g. *zukyuun* 'sniping') and /o/ following /d/ (e.g. *dokyuun* 'sniping with a bang'). Mimetics' contribution to the soundscape of Japanese has also been noted for haiku/tanka poetry (Tsujimura 2022). All these findings indicate that mimetics are surely part of the linguistic and cultural systems of Japanese.

Text corpora have also revealed some important syntactic and semantic characteristics of mimetics. Using a novel corpus called the Aozora Bunko Corpus, and the Nagoya University Conversation Corpus (NUCC) (Fujimura et al. 2012), Akita (2012) found that mimetic adverbs, which generally have highly specific, depictive meanings, tend to form strong collocations with a more restricted semantic range of verbs and nouns than do non-mimetic adverbials. For example, the mimetic *gabugabu* 'swilling' collocates strongly with the verb *nom-u* 'to drink' and the noun *sake* 'sake', whereas the non-mimetic adverbial *awate-te* 'hurriedly' is found with various collocates, such as *mi-ru* 'to look', *uti-kes-u* 'to deny', *kuti* 'mouth', and *ko* 'child'. Tamaoka et al. (2011) further showed that mimetic-verb collocations are stronger in newspapers than in novels, whose high creativity allows writers to readily create new collocations. These results have cross-linguistic significance, as the high collocability of expressive lexemes with certain words, especially verbs, has been reported without quantitative evidence in many languages (Childs 1994).

Related to this is Toratani's (2017) investigation of the relative positioning of reduplicated adverbial mimetics in sentences. Mimetics with total reduplication are optionally followed by the quotative marker *-to*. However, counting adverbial mimetics in eight novels, Toratani found that, unlike quotative-marked forms (e.g. *tobotobo-to* 'ploddingly'), zero-marked forms (e.g. *tobotobo* 'ploddingly'), which

STUDYING JAPANESE MIMETICS   175

are phonologically constrained, strongly prefer the immediately preverbal position. This result suggests that zero-marked mimetics form a tight, idiom-like unit with their verbal collocates (e.g. *tobotobo aruk-u* 'to walk ploddingly') (Akita and Usuki 2016).

Another quantitative investigation using the NUCC revealed Japanese mimetics' preference for particular sentence types. Examining the scripts of twenty-seven informal conversations between friends (28,277 sentences in total), Akita (2017a) found that prototypical mimetics are more likely than quasi-mimetics to localise in affirmative-declarative sentences, while quasi-mimetics are often attested in negative, interrogative, and imperative sentences as well. Expressive lexemes in some languages, such as Hausa (Afro-Asiatic; Newman 1968) and Kisi (Niger-Congo; Childs 1994), are said to be incompatible with negation (and interrogation and command). Akita's results indicate that the same is not true for Japanese mimetics but that this language also has this sentence-type restriction as a relative preference. This observation made Akita argue that Japanese mimetics are more deeply integrated into the linguistic system than expressive lexemes in languages such as Hausa and Kisi. This possibility is further supported by the additional finding that non-affirmative-declarative sentences are particularly frequent with adjectival mimetics, which some researchers claim to be more prosaic-like than adverbial mimetics (Kita 1997; Baba 2003; Dingemanse and Akita 2017).

9.4.2 Variations

Corpora have also revealed that the use of mimetics varies considerably across different types and parts of discourse, dialects, eras, and even individuals. Understanding these variations will help us to plan our research projects and, more importantly, compare the pragmatic functions of Japanese mimetics with those of expressive lexemes in other languages.

The Balanced Corpus of Contemporary Written Japanese (BCCWJ) is arguably the most widely used corpus of Japanese. Due to its balanced design, this corpus gives us information about the frequency of mimetics in different types of discourse. Figure 9.1 shows the log10 frequency of 801 mimetics, a subset of Kakehi et al. (1996), per million words in the twelve types of discourse that constitute the BCCWJ.

According to this figure, mimetics are particularly frequent in verses, again suggesting their high compatibility with creative discourse. (Schourup's (1993) smaller study of 365 mimetic tokens show that, not surprisingly, mimetics are also frequent in children's books, novels for students, sports newspapers, balloons of manga, and informal conversation.) Although mimetics are also used in formal speech, such as the minutes of the Diet, they are rare in white books and completely absent in law books.

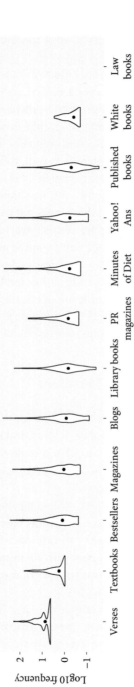

Figure 9.1 Log10 frequency of 801 mimetics per million words in BCCWJ (The width of the violin plots represents the relative number of mimetics at different frequencies of use. Dots represent the means.)

Using the Aozora Bunko Corpus (a corpus of out-of-copyright novels) and the NUCC, Park (2019: Ch. 5) further showed that mimetics are more likely to be realised as part of the predicate in spoken discourse than in written discourse. It appears that the high flexibility of spoken register, especially informal conversation, facilitates the integration of mimetics into the core of sentence structure (see Akita 2017a for a related discussion).

The token frequency of mimetics also differs within discourse. Using the online minutes of the Diet of Japan from 1947 to 2011, Akita et al. (2012) counted mimetic and non-mimetic adverbials in ten equal parts of all turns that consist of ten or more consecutive sentences. They showed that mimetics increase as one's speech goes on, whereas the frequency of non-mimetic adverbials does not increase or decrease remarkably. This tendency was replicated in my search of sixty-four transcribed interviews about war experience (18,906 sentences in total) from the NHK World War II Archive. Prototypical mimetics clearly increased as the interviews proceeded, whereas quasi-mimetics exhibited only a small increase.

The minutes of the Diet consist of utterances by politicians from different parts of Japan, although many of them do not use their dialects at the Diet. Sorting the data by the politician's hometown, Hirata-Mogi et al. (2015) examined the stereotype of people from West Japan, especially the Kansai region, which many comedians come from, as frequent mimetic users. They found that although the overall uses of mimetics did not differ considerably across regions, CVCCVri mimetics, such as *hakkiri* 'clear' and *zikkuri* 'slow and careful', were particularly frequent among Kansai-born politicians. On the other hand, Takamaru et al. (2014) demonstrated the overrepresentation of mimetics in West Japan by using the online minutes of 403 local assemblies (approximately 300 million words in total), where politicians more often use their own dialects. Despite these pioneering reports, it remains an open question whether the frequency of mimetics in everyday speech shows similar dialectal variations. In fact, based on a questionnaire survey that asked people from different parts of Japan how they describe given scenes, such as crying noisily, Kobayashi (2018) proposes a more detailed picture of the dialectal variations of mimetics. He argues that West Japanese speakers use more mimetics for intensification, such as *gaaaaQ* 'going on and on', whereas East Japanese speakers use more mimetics for specific situations, such as *poyapoya* 'soft and thin (of an infant's hair)'.

Corpora with speakers' information allow us to observe even more detailed speaker variations, such as gender and age variations. For example, in the 214 edited interviews with victims and rescuers in the NHK Great East Japan Earthquake Archive (10,413 sentences in total) used in Dingemanse and Akita (2017), female and young speakers tended to use mimetics more frequently than male and older speakers (Akita 2017b). However, since the data are limited in size and topics, these variations would need re-examining with other corpora. Moreover, the earthquake corpus also shows that mimetics are particularly frequent in emotional speech immediately after the earthquake and tsunami disaster. This additional result suggests that we need to investigate how different factors contribute to the use of mimetics.

Due to their long history, the minutes of the Diet can also be utilised for diachronic studies. A quantitative examination of the data from 1947 to 2011 (1,333,265 mimetic tokens; Akita et al. 2014) revealed that mimetics, especially CVCCVri forms with quotative marking (e.g. *hakkiri-to* 'clearly'), increased over time. Moreover, NINJAL's Corpus of Historical Japanese, covering the eighth to the twentieth centuries, gives us a glimpse into the earlier history of Japanese mimetics. For example, according to this corpus, both zero-marking (e.g. *yoroyoro* 'staggeringly' (*Ōkura Toraaki Book*, 1642)) and 'do'-verb formation (e.g. *tazitazi-su-ru* 'to totter' (*Ōkura Toraaki Book*, 1642)) gradually increased from the twelfth to the twentieth century (see also Kawase 2005, 2006). However, the limitations of the historical sources and their non-uniformity in text types, ranging from poetry to missionary writings, essays, and magazines, prevent us from getting conclusive evidence for these diachronic changes.

The development of mimetics over time within individuals is another subject matter in corpus-based studies. Currently, twelve corpora of child Japanese are available on the Child Language Data Exchange System (CHILDES). Several studies have used Noji's (1973–1977) longitudinal diary record of the speech of a monolingual male child named Sumihare to investigate his acquisition of mimetics (Tsujimura 2005; Akita 2009; Murasugi 2017). It was found that the boy acquired phonomimes first, followed by phenomimes and finally psychomimes, suggesting that the more iconic, the easier to learn (Perry et al. 2015). Another important observation is that Sumihare made extensive use of mimetic 'do'-verbs, such as *pai-si-ta* '[I] tossed [my pajamas]' [1;6] before learning to use adult-like combinations of mimetic adverbs and prosaic verbs, such as *patiin-to nagut-tyaru-wai-ne* '[I]'ll hit [him] with a slapping sound' [3;9].

9.4.3 Multimodality

Multimodal corpora that contain both transcripts and audiovisual information are not in wide use yet in Japanese linguistics. Therefore, what we know about the multimodal features of mimetic utterances is still relatively limited. This situation is in stark contrast to fieldwork-based studies in some African and American languages where expressive lexemes are collected from video recordings (Dingemanse 2011; Mihas 2013; Nuckolls 2019).

The earthquake corpus introduced in Section 9.4.2 has audiovisual components. Dingemanse and Akita (2017) utilised them for their examination of the relationship between morphosyntax, expressivity ('expressiveness' in their terms), and gesture noted in several languages (Dingemanse 2017; Akita and Dingemanse 2019). They quantitatively showed that the more integrated a mimetic is with sentence structure, the less likely it is to have expressive, 'wild' features in its morphology and prosody, ending up in a 'tame' form (Rhodes 1994). For example, non-predicative, quotative-adverbial mimetics often involved multiplication (e.g. *gagagagagagagagaQ-to* 'with a repeated rattling sound'), lengthening (e.g. *guuQ-to* '(going down) rapidly'), marked voice quality (e.g. *paaQ-to* [pḁːtːo] 'with a rush'), and distinctly high pitch, all of which were much less frequent with predicative mimetics (e.g. *hoQ-to-si-ta* '[I] got relieved'). Zero-marked adverbial mimetics behaved in an intermediate fashion. Dingemanse and Akita (2017) also found that the morphosyntactic integration of mimetics is inversely correlated with their synchronisation with iconic gesture strokes (for a similar report based on a multimodal corpus of TV shows, see Son 2010). These results illustrate that Japanese data can quantitatively substantiate the proposals that are made qualitatively in other languages.

Expressivity and gesture synchronisation also differ between prototypical mimetics and quasi-mimetics. Using the earthquake corpus, Akita (2019b) showed that utterances of prototypical mimetics are more likely than those of quasi-mimetics to involve expressive features and iconic gestures. Furthermore, it was found that prototypical mimetics are more likely than quasi-mimetics and non-mimetic verbs to be accompanied by the speaker's obvious change in facial expression and eye contact with the hearer. These findings suggest the need for more research on the interactional functions of expressive lexemes as compared with other lexical classes.

9.4.4 Limits of corpus-based approaches

To conclude Section 9.4, corpora enable us to explore and examine various hypotheses about the form and function of mimetics and their linguistic, paralinguistic, and non-verbal correlates. However, it should be noted that the use of mimetics is so sensitive to various factors, from discourse type to communication setting and possibly one's personality traits, that a generalisation made in one (sub-)corpus might not hold in another. For example, the relative position of quotative- and zero-marked mimetics found in novels (Section 9.4.1) is not replicated in the earthquake corpus (Akita and Usuki 2016). It appears that the spoken register gives the speaker more freedom to choose different marking. Likewise, expressive forms of mimetics (Section 9.4.3) are far more frequent in the earthquake corpus than in the World War II corpus and the NUCC (Akita 2017b). This contrast is obviously attributed to the emotional nature of many earthquake interviews. Furthermore, it appears that Sumihare in the Noji corpus is a notably frequent mimetic user compared to the other Japanese children on CHILDES.

180   KIMI AKITA

On top of the variation issues, obtaining all mimetics from a large corpus is difficult for two reasons. First, as native speakers can readily create new mimetics, a ready-made list of search items may not suffice. Second, non-reduplicated mimetics, especially short ones, often cause morphological analysis errors. For example, *buriQ-to* 'pfft (sound of a fart)' may be misanalysed into the noun *buri* 'yellowtail' or the suffix *-buri* 'since' and the colloquial quotative *-tto*.

Thus, having developed corpora alone does not guarantee comprehensive research. To answer some research questions, we will need to consider how to minimise the irrelevant variations in the use of mimetics and how to get all mimetic tokens from the data set. One way of compensating for these crucial limitations of corpus-based studies will be to conduct experiments, as described in the next section.

9.5 Experiments

Experimental methods have also been employed to elicit mimetics from Japanese speakers, especially in recent psycholinguistic studies. These studies are designed to address relatively specific research questions, such as when people use mimetics and how similar mimetics are across dialects.

Baba (2003) used four speech settings (three role-plays and one monologue) to see under what circumstances Japanese speakers often use mimetics. She found that mimetics are particularly frequent in subjective and interactive speech settings, such as when one tells one's friend the story of a comic strip from the main character's perspective. On the other hand, politeness was not found to be a relevant factor.

Akita and Matsumoto (2020) created thirty short videos in which someone or something moves from one place to another and asked Japanese speakers to describe each of them. They found that mimetic adverbials with expressive features (see Section 9.4.3), such as *piiiiiit-te* 'with a long whistle' and *gatagatagatagatagatagata-to* 'with a repetitive rattling sound', made a remarkable contribution to the expressive power of sound descriptions (see also Iwasaki 2017 for the use of mimetics for motion events by L2 learners of Japanese).

Experiments are also used to elicit mimetics from parents. Ogura et al. (1997) conducted longitudinal observations of two mother–child pairs. The mothers and their children visited a university's playroom nearly once a month and interacted with each other while playing house or playing with dolls. Both mothers decreased mimetics and motherese words slightly earlier than their children did, indicating that they adjusted their verbal input according to their children's cognitive or linguistic development. Saji and Imai (2013) used a more restricted experimental setting, in which parents explained twelve short animated drawings of various actions to their children or the adult experimenter. As a result, the parents of two-year-olds used more mimetics than parents of three-year-olds, both using even fewer mimetics to the experimenter. In Section 9.4.2, I mentioned Sumihare's preference for higher iconicity in the beginning of his acquisition of mimetics. The two experimental results here are consistent with this corpus-based insight: the iconicity of mimetics helps children to start learning language, and parents believe so (Imai et al. 2008; Nielsen and Dingemanse 2021).

Finally, McLean (2021) conducted a field experiment using a stimulus kit to elicit mimetics for fifty-six sensory perceptions from seven varieties of Japonic. The stimulus kit included videos (for audition and vision), drawings (for vision and interoception), objects with different textures (for tactition), liquids (for gustation), and fragrances (for olfaction). Examining how often these sensory perceptions are represented by mimetics across Japonic varieties, McLean revised Dingemanse's (2012) implicational hierarchy for the possible semantic range of expressive lexicons as follows: SOUND < MOVEMENT < FORM < TEXTURE < OTHER SENSORY PERCEPTIONS (e.g. COLOUR, TASTE, SMELL, INTEROCEPTION). This hierarchy predicts that if (a variety of) a language has expressive lexemes for one type of sensory perception (e.g. *tuntikanti* 'uneven' (FORM) in Ishigaki), it also has expressive lexemes for the sensory perceptions located lower in the hierarchy (e.g. ʃonʃonʃon 'cicada call' (SOUND) in Ishigaki), but not vice versa.

The experimental methods sketched here allow researchers to elicit mimetics in controlled settings and answer their specific research questions. It is also often possible to reuse the same experimental stimuli to test these research questions in other languages. However, it should be noted that the variation issue raised in Section 9.4 also applies to experiments. In general, people need casual settings to use mimetics. Therefore, they might refrain from using mimetics when they are forced to speak to an unfamiliar experimenter. One solution would be to recruit experimental participants in pairs so that they can speak to their familiar partner.

9.6 Conclusion

The study of Japanese mimetics has a long history made by native speaker linguists' introspection, various dictionaries and corpora, and experiments. These advanced research environments and methods have enabled Japanese linguistics to make important descriptive and theoretical contributions to expressivity research. However, these advantages have also kept Japanese linguists away from natural, multimodal conversation data, which are crucial for uncovering the essential properties of mimetics as an interactional device (Dingemanse 2011). This ironic situation is expected to be improved soon by the development of multimodal conversation corpora, such as NINJAL's Corpus of Everyday Japanese Conversation. Moreover, there is a surge of interest in mimetics among Japanese dialectologists (Kobayashi 2018). Together with the traditional historical studies

References

Akita, Kimi (2005–2010). A bibliography of sound-symbolic phenomena in Japanese. Available at https://sites.google.com/site/akitambo/Home/biblio/bib?authuser=0. Accessed 23 September, 2022.

Akita, Kimi (2009). *A grammar of sound-symbolic words in Japanese: theoretical approaches to iconic and lexical properties of mimetics*. PhD dissertation, Kobe University.

Akita, Kimi (2012). Toward a frame-semantic definition of sound-symbolic words: A collocational analysis of Japanese mimetics. *Cognitive Linguistics* 23(1): 67–90.

Akita, Kimi (2013). Constraints on the semantic extension of onomatopoeia. *Public Journal of Semiotics* 5(1): 21–37.

Akita, Kimi (2017a). The linguistic integration of Japanese ideophones and its typological implications. *Canadian Journal of Linguistics* 62(2): 314–334.

Akita, Kimi (2017b). NHK ākaibusu no onomatope: Mihappyō deēta [Mimetics in the NHK corpora: Unpublished data]. Available at https://sites.google.com/site/akitambo/Home/pub?authuser=0. Accessed 23 September 2022.

Akita, Kimi (2019a). Ideophones. In Mark Aronoff (ed.), *Oxford Bibliographies in Linguistics*. New York: Oxford University Press.

Akita, Kimi (2019b). Mimetics, gaze, and facial expression in a multimodal corpus of Japanese. In Kimi Akita and Prashant Pardeshi (eds), *Ideophones, mimetics and expressives*, 229–247. Amsterdam and Philadelphia: John Benjamins.

Akita, Kimi and Dingemanse, Mark (2019). Ideophones (mimetics, expressives). In Mark Aronoff (ed.), *Oxford Research Encyclopedia of Linguistics*. Oxford: Oxford University Press.

Akita, Kimi and Matsumoto, Yo (2020). A fine-grained analysis of manner salience: Experimental evidence from Japanese and English. In Yo Matsumoto and Kazuhiro Kawachi (eds), *Broader Perspectives on Motion Event Descriptions*. Amsterdam and Philadelphia: John Benjamins, 143–179.

Akita, Kimi, Nakamura, Satoshi, Komatsu, Takanori, and Hirata, Sachiko (2012). Onomatope no intarakushonsei ni kansuru ryōteki kōsatu [A quantitative study of the interactional function of mimetics]. In *Proceedings of the 26th Annual Conference of the Japanese Society for Artificial Intelligence*, 13 June 2012. 2N1–OS–8c–5.

Akita, Kimi, Nakamura, Satoshi, Komatsu, Takanori, and Hirata-Mogi, Sachiko (2014). A quantitative approach to mimetic diachrony. In Mikio Giriko, Naonori Nagaya, Akiko Takemura, and Timothy J. Vance (eds), *Japanese/Korean Linguistics, Vol. 22*. Stanford: CSLI, 181–195.

Akita, Kimi and Usuki, Takeshi (2016). A constructional account of the 'optional' quotative marking on Japanese mimetics. *Journal of Linguistics* 52(2): 245–275.

Ameka, Felix K. (2001). Ideophones and the nature of the adjective word class in Ewe. In Friedrich K. Erhard Voeltz and Christa Kilian-Hatz (eds), *Ideophones*. Amsterdam and Philadelphia: John Benjamins, 25–48.

Asano, Tsuruko (ed.) (1978). *Giongo/gitaigo jiten* [A Dictionary of Mimetics]. Tokyo: Kadokawa.

Atoda, Minoko and Hoshino, Kazuko (1995). *Giongo/gitaigo tsukaikata jiten* [A Dictionary of the Usage of Mimetics]. Tokyo: Sotakusha.

Baba, Junko (2003). Pragmatic function of Japanese mimetics in the spoken discourse of varying emotive intensity levels. *Journal of Pragmatics* 35(12): 1861–1889.

Badenoch, Nathan and Osada, Toshiki (eds) (2019). *A Dictionary of Mundari Expressives*. Tokyo: Research Institute for Languages and Cultures of Asia and Africa, Tokyo University of Foreign Studies.

Chang, Andrew C. (1990). *A Thesaurus of Japanese Mimesis and Onomatopoeia: Usage by Categories*. Tokyo: Taishukan.

Childs, G. Tucker (1994). African ideophones. In Leanne Hinton, Johanna Nichols, and John J. Ohala (eds), *Sound Symbolism*. Cambridge: Cambridge University Press, 178–204.

Diffloth, Gérard (1972). Notes on expressive meaning. *Chicago Linguistic Society (CLS)* 8: 440–447.

Dingemanse, Mark (2011). *The meaning and use of ideophones in Siwu*. PhD dissertation, Radboud University.

Dingemanse, Mark (2012). Advances in the cross-linguistic study of ideophones. *Language and Linguistics Compass* 6(10): 654–672.

Dingemanse, Mark (2015). Ideophones and reduplication: depiction, description, and the interpretation of repeated talk in discourse. *Studies in Language* 39(4): 946–970.

Dingemanse, Mark (2017). Expressiveness and system integration: on the typology of ideophones, with special reference to Siwu. *STUF—Language Typology and Universals* 70(2): 119–141.

Dingemanse, Mark (2019). 'Ideophone' as a comparative concept. In Kimi Akita and Prashant Pardeshi (eds), *Ideophones, Mimetics and Expressives*. Amsterdam and Philadelphia: John Benjamins, 13–33.

Dingemanse, Mark and Akita, Kimi (2017). An inverse relation between expressiveness and grammatical integration: on the morphosyntactic typology of ideophones, with special reference to Japanese. *Journal of Linguistics* 53(3): 501–532.

Fujimura, Itsuko, Chiba, Shoju, and Ohso, Mieko (2012). Lexical and grammatical features of spoken and written Japanese in contrast: exploring a lexical profiling approach to comparing spoken and written corpora. In Heliana Mello, Massimo Pettorino, and Tommaso Raso (eds), *Proceedings of the VIIth GSCP International Conference, Speech and Corpora*, 393–398. Belo Horizonte, Brazil: Universidade Federal de Minas Gerais. 29 February to 2 March.

Gomi, Taro (1989) [2004]. *Nihongo gitaigo jiten* [A Dictionary of Japanese Mimetics]. Tokyo: The Japan Times.

Guo, Huajiang (2019). *A New Japanese-Chinese Dictionary of Mimetics*. 2nd edition. Shanghai: Shanghai Translation.

Hamano, Shoko (1998). *The Sound-symbolic System of Japanese*. Tokyo: Kurosio.

Hida, Yoshifumi and Asada, Hideko (eds) (2002). *Gendai giongo/gitaigo yōhō jiten* [A Dictionary of Contemporary Mimetic Usage]. Tokyo: Tokyodo.

Hirata, Sachiko, Nakamura, Satoshi, Komatsu, Takanori, and Akita, Kimi (2015). Kokkai kaigiroku kōpasu o mochiita onomatope shiyō no chiiki hikaku [Cross-regional comparison of mimetic word uses based on the minutes of the Diet of Japan]. *Journal of the Japanese Society for Artificial Intelligence* 30(1): 274–281.

Imai, Mutsumi, Kita, Sotaro, Nagumo, Miho, and Okada, Hiroyuki (2008). Sound symbolism facilitates early verb learning. *Cognition* 109(1): 54–65.

Iwasaki, Noriko (2017). Use of mimetics in Motion event descriptions by English and Korean learners of L2 Japanese: Does language typology make a difference? In Noriko Iwasaki, Peter Sells, and Kimi Akita (eds), *The Grammar of Japanese Mimetics: Perspectives from Structure, Acquisition, and Translation*. London: Routledge, 193–218.

Kakehi, Hisao (1986). The function and expressiveness of Japanese onomatopes. *Bulletin of the Faculty of Letters* (Kobe University) 13: 1–12.

Kakehi, Hisao, Tamori, Ikuhiro, and Schourup, Lawrence (1996). *Dictionary of Iconic Expressions in Japanese*. Berlin and New York: Mouton de Gruyter.

Kawase, Suguru (2005). Shōchōshi o dōshika suru keishiki no hensen [The historical change of mimetic verbalisers]. *Gobun Kenkyū* (Kyushu University) 99: 11–24.

Kawase, Suguru (2006). Shōchōshi no *to* datsuraku ni tsuite no tsūjiteki kōsatu [A diachronic study of *to*-drop in mimetics]. *Gobun Kenkyū* (Kyushu University) 100/101: 16–29.

Kita, Sotaro (1997). Two-dimensional semantic analysis of Japanese mimetics. *Linguistics* 35(2): 379–415.

Kobayashi, Takashi (ed.) (2018). *Kansei no hōgengaku* [The Dialectology of Emotion]. Tokyo: Hituzi Syobo.

Lovestrand, Joseph (2022). Ideophones, expressiveness and system integration in Barayin. Paper presented at *Workshop on Typology of Ideophones*, 25 June, York University and Nagoya University.

McLean, Bonnie (2021). Revising an implicational hierarchy for the meanings of ideophones, with special reference to Japonic. *Linguistic Typology* 25(3): 507–549.

Mester, R. Armin and Itô, Junko (1989). Feature predictability and underspecification: Palatal prosody in Japanese mimetics. *Language* 65(2): 258–291.

Mihas, Elena (2013). Composite ideophone-gesture utterances in the Ashéninka Pereré 'community of practice', an Amazonian Arawak society from Central-Eastern Peru. *Gesture* 13: 28–62.

Murasugi, Keiko (2017). Mimetics as Japanese root infinitive analogues. In Noriko Iwasaki, Peter Sells, and Kimi Akita (eds), *The Grammar of Japanese Mimetics: Perspectives from Structure, Acquisition, and Translation*. London: Routledge, 131–147.

Nasu, Akio (2004). Shinzō onomatope no on'in kōzō to bunsetsu no muhyōsei [Phonological structure of mimetic neologisms and segmental unmarkedness]. *Japanese Linguistics* 16: 69–91.

Newman, Paul (1968). Ideophones from a syntactic point of view. *Journal of West African Languages* 5: 107–117.

Nielsen, Alan K. S. and Dingemanse, Mark (2021). Iconicity in word learning and beyond: a critical review. *Language and Speech* 64(1): 52–72.

Noji, Junya (1973–1977). *Yōjiki no gengo seikatsu no jittai, I–IV* [A Field Study of Infant Language Life, Vol. I–IV]. Hiroshima and Tokyo: Bunka Hyoron.

Nuckolls, Janis B. (2019). The sensori-semantic clustering of ideophonic meaning in Pastaza Quichua. In Kimi Akita and Prashant Pardeshi (eds), *Ideophones, Mimetics and Expressives*. Amsterdam and Philadelphia: John Benjamins, 167–198.

Ogura, Tamiko, Yoshimoto, Yoshie, and Tsubota, Minori (1997). Hahaoya no ikujigo to kodomo no gengo hattatsu, ninchi hattatsu [Babytalk and children's linguistic and cognitive development]. *Bulletin of the Faculty of Human Development* 5(1): 1–14.

Ono, Masahiro (ed.) (2007). *Giongo/gitaigo 4500: Nihongo onomatope jiten* [4500 Mimetics: A Dictionary of Japanese Onomatopoeia]. Tokyo: Shogakukan.

Park, Jiyeon (2019). *Onomatope no gengoteki tōgōsei ni kansuru nikkan taishō kenkyū* [A Study of the System Integration of Mimetics in Japanese and Korean]. PhD dissertation, Nagoya University.

Perry, Lynn K., Perlman, Marcus, and Lupyan, Gary (2015). Iconicity in English and Spanish and its relation to lexical category and age of acquisition. *PLoS ONE* 10(9): e0137147.

Rhodes, Richard (1994). Aural images. In Leanne Hinton, Johanna Nichols, and John J. Ohala (eds), *Sound Symbolism*. Cambridge: Cambridge University Press, 276–292.

Saji, Noburo and Imai, Mutsumi (2013). Goi kakutoku ni okeru ruizōsei no kōka no kentō: oya no hattatsu to kodomo no rikai no kanten kara [A study of the effect of iconicity on lexical acquisition: from the perspectives of parents' utterances and children's comprehension]. In Kazuko Shinohara and Ryoko Uno (eds), *Onomatope kenkyū no shatei: Chikazuku oto to imi* [Sound Symbolism and Mimetics: Rethinking the Relationship Between Sound and Meaning in Language]. Tokyo: Hituzi Syobo, 151–166.

Schourup, Lawrence (1993). Nihongo no kaki kotoba/hanashi kotoba ni okeru onomatope-no bunpu ni tsuite [On the distribution of mimetics in written and spoken Japanese]. In Hisao Kakehi and Ikuhiro Tamori (eds), *Onomatopia: Gion-/gitaigo no rakuen* [Onomatopoeia: A Utopia of Mimetics]. Tokyo: Keiso Shobo, 77–100.

Sells, Peter (2017). The significance of the grammatical study of Japanese mimetics. In Noriko Iwasaki, Peter Sells, and Kimi Akita (eds), *The Grammar of Japanese Mimetics: Perspectives from Structure, Acquisition, and Translation*. London: Routledge, 7–19.

Sohn, Ho-min (1994). *Korean*. London: Routledge.

Son, Youngsuk (2010). Giongo/gitaigo to miburi: terebi hōsō no maruchimedia kōpasu ni yoru keiryōteki bunseki [Onomatopoeias and gestures: a multimedia corpus-based quantitative study of Japanese television broadcasts]. *Mathematical Linguistics* 27: 131–153.

Takamaru, Keiichi, Uchida, Yuzu, Ototake, Hokuto, and Kimura, Yasutomo (2014). Chihō gikai kaigiroku kōpasu o mochiita onomatope no bunseki [Analysis of onomatopoeias in the corpus of regional assembly minutes]. In *Proceedings of the Sixth Workshop on Japanese Corpus Linguistics*, 83–92. Sapporo.

Takeda, Koko (2012). *Tōhoku hōgen onomatope (giongo/gitaigo) yōreishū: Aomori ken, Iwate ken, Miyagi ken, Fukushima ken* [A Booklet of Examples of Mimetics in Tohoku Dialects: Aomori, Iwate, Miyagi, and Fukushima Prefectures]. Tokyo: National Institute for Japanese Language and Linguistics.

Tamaoka, Kazuo, Kiyama, Sachiko, and Miyaoka, Yayoi (2011). Shinbun to shōsetsu no kōpasu ni okeru onomatope to dōshi no kyōki patān [Collocation patterns of sound-symbolic words and verbs in corpora of a newspaper and novels]. *Gengo Kenkyū* 139: 57–84.

Tamori, Ikuhiro (2010). *Kenji onomatope no nazo o toku* [Solving the Mystery of Kenji's Mimetics]. Tokyo: Taishukan.

Tamori, Ikuhiro and Schourup, Lawrence (1999). *Onomatope: Keitai to imi* [Mimetics: Form and Meaning]. Tokyo: Kurosio.

Toratani, Kiyoko (2017). The position of to/Ø-marked mimetics in Japanese sentence structure. In Noriko Iwasaki, Peter Sells, and Kimi Akita (eds), *The Grammar of Japanese Mimetics: Perspectives from Structure, Acquisition, and Translation*. London: Routledge, 35–72.

Tsujimura, Natsuko (2005). Mimetic verbs and innovative verbs in the acquisition of Japanese. *Berkeley Linguistics Society (BLS)* 31: 371–382.

Tsujimura, Natsuko (2022). *Expressing Silence: Where Language and Culture Meet in Japanese*. Maryland: Lexington Books.

Yamaguchi, Nakami (2002). *Inu wa 'biyo' to naite ita: Nihongo wa giongo/gitaigo ga omoshiroi* [Dogs Used to Say 'biyo': It is Mimetics That Are Interesting in Japanese]. Tokyo: Kobunsha.

Yamaguchi, Nakami (ed.) (2003) [2015]. *Giongo/gitaigo jiten* [A Dictionary of Mimetics]. Tokyo: Kodansha.

Corpora

Aozora Bunko Corpus (1998). Available at www.aozora.gr.jp/. Accessed 23 September 2022.

Balanced Corpus of Contemporary Written Japanese (2011). Tokyo: National Institute for Japanese Language and Linguistics.

Corpus of Everyday Japanese Conversation (2018). Tokyo: National Institute for Japanese Language and Linguistics. Available at www2.ninjal.ac.jp/conversation/cejc/design.html. Accessed 23 September 2022.

Corpus of Historical Japanese (2021). Tokyo: National Institute for Japanese Language and Linguistics. Available at https://clrd.ninjal.ac.jp/chj/overview-en.html. Accessed 23 September 2022.

Nagoya University Conversation Corpus Aichi: Nagoya University. Available at https://mmsrv.ninjal.ac.jp/nucc/. Accessed 23 September 2022.

NHK Great East Japan Earthquake Archive (2012). Tokyo: Japan Broadcasting Corporation. Available at https://www.nhk.or.jp/archives/saigai/special/311shogen/. Accessed 23 September 2022.

NHK World War II Archive (2010). Tokyo: Japan Broadcasting Corporation. Available at https://www.nhk.or.jp/archives/sensou/. Accessed 23 September 2022.

PART III
TECHNIQUES

10

Is there an aesthetic component of language?

Harshit Parmar and Jeffrey P. Williams

10.1 Introduction

Language processing is a complex task performed by the brain. Studies suggest that a number of functional brain regions are involved in understanding different aspects of language (Hickok 2009). Language being an important social aspect of an individual, the language regions have been studied extensively using functional neuroimaging tools. Identification of language regions has been a crucial factor for pre-surgical procedures as well. For pre-surgical procedures, language regions have been identified using both task (Benjamin et al. 2017) and resting state (Tie et al. 2014) fMRI paradigms. The temporal and spatial reliability of these language regions has been successfully tested with multiple longitudinal studies (Zhu et al. 2014; Nettekoven et al. 2018).

Within the language regions, aspects of grammar are interpreted in different locations. Semantic processing regions differ from syntactic processing (Rüschemeyer et al. 2005) and so do the nominal and verbal processing regions (Sahin et al. 2006). But collectively, most of the language processing regions lie either within the Broca's area or the Wernicke's area of the brain. However, some aspects of language are processed differently by the brain. For example, grammar norm violations are in fact processed partially outside the classic language regions (Hubers et al. 2016). Along with that, taboo words (cursing or swearing), which are also part of every language, are processed differently from non-taboo words inside the brains of bilinguals (Sulpizio et al. 2019). Apart from involving more brain regions, processing times for taboo words was also shown to be longer than for neutral words (Sulpizio et al. 2019). It is thus plausible to think that there could be other aspects of language which are interpreted in a different way inside the brain. One such aspect of language is the category of expressives. Expressives are very prevalent in South Asian languages (cf. Williams 2020) and, most importantly for our study, are thought to belong to a special category of grammar (cf. Diffloth 1972; Zwicky and Pullum 1987).

Harshit Parmar and Jeffrey P. Williams, *Is there an aesthetic component of language?*. In: *Capturing Expressivity.*
Edited by: Jeffrey P. Williams, Oxford University Press. © Harshit Parmar and Jeffrey P. Williams (2025).
DOI: 10.1093/oso/9780192858931.003.0010

The proposed study seeks to provide preliminary data to assist in answering the question 'Is there an aesthetic component of language?' The idea of an aesthetic component of language was first proposed in modern linguistics by Gérard Diffloth in 1972, in his seminal article 'Notes on Expressive Meaning.' (Diffloth 1972). In that article, Diffloth made the claim that features of grammar, such as expressives, belonged to a discrete and separate category, or component of language, that he called 'esthetic'. The esthetic/aesthetic component existed separately from other components of grammar, leading us to speculate that there might be some different localization for the brain activity associated with the production and interpretation of expressives.

In the following section we outline expressivity and provide examples of expressives to give the relevant linguistic background to our neuropsychological study of expressives in Gujarati and Hindi (Indo-Aryan languages).

10.1.1 Expressivity and expressives

We can assume, relatively non-controversially, that grammar comprises representations guided by principles and rules. The exact shape of these components is still in debate, but overall, principles set the stage for the production of semantic–syntactic strings through an orderly application of a rule component. Expressivity certainly plays a part in this sort of structure, also being governed by both principles and rules and shaped by representational constraints.

10.1.1.1 Expressivity

Expressivity is no different from other properties of human language that find articulation in the grammar through principles and rules. Expressivity is governed by a principle of expressivity that is universal in human language, which states the following: a systematic feature of human language is the ability to articulate and communicate perception of natural and social worlds (Williams 2025). We refer to this feature as the principle of expressivity.

The principle of expressivity is manifested through the grammatical resources of human languages. The grammar of each language has its own set of structures that can be employed by speakers to reflect on perceptions of actions, activities, and social positions of individuals. This accounts for the variation we find across languages in terms of what structurally constitutes expressivity. In this chapter we examine the principle of expressivity in Gujarati (Indo-Aryan) and Hindi (Indo-Aryan) through a pilot study.

10.1.1.1.1 Expressives

Expressives are shape-shifting forms whose functions cross-cut grammatical categories and classes but, in general, serve to allow the speaker to provide metacommentary on an argument in the discourse. As the name conveys, expressives allow speakers to 'express' an opinion, an attitude, a perception, or other psychological state regarding a topic in a situated discourse (Williams 2021). As Tuvasson states, '[e]xpressives typically package multiple aspects of a sensory event in a single word' (Tuvasson 2011: 88).

The concept of expressives, sometimes referred to as ideophones, is a relatively young one in linguistics. One of the earliest descriptions of an expressive can be found in the writings of the psychologist-phoneticist Edward Wheeler Scripture (1864–1945). In his *Elements of Experimental Phonetics*, Scripture used the term *ideogram* for the holistic perception of a printed word. He states, 'printed words are perceived in wholes as ideograms and not as combinations ... ... words may be perceived under conditions that exclude any perception of the single elements' (Scripture 1902: 128). Scripture goes further to create a parallel between the 'image' of the printed word and that of the auditory word:

> It may be suggested that auditory words and phrases form 'ideophones', just as printed ones form 'ideograms'. Further distinctions may be made of ideograms and ideophones into sensory (visual words and auditory words) and motor ones (written words and spoken words). In all probability the most prominent features of a phonetic unit are first perceived, and the details are gradually filled in. (Scripture 1902: 132)

For Scripture, then, an expressive is a unit of sound that is perceived as a whole rather than as a combination of some parts; and this whole represents one idea. This condition is what has driven linguists to consider expressives as somehow special in terms of their linguistic categorization.

There are several types or forms of expressives found in the grammars of human languages. It is beyond the scope of the present chapter and reported study to go into these in any detail. The particular kind of expressives that we employed in our study are reduplications and echo words and we will define and illustrate those in the following sections.

10.1.1.1.2 Reduplication

Reduplication is a word-formation process involving the copying of a base or root form and collocating the two together. Theoretically, there is disagreement as to whether reduplication is a form of compounding or a form of affixation. That debate need not trouble us here and is not relevant for the present study. Examples of reduplication from our data set include the following examples, from Gujarati and Hindi respectively:

આ ઘાવ **ધીમે ધીમે** રુઝાઇ જશે
Aa ghaav **dheeme dheeme** rujai jase.
'The wound will heal slowly.'

मुझे **गरम गरम** पकोड़े खाने हैं ।

Muje **garam garam** pakode khaane hai.

'I want to eat hot fritters.'

In each example, the first sentence is a sentence with expressive (**highlighted**) in the native script, the second one is the Romanized pronunciation, and the third sentence is the translation in English.

10.1.1.1.3 Echo words

Echo-words are the result of a special word-formation process involving the formation/generation of rhyming words through copying, change, and collocation. Rhyming is a tricky term to use in a universal fashion, since the conceptualization of what it means to rhyme is governed by local grammatical conditions. Abbi defines an echo word as '... a partially repeated form of the base word—partially in the sense that either the initial phoneme (which can be either a consonant or a vowel) or the syllable of the base is replaced by another phoneme or another syllable' (Abbi et al. 1992: 20). Examples from our data set of echo words include the following:

ध્યાન રાખજો, **હડકુ બડકુ** તુટી ના જાય

Dhyan rakhjo, **hadku badku** tuti naa jaay.

'Be careful not to break your bone.'

वहाँ के रास्ते बहुत **तेढे मेढे** है ।

Vaha ke raaste bahut **tedhe medhe** hai.

'The roads there are very uneven.'

The aim of this study is to verify whether expressives are actually being perceived differently from standard grammar or not. The perception of expressives was achieved through identifying by task functional Magnetic Resonance Imaging (fMRI). Difference in brain activation was obtained for response to sentences with and without expressives. The idea is to reduce the common aspects between expressives and non-expressives as much as possible and focus only on the difference. Apart from that, reading and translation paradigms were used. It is our assumption that response to just reading a sentence should not be affected by the presence or absence of expressives. The act of reading is just vocalizing the symbols and should be almost independent of intricate elements of language. In translation, the meaning of the sentence must be understood and thus can be an indirect measure of perception. Two separate languages were used in the experimental paradigm to see if the perception difference of expressives was the same across the native and secondary languages.

The next section details the methodology of the experiment, with information on the experiment design and the analysis process. Results are presented in the

IS THERE AN AESTHETIC COMPONENT OF LANGUAGE?

third section, followed by the discussion of the results in the fourth section. The fifth section discusses some of the limitations and challenges of the current study.

10.2 Methodology

10.2.1 Functional experiment

The fMRI measures brain activity from the entire brain. To isolate brain activation corresponding to a specific condition, a contrast fMRI experiment design is used. An fMRI contrast refers to an experiment design where everything except the cognitive process under study is changed between different experiment conditions during a task. The concept of contrast plays a central role in analyzing fMRI data, as it involves comparing brain activity under different experimental conditions to highlight significant differences. For instance, a simple contrast might compare brain activation during a task (e.g., viewing images) to a control condition (e.g., viewing a blank screen), while complex contrasts might involve weighted combinations of multiple conditions. These comparisons are analyzed statistically, often using a General Linear Model (GLM), to produce contrast maps that pinpoint regions of significant activation. By combining experimental design with contrast analysis, fMRI experiments provide insights into how specific brain regions support cognitive and sensory functions.

The functional experiment to identify the cognitive process of expressives involves two phases: a reading phase and a translation phase. Each phase consists of a mixed event-related and block-task *f*MRI experiment design. The entire functional experiment was divided into multiple blocks based on the language of the sentence and the presence or absence of expressives in the sentence. Each block can be categorized into one of the four categories—Gujarati expressives (GE), Gujarati non-expressives (GNE), Hindi expressives (HE), and Hindi non-expressives (HNE). For the reading phase, a sentence appeared on the screen in either Hindi or Gujarati and the participant had to read the sentence aloud. Instructions were given to the participants before entering the MRI scanner on how to speak from the diaphragm in order to minimize the head motion. (Head motion introduces motion artefacts into *f*MRI data.) Once the participant had finished reading a sentence, they would indicate with a button press and the next sentence would appear on the screen immediately after the button press. The button was pressed using the index finger of the right hand. A total of five sentences were presented together in a single block. At the end of each block, there was a blank screen with a small cross in the middle of the screen. The participants were instructed not to do anything while the screen was blank and to focus on the cross. The blank screen lasted for ten seconds before the first sentence from the next block was displayed on the screen. Within each block, sentences from the same categories were displayed. The entire reading phase consists of sixteen blocks, with four in each category. The order of the blocks was randomized for each participant. The graphic representation of the experiment paradigm is shown in Figure 10.1. The top portion shows one of the example screenshots for each group. The middle portion shows the timeline representation, with different colours representing blocks of different categories. Each block consists of five separate sentences and the duration for each sentence is decided by the user with a button press.

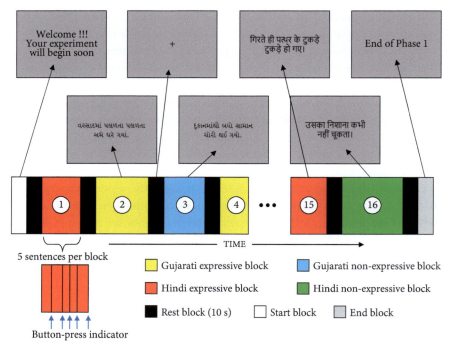

Figure 10.1 Graphic representation for the experiment design

For the translation phase, the sentences were displayed on the screen in Hindi or Gujarati and the participants had to translate the sentences to English and speak out loud the English translation. The participants were advised that there is no correct or incorrect translation and they had to translate the sentences the way they felt was correct. Audio recording of the reading and translation phase was intended originally. However, it was decided prior to the scans that the loud noise of the MRI machine would not allow for good-quality sound recording. Thus, no sound recording was made for the speech in both phases. A few of the participants opted to participate in only one language instead of both. For those participants, the experiment design was kept the same with only two categories (in the language of their choice) and five blocks per category. Lastly, the duration for which each sentence appeared on the screen had an upper bound in case there was some error

IS THERE AN AESTHETIC COMPONENT OF LANGUAGE? 195

in button press or some participants deliberately didn't press the buttons. In case the button was not pressed, a new sentence would appear on the screen after ten seconds for the reading phase and after fifteen seconds for the translation phase. The upper bound in time was set assuming the slowest reading speed to be 40 words per minute (w.p.m.), (average reading speed being 120–150 w.p.m.).

10.2.2 Participants

The participants were healthy adults who could read, understand, and speak Hindi and/or Gujarati along with English. Prior to the experiment, approval was obtained from the Institution Review Board (IRB) of Texas Tech University and signed consent was obtained from all the participants. All the participants were also screened for MRI safety through the use of an MRI safety screening form. The total number of participants was ten (four F and six M) with an average (standard deviation) age of 31.2 (9.2) years. Apart from English, a total of eight participants knew both Gujarati and Hindi, while one participant knew only Hindi, and one participant knew only Gujarati. One participant knew both Hindi and Gujarati but opted to participate only for the Hindi experiment. Before the MRI scanning, the participants were asked to read from a fictional novel in Gujarati and Hindi for exactly one minute to measure their natural reading speed. The average reading speed across participants for Gujarati was 129 w.p.m. (min = 100 w.p.m. and max = 165 w.p.m.) and for Hindi also it was 129 w.p.m. (min = 90 w.p.m. and max = 175 w.p.m.). No prior information was given to any participant about expressives, to avoid any bias in the data. The participants also practised on a demo task prior to entering the MRI scanner. All the sentences for the demo were without expressives, again to avoid any prior knowledge about the construct to be studied.

10.2.3 MRI scan parameters

The MRI scanning was performed on a 3T Siemens Skyra scanner. One high-resolution anatomical scan and two separate functional scans were performed on each subject. The anatomical scans were performed using a sagittal MPRAGE pulse sequence. The echo time (TE) and repetition time (TR) for anatomical scans are 2.49 milliseconds and 1,900 milliseconds, respectively. The resolution of sagittal images is 1 mm × 1 mm with a slice thickness of 0.9 mm. Two separate functional scans were acquired, one for the reading phase and one for the translation phase. The functional images were acquired using a multiband echo planar imaging (MB-EPI) pulse sequence (Setsompop et al. 2012). Because of the multiband pulse sequence, six axial slices were acquired at a time, allowing a lower TR value of 545 milliseconds. For each functional volume, forty-eight axial slices of

3.3 mm thickness were acquired with an in-plane resolution of 3.25 mm × 3.25 mm. The experiment was self-paced, and thus different participants took different amount of time to complete it. The total number of functional volumes for reading phase range from 514 (4 min 40 sec) to 1036 (9 min 24 sec) and for translation phase range from 791 (7 min 11 sec) to 1490 (13 min 32 sec).

10.2.4 Behavioural data analysis

The first step in the analysis was to check if there is any difference in response time for expressives and non-expressives. The time to read/translate each sentence was known from the button-press timing. Response time for each sentence was computed using the total time taken and the number of syllables in the sentence. The total number of syllables was calculated for each sentence. To account for the differences in syllable length, the read/translate times were weighted (divided) according to the syllable count. Hindi and Gujarati are both syllabary languages, thus it is more suitable to weight according to the number of syllables rather than the number of words or characters. A paired t-test was conducted between the response times for reading and translating the sentences with and without expressives in them. First, a paired t-test was conducted independently for all participants and then a group-level paired t-test was conducted using the average response time per participant. For all the t-tests, a p value was computed and only the tests with p value less than 0.05 were considered statistically significant.

Correlation was also computed between the average response time of the participants and their reading speed. Correlation was computed in all four categories for both reading and translation. Next, the difference between the reading and translation response times was analysed. A paired t-test was performed between response times of reading vs translation for all participants. Independent t-tests were conducted for each of the four categories (GE, GNE, HE, and HNE).

10.2.5 Functional data analysis

The functional data analysis begins with the preprocessing of the data. The preprocessing of the functional data was carried out using the SPM12 toolbox (Ashburner et al. 2014) and in-house MATLAB script. The very first step was to convert and merge the raw DICOM files for all of the functional TRs into a single Nifti file. The preprocessing steps that were then applied to the Nifti file were: motion correction, co-registration, spatial normalization, spatial segmentation, masking, temporal signal drift reduction, and spatial smoothing. The details of each of the preprocessing steps and its needs are given in 10.7 Appendix A.

Preprocessing was followed by subject-level analysis, also known as first-level analysis. The first-level analysis was performed using the GLM framework in the SPM12 toolbox, using different regressors for each of the four categories. Motion parameters estimated in the preprocessing were also used as nuisance regressors. Subject-wise activation regions were identified for different contrasts. The resulting activation maps were combined across subjects to obtain the group-level activation pattern. The group-level inference was also performed using the SPM 12 toolbox. The group-level analyses for various contrasts were then analysed individually to draw inferences about the perception of expressives and other aspects of the study. The spatial locations of the activation regions were identified using the Brodmann atlas (Maldjian et al. 2003) and meta-analysis database from Neurosynth [https://neurosynth.org]. An in-depth description of the functional data analysis is given in 10.8 Appendix B.

10.3 Results

10.3.1 Behavioural data analysis

The behavioral analysis examines response times and accuracy to evaluate task performance and participant engagement. By analyzing these measures, we can gain insights into how participants process and respond to the experimental tasks, providing a clear understanding of behavioral patterns and performance variability across conditions.

The response times for expressives and non-expressives (E vs NE) were compared using a paired t-test at both subject and group levels. There was no significant difference ($p < 0.05$) in the response times for participant-level and group-level analysis, except for some participants in Hindi reading. The detailed behavioural analysis results for response times are shown in 10.9 Appendix C. For the reading phase, a strong correlation was observed between the response times and the reading speed across all participants. However, such correlation was not observed for the translation phase. Finally, a significant difference ($p < 0.05$) in the response time was observed between reading and translation phases for all four categories. The detailed analysis for reading speed and response time is also given in 10.9 Appendix C. In summary, the behavioural analysis did not yield any significant difference for response times between sentences with and without expressives for either language.

10.3.2 Functional results

The spatial clusters corresponding to the main contrast E vs NE are shown in Figure 10.2A. The contrast computes spatial regions showing significant activation

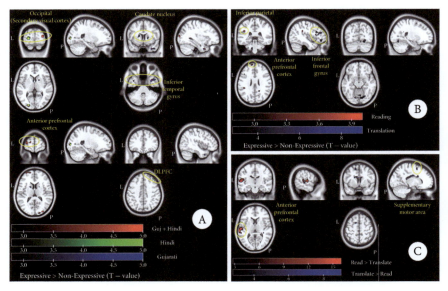

Figure 10.2 (A) Spatial clusters for contrasted E vs NE (reading + translation) for combinations of different languages. (B) Spatial clusters of E vs NE contrast for reading and translation separately. (C) Spatial cluster for contrasted R>T and T>R

for reading and translation combined. The same contrast is computed for three separate cases: Gujarati alone, Hindi alone, and both languages combined. The spatial brain-activation regions corresponding to each of the three cases are shown in the figure with different colour coding. Overlapping regions are represented by overlapping colours. The cluster-level information for all three cases is shown in Table 10.1. Table 10.1 also shows the cluster-level information for the contrast NE vs E. The colour coding for each of the cases is as below.

The voxel with the most significant activation is within the occipital cortex. The clusters for both languages combined show some similarities to and some differences from the clusters of individual languages. For instance, the right inferior temporal gyrus shows significant activation for the contrast of Gujarati and both languages combined, and not for Hindi. Considering that most of the participants (nine out of ten) have Gujarati as their mother tongue (L1 language) this might be an indication of the processing region for L1 and not L2 (Hindi). Similar, occipital gyrus and DLPFC activation is observed only for Hindi and both languages combined. In differences, the caudate nucleus is activated only for Gujarati while parts of the supramarginal gyrus are active only for Hindi.

Apart from the difference language-wise, the E vs NE contrast was also tested for reading and translation separately. Figure 10.2B shows the spatial-activation regions, while Table 10.1 shows the cluster-level information. From the figure and the table, it can be observed that the difference between expressives for reading is

Table 10.1 Cluster level information for all the contrasts shown in Figure 10.2

Region Name	L/R	BA	MNI coordinate			T	Region Name	L/R	BA	MNI coordinate			T
			X	Y	Z					X	Y	Z	
Expressive > Non-expressive	*Gujarati and Hindi*			*Read and Translate*			*Non-expressive > Expressive*	*Gujarati and Hindi*			*Read and Translate*		
Occipital (secondary visual)	R	18	*30*	*−91*	*11*	4.94	Temporal gyrus	R	21–22	*42*	*−28*	*−4*	9.08
		18	*18*	*−97*	*14*	3.66	Middle temporal gyrus	R	21	*57*	*−4*	*−22*	8.22
DLPFC	R	46	*45*	*35*	*38*	4.93	Superior temporal gyrus	R	22	*42*	*−58*	*20*	6.86
Anterior prefrontal cortex	L	10	*−30*	*62*	*14*	4.42							
		10	*−15*	*62*	*14*	3.8							
Occipital	L	18	*−24*	*−91*	*2*	4.32							
Inferior temporal gyrus	R	20	*33*	*9*	*−37*	3.83							
Expressive > Non-expressive	*Gujarati*			*Read and Translate*			*Expressive > Non-expressive*	*Hindi*			*Read and Translate*		
	R	45	*18*	*2*	*−10*	5.95	Occipital	L	18	*−24*	*−91*	*2*	6.06
			18	*8*	*5*	3.89	Occipital	R	18	*21*	*−94*	*11*	3.4
Inferior temporal gyrus	L	20	*−39*	*5*	*−34*	5.04				*36*	*−88*	*17*	3.16
	R	36	*30*	*5*	*−37*	4.67	DLPFC	R	46	*42*	*35*	*41*	5.51
Caudate nucleus	L		*−15*	*5*	*14*	4.5	Supramarginal gyrus	L	40	*−42*	*−49*	*44*	5.34

Continued

Table 10.1 *Continued*

Region Name	L/R	BA	X	Y	Z	T	Region Name	L/R	BA	X	Y	Z	T
MNI coordinate heads above X Y Z												
Expressive > Non-expressive **Gujarati + Hindi** **Reading**							***Read > Translate*** **Gujarati + Hindi**						
Inferior parietal	L		−42	−37	26	3.88	Superior Temporal Gyrus	L	22	−60	−19	8	32.37
Anterior prefrontal cortex	L	10	−12	62	23	3.6		R	22	69	−10	5	11.09
Expressive > Non-expressive **Gujarati + Hindi** **Translation**							***Translate > Read*** **Gujarati + Hindi**						
	R		18	−46	23	9.47		L		−9	−4	26	9.24
Occipital	R	18	24	−70	−13	7.38		R		12	−7	26	7.49
Occipital	L	18	−12	−79	−10	7.26	DLPFC	L	48	−36	23	26	4.85
Inferior frontal gyrus	L	45	−42	38	20	6.61		R	48	30	−34	14	4.24
	L		−42	41	−16	5.58	Sup motor	L	6	−15	5	59	4.2
Inferior temporal gyrus	L	20	−42	5	−28	5.5							

Different contrasts are indicated in **bold + italics**. The table also shows the activation regions' names, their Brodmann area, and the MNI coordinates (in mm) for the peak activation within the cluster along with its t-value.

very much less than for translation. There is also no overlapping region between reading and translation. To confirm the claim, two separate contrasts were tested— Reading > Translate and Translate > Reading. The spatial regions of both the contrasts are shown in Figure 10.2C and the cluster-level information is shown in Table 10.1. Again, for reading, a smaller activation region is obtained than for translation. This suggests that the very act of translation involves more brain regions.

10.4 Discussion

The behavioural analysis suggests that there is no significant difference in the response times between expressives and non-expressives. For reading, it can be understood that sentences with expressives and non-expressives would be read in a similar fashion. However, there being no difference in the response times for translation was unexpected. One possible explanation for this could be the small compositional component of expressives in a sentence. In a typical sentence with six to eight words, only a couple of words are expressives. Thus, the rest of the sentence would be translated as if there were no expressives present in it. Beyond this, however, for some of the expressives, there is no corresponding translation in English, which may induce a slightly larger change. Also, the response times for reading Gujarati and Hindi are similar, while Hindi translation takes a bit longer than Gujarati translation. Given that nine out of ten participants were native Gujarati speakers, it is safe to assume that they would be more proficient in Gujarati than in Hindi.

The main E vs NE contrast suggests the involvement of some of the brain regions in processing expressives differently from non-expressives. Usually the language-related areas, Broca and Wernicke areas in particular, are left-lateralized (Zahn et al. 2000; Tie et al. 2014; Zhu et al. 2014). However, many significant activation areas for the E vs NE contrast are found in the right hemisphere. Right hemisphere activation is often seen when processing figurativeness and the metaphorical aspect of the language (Diaz et al. 2011; Diaz and Hogstrom 2011). The right hemisphere activation of the E vs NE contrast may suggest that expressives are being perceived as more figurative and creative aspects of the language. Results also show a language-dependent region of activation. In the case of bilinguals, slightly different brain regions are involved in understanding L1 and L2 languages (Tie et al. 2014; Reverberi et al. 2018). Most of the participants (nine out of ten) are native Gujarati speakers (L1) with Hindi and English as their secondary languages (L2). Thus, it is very possible that difference in the activation regions for Gujarati and Hindi is caused by differences in understanding L1 and L2.

In the case of L1, the E vs NE contrast shows significant activation in the right inferior temporal gyrus and the caudate nucleus. Previous study has shown the involvement of the caudate nucleus in the language-switch circuitry (Wang et al. 2007; Hosoda et al. 2012), especially in the forward switch from L1 to L2. The caudate nucleus is also shown to be involved in understanding the same concept in different languages (Abutalebi et al. 2008). Activation in parts of the right inferior temporal gyrus and right temporal pole has been shown to be associated with creative and unique perception. Asari et al. used vocal responses from the participant, which is similar to our experimental protocol. The same study also shows the involvement of the regions of the left anterior prefrontal cortex in creative mental activity. Activation of both the left inferior prefrontal cortex and the right inferior temporal gyrus for E vs NE contrast is yet another indication that expressives are being perceived as a more creative aspect of language.

For L2, the main regions of interest for E vs NE contrast are within the occipital lobe, dorsolateral prefrontal cortex (DLPFC), and supramarginal gyrus. Some early fMRI studies have suggested the involvement of the occipital gyrus in word encoding (Kelly et al. 1998). Recent studies have shown the involvement of the occipital gyrus areas in differentiating semantic concepts across different languages (Van de Putte et al. 2017) and language switch for bilinguals (Hosoda et al. 2012). The DLPFC activation in the linguistic context is associated with verbal working memory (Veltman et al. 2003). The act of translation requires the working-memory aspect, which also explains the DLPFC activation only for the Translate > Reading contrast and not the other way around.

Comparison of the E vs NE contrast for reading and translation also gives an insight into how expressives are perceived by the brain. For reading, there isn't much difference in brain activity for expressives and non-expressives. The cluster size and T-values are both smaller than for translation. Intuitively, reading a sentence with or without an expressive shouldn't be very different. However, for translation, the presence or absence of expressives does make a difference. Apart from the occipital and the inferior temporal gyrus, which have been discussed earlier, significant activation is observed in the inferior frontal gyrus (IFG). The IFG shows greater activation in encoding the L2 language (Abutalebi et al. 2008.Reverberi et al. 2018). The IFG is also involved in language-switch circuitry, which is a crucial aspect of translation (Hosoda et al. 2012). Apart from that, a study has shown higher activation of the IFG for semantically incorrect statements (Rüschemeyer et al. 2005). Considering the comparative paucity of expressives in vernacular English as well as the degree of cultural knowledge associated with expressivity, it is possible that a direct word-for-word translation of expressives may result in a semantically incorrect statement, resulting in higher activation of the IFG for expressive translation.

Activation in parts of the left IFG have been associated with creative thinking in various studies. Japardi et al. have shown a higher activation in the left IFG for the Big-C group of people than for others (Japardi et al. 2018). 'Big-C creative' refers to individuals with much higher creative-thinking abilities. Abraham et al. have shown the involvement of the left IFG in creative conceptual expansion (Abraham et al. 2018), while Marron et al. have shown the involvement of the IFG with free creative association. Along with the left IFG, both these studies also identify regions near the temporal poles to be involved in creative tasks. Regions near the inferior temporal gyrus and temporal poles have also been associated with evaluation of aesthetic value for art (Kirk et al. 2009). Thus, observing activations in the IFG, inferior temporal gyrus, and some other regions discussed earlier, may indicate that expressives are perceived as an aesthetic and creative aspect of grammar.

Another important contribution of this research is the fMRI for translation in bilinguals. Translation was compared against reading as a baseline. In the reading phase, the participants read out aloud the sentences displayed on the screen. In the translating phase, the participants read the sentence and then speak out the translation. Irrespective of whether expressives are present or not, the contrast of Translate > Read reveals the regions involved in the process of translation. The brain regions involved in the process of translation lie within the DLPFC and the supplementary motor area (SMA), as shown in Table 10.1 and Figure 10.2. The function of the DLPFC has been discussed earlier in verbal working memory. Along with the DLPFC, the SMA is also shown to be involved in the verbal working memory (Veltman et al. 2003) and in forward language switch (Wang et al. 2007; Abutalebi et al. 2008). On the other hand, the Read > Translate contrast shows activation in areas of the superior temporal gyrus, which is part of the famous Wernicke's area (Zhu et al. 2014). The superior temporal gyrus is shown to be involved in detection of syntactic anomaly (Rüschemeyer et al. 2005). This might suggest that less attention is focused on the syntactic correctness, or grammaticality, of a sentence when it is viewed for translation. Thus, the key neurological processes of translation can be summarized as follows: first, the given sentence is read, but less attention is given to its exact correctness. Secondly, the sentence is stored in the verbal working memory. At the same time, the forward language-switch regions mentally translate the sentence. Finally, the translated sentence is spoken out. (Because both 'Read' and 'Translate' phases involve speaking, the vocal regions are not identified in either the Read > Translate or the Translate > Read contrast.).

10.5 Limitations

The study described in this chapter is an explorative study to find the neurological effects of expressives. As expressives are only a couple of words in a sentence, the difference between a sentence with and one without expressives is very small. This small difference leads to a smaller effect inside the brain when reading. For translation, the majority of the difference lies in the translation of expressives when there is no corresponding translation for expressives in the other language. However, in translation as well the rest of the sentence can be translated easily. Thus, a difference of only a couple of words between sentences with and without expressives leads to relatively smaller differences in activation pattern. Another limitation is the inter-subject variability. Variability factors like age, gender, handedness, reading speed, etc. can be controlled. It is a little difficult to control for abstract aspects of language proficiency like the knowledge about grammar and vocabulary. The inter-subject variability, along with smaller effect size, makes it challenging to detect smaller activation regions across subjects with stringent statistical thresholds.

Limitation was also posed by the MRI hardware itself. First, the participants were not allowed to move their heads, especially the lower jaw, while speaking. The participants could only speak with a lower amplitude than usual without getting uncomfortable. Secondly, the MRI scanner is very loud because of the constantly changing gradients. Altogether, the audio recording of the participants would be difficult to interpret. In such a scenario, the correctness of translation and reading cannot be quantified accurately. It can only be assumed that the participants performed the task correctly.

10.6 Conclusion

The results suggest that there are certain regions involved in processing the expressives differently from the non-expressives. Also, most of the significant difference between expressives and non-expressives arises when translating the expressives into a language not having a direct correlation with the expressives, rather than just reading the expressives. Activation in some of the brain regions suggests that expressives are not processed completely at typical language-processing regions. Also, the expressives may be perceived as a more creative and aesthetic part of language by the brain. Apart from that, the cognitive process of language translation was also discussed.

10.7 Appendix A

fMRI preprocessing

Preprocessing is an important step for fMRI data analysis. Preprocessing reduces the effect of noise and artefact, which may result in incorrect inference. During the scans, the participants tend to move a bit. The head motion introduces motion artefacts into the data. These motion artefacts are reduced by motion correction. The head motion of the participants is estimated and then functional volume at each TR is corrected for the motion. The motion is corrected with 3D rigid-body affine transformation, using six degrees of freedom (three translational and three rotational). Motion correction of both phases of functional data is done at one time to avoid any spatial mismatch between the two phases. After motion correction, the high-resolution anatomical and low-resolution functional volumes are co-registered together. The co-registration step allows mapping of the results of the low-resolution functional images on to the high-resolution anatomical volume after the analysis.

Every participant's brain is of a different shape and size from the others. To compare the results across multiple participants, all the brains should be of the same shape and size. The normalization step maps the functional volume of each participant on to a standard brain atlas. Thus, the brain shape and size for all participants are similar and functional results can be compared across multiple participants. The functional brain data for all participants were normalized to the MNI brain atlas (Fonov et al. 2009) with a spatial resolution of 3 mm x 3 mm x 3 mm. The normalized functional volume is then segmented into, primarily, grey matter, white matter, cerebrospinal fluid (CSF), skull, and other soft tissue like skin and muscles. The grey matter, white matter, and CSF segments are used to create a binary brain mask which eliminates all the area outside the brain from further analysis. Masking is important, as it reduces the total number of voxels to be analysed. A typical brain volume with a resolution of 3 mm x 3 mm x 3 mm has about 150,000 voxels. Out of these 150k voxels, only about 50,000–70,000 voxels are inside the brain region. Thus, discarding the extra voxels from further analysis increases computation and time efficiency.

After masking, only the voxels inside the brain region are used for further analysis. The next preprocessing step is the reduction of temporal signal drift. Owing to scanner instabilities, there is a very low-frequency temporal artefact introduced in the fMRI data. This artefact has a global effect and introduces noise in all the voxels across the brain. The temporal signal drift was estimated and reduced using a principal components analysis (PCA) technique (Parmar et al. 2019). The last preprocessing step is spatial smoothing. In spatial smoothing, a 3D Gaussian filter with a full-width half maximum (FWHM) of 8 mm was used to smooth the functional data.

10.8 Appendix B

Functional data analysis

The preprocessed functional was analysed to obtain spatial activation regions for different fMRI contrast. The analysis was done in two parts—subject-level analysis and group-level analysis. For subject-level analysis the general linear model

(GLM) framework was used to obtain information activation regions for each participant. Activation regions corresponding to multiple contrast were obtained for each subject. Then, in the group-level analysis, the activation maps for all participants were combined.

The subject-level analysis was performed using SPM12's *'First Level Analysis'*. Two separate GLM models were used for each participant—one for the reading phase and one for the translation phase. The timings for button press were used to generate onset time and duration for four categories (GE, GNE, HE, and HNE). For each category three separate regressors were used in the design matrix

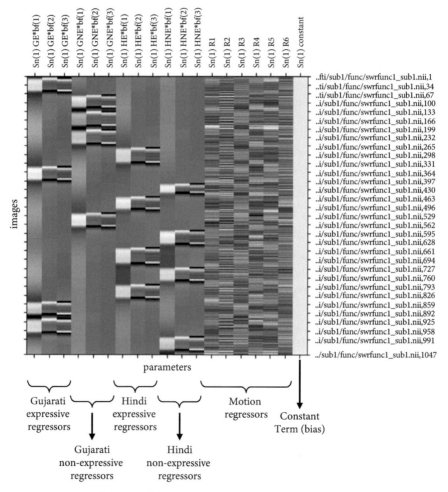

Figure 10.3 Visualization of design matrix for first-level analysis. The columns correspond to regressors while the rows correspond to time points. Higher amplitudes are represented with a lighter shade of grey, while lower amplitudes are represented using darker shades of grey.

of the GLM. The first regressor corresponds to the predicted response obtained by convolving the onset time and duration with canonical double-gamma haemodynamic response function (HRF). The second and third regressors were obtained from time and dispersion derivatives of the first regressor. The derivative regressors are used to account for any subject-level variation in the HRF. The six estimated motion parameters were also used as nuisance regressors in the design matrix. The visualization of the entire design matrix for the reading phase of participant 1 is shown in Figure 10.3. In the visualization, the rows correspond to TRs while the columns correspond to regressors. The bright regions show higher amplitude, while the dark regions show lower amplitude.

$$Y = X\beta + \varepsilon \qquad \text{Equation B1}$$

$$\beta \approx \left(X^T X\right)^{-1} \left(X^T Y\right) \qquad \text{Equation B2}$$

The constructed design matrix is used with the GLM model to estimate the contribution (weights) of each of the regressors. The basic structure of the GLM model is shown in Equation B1. In the equation, Y is the matrix of observed time series. Each column is a time series from a different voxel inside the brain. The matrix X is the design matrix constructed from the timing information and β is the matrix of weights that is to be estimated using Equation B2. The rows of β correspond to weights corresponding to a regressor while the columns correspond to voxels of the brain. After the estimation of β, the weights corresponding to each regressor are converted to 3D volume. In-house MATLAB script was used to combine the 3D weight volumes for all subjects according to different contrasts. Some of the different contrasts tested are shown in Table 10.2. The volumes for different contrasts are saved for each participant.

Table 10.2 Weights for regressors corresponding to different contrasts

NAME	READING				TRANSLATION			
	GE	GNE	HE	HNE	GE	GNE	HE	HNE
$E > NE$	1	−1	1	−1	1	−1	1	−1
$NE > E$	−1	1	−1	1	−1	1	−1	1
$E > NE$ (Gujarati)	1	−1	0	0	1	−1	0	0
$E > NE$ (Hindi)	0	0	1	−1	0	0	1	−1
$E > NE$ (Read)	1	0	1	0	−1	0	−1	0
$E > NE$ (Translate)	−1	0	−1	0	1	0	1	0
Read > Translate	1	1	1	1	−1	−1	−1	−1
Translate > Read	−1	−1	−1	−1	1	1	1	1

208 HARSHIT PARMAR AND JEFFREY P. WILLIAMS

The group-level analysis was performed using SPM12's 'Second Level Analysis' option. The input to the second-level analysis were the saved contrast volumes for all of the participants. The second-level analysis combines the contrast volume for all the participants and thresholds it according to the specified statistical significance. The spatial clusters were also thresholded according to the random field theory (RFT) to eliminate noisy single-voxel clusters (Friston et al. 1994). No significant group-level clusters were identified at an uncorrelated p-value threshold of 0.001. Thus, the threshold was lowered to 0.005. The thresholded activation maps for all the contrast were saved for inference.

10.9 Appendix C

Behavioural data analysis results

Table 10.3 shows the calculated p-value for the subject-level paired t-test. Each row corresponds to a subject, while each column corresponds to a category. The four different categories of E vs NE are as follows—Gujarati reading, Hindi reading, Gujarati translation, and Hindi translation. The category-subject pair for which there is a significant difference ($p < 0.05$) in the response time between expressive and non-expressives is **bold and underlined**. The participants that didn't perform the task in any particular category are highlighted in **light grey**. It can be observed that for most of the cases, there isn't a significant difference in response times between E vs NE. The above statement is confirmed from the group-level paired t-test results. The group-level p-values for all four categories are as follows: *p (Gujarati reading)* = 0.4142; *p (Hindi reading)* = 0.1908; *p (Gujarati translation)* = 0.4207; and *p (Hindi translation)* = 0.5402. The p-values clearly suggest that there is no significant difference (*p<0.05*) in the response time between expressives and non-expressives for either reading and translation. The response times across different subjects for both reading and translation are shown as box plots in Figure 10.4.

The correlation is also computed between the response times and the reading speeds of the participants. Figure 10.5 shows the plots for reading speed vs response time. For all four categories in reading, a strong negative correlation is observed between reading speed and response time. A negative correlation suggests that for higher reading speed participants will have a lower response time, which is obvious. However, the correlation between reading speed and response time for translation is different for Gujarati and Hindi. For Gujarati, there is a positive correlation, suggesting that on average shorter sentences take a longer time to translate than longer ones. This is true, irrespective of the presence of

IS THERE AN AESTHETIC COMPONENT OF LANGUAGE?

Table 10.3 Subject level p-value for paired t test

	Paired t-test for E vs NE			
Participant	Gujarati reading	Hindi reading	Gujarati translation	Hindi translation
1	0.239	0.120	0.485	0.595
2	0.064	NA	0.560	NA
3	0.607	**0.001**	0.806	0.162
4	0.622	**0.001**	0.935	0.898
5	NA	0.388	NA	0.070
6	0.259	**0.019**	0.940	0.257
7	0.327	0.644	0.635	0.281
8	0.495	**0.026**	0.907	**0.040**
9	NA	0.480	NA	0.874
10	0.172	**0.047**	0.703	0.180

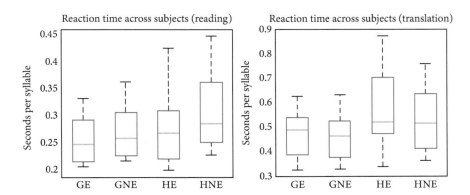

Figure 10.4 Reaction times for reading and translation

expressives or not. On the other hand, there is no correlation in the reading speed and translation response time in Hindi.

The average response time for reading and translation for all four categories is shown in Figure 10.6. A paired t-test was also performed between the reading and translation response times. For all four cases, there is a significant increase ($p<0.05$) in the response times when going from reading to translation. The p-values for the paired t-test of all four categories are as follows: *p (Gujarati expressives)* = 0.0013; *p (Gujarati non-expressives)* = 0.0042; *p (Hindi expressives)* = 0.0004; and *p (Hindi non-expressives)* = 0.0016.

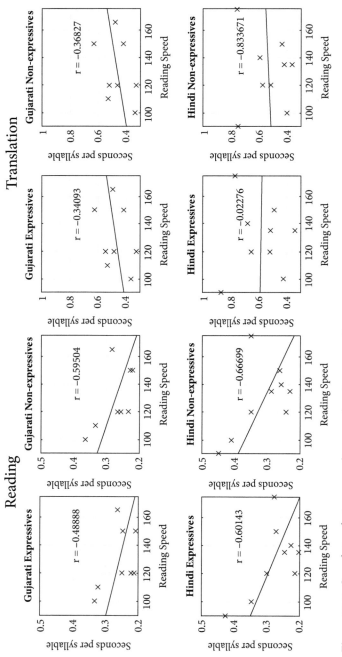

Figure 10.5 Correlation between reading speed and response time

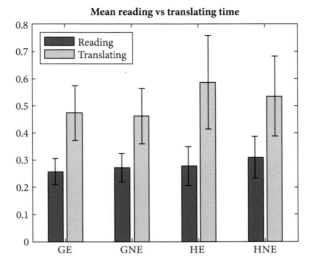

Figure 10.6 Comparison of response times for reading and translation

References

Abbi, Anvita (1992). 'Contact, conflict and compromise: the genesis of reduplicated structures in South Asian languages.' In Dimock, Edward C., Kachru, Braj B., and Krishnamurti, Bh. (eds), *Dimensions of Sociolinguistics in South Asia*, Delhi: South Asia Books, 131–148.

Abraham, Anna, Rutter, Barbara, Bantin, Trisha, and Hermann, Christiane (2018). Creative conceptual expansion: a combined fMRI replication and extension study to examine individual differences in creativity. *Neuropsychologia* 118: 29–39.

Abutalebi, Jubin, Annoni, Jean-Marie, Zimine, Ivan, Pegna, Alan J., Seghier, Mohamed L., Lee-Jahnke, Hannelore, Lazeyras, François, Cappa, Stefano F., and Khateb, Asaid (2008). Language control and lexical competition in bilinguals: an event-related fMRI study. *Cerebral Cortex* 18(7): 1496–1505.

Akita, Kimi (2015). Sound symbolism. In Jan-Ola Östman and Jef Verschueren (eds), *Handbook of Pragmatics*. Amsterdam: John Benjamins, 1–24.

Ashburner, John, Barnes, Gareth, Chen, Chun-Chuan, Daunizeau, Jean, Flandin, Guillaume, Friston, Karl, Kiebel, Stefan, et al. (2014). *SPM12 manual.*, London: Wellcome Trust Centre for Neuroimaging.

Benjamin, Christopher F., Walshaw, Patricia D., Hale, Kayleigh, Gaillard, William D., Baxter, Leslie C., Berl, Madison M., Polczynska, Monika, et al. (2017). Presurgical language fMRI: Mapping of six critical regions. *Human Brain Mapping* 38(8): 4239–4255.

Diaz, Michele T., Barrett, Kyle T., and Hogstrom, Larson J. (2011). The influence of sentence novelty and figurativeness on brain activity. *Neuropsychologia* 49(3): 320–330.

Diaz, Michele T. and Hogstrom, Larson J. (2011). The influence of context on hemispheric recruitment during metaphor processing. *Journal of Cognitive Neuroscience* 23(11): 3586–3597.

Diffloth, Gérard (1972). Notes on expressive meaning. *Chicago Linguistic Society* 8: 440–447.

Diffloth, Gérard (1976). Expressives in Semai. *Oceanic Linguistics Special Publications* 13: 249–264.

Diffloth, Gérard (1980). Expressive phonology and prosaic phonology in Mon-Khmer. In Theraphan L. Thongkum (ed.), *Studies in Mon-Khmer and Thai Phonology and Phonetics in Honor of E. Henderson*. Bangkok: Chulalongkorn University Press, 49–59.

Dingemanse, Mark (2012). Advances in the cross-linguistic study of ideophones. *Language and linguistics compass* 6(10): 654–672. DOI: https://doi.org/10.1002/lnc3.361.

Dingemanse, Mark (2015). Ideophones and reduplication: Depiction, description, and the interpretation of repeated talk in discourse. *Studies in language* 39(4): 946–970. DOI: https://doi.org/10.1075/sl.39.4.05din.

Dingemanse, Mark (2018). Redrawing the margins of language: Lessons from research on ideophones. *Glossa: a Journal of General Linguistics* 3(1): .4. DOI: http://doi.org/10.5334/gjgl.444

Friston, Karl J., Worsley, Keith J., Frackowiak, Richard S. J., Mazziotta, John C., and Evans, Alan C. (1994). Assessing the significance of focal activations using their spatial extent. *Human Brain Mapping* 1(3): 210–220.

Fonov, Vladimir S., Evans, Alan C., McKinstry, Robert C., Almli, C. R., and Collins, D. L. (2009). Unbiased nonlinear average age-appropriate brain templates from birth to adulthood. *NeuroImage* 47: S102.

Hansen, Samuel J., McMahon, Katie L., and de Zubicaray, Greig I. (2019). The neurobiology of taboo language processing: fMRI evidence during spoken word production. *Social Cognitive and Affective Neuroscience* 14(3): 271–279.

Hickok, Gregory (2009). The functional neuroanatomy of language. *Physics of Life Reviews* 6(3): 121–143.

Hosoda, Chihiro, Hanakawa, Takashi, Nariai, Tadashi, Ohno, Kikuo, and Honda, Manabu (2012). Neural mechanisms of language switch. Journal of Neurolinguistics 25(1): 44–61.

Hubers, Ferdy, Snijders, Tineke M., and De Hoop, Helen (2016). How the brain processes violations of the grammatical norm: An fMRI study. *Brain and Language* 163: 22–31.

Japardi, Kevin, Bookheimer, Susan, Knudsen, Kendra, Ghahremani, Dara G., and Bilder, Robert M. (2018). Functional magnetic resonance imaging of divergent and convergent thinking in Big-C creativity. *Neuropsychologia* 118: 59–67.

Kirk, Ulrich, Skov, Martin, Hulme, Oliver, Christensen, Mark S., and Zeki, Semir (2009). Modulation of aesthetic value by semantic context: An fMRI study. *NeuroImage* 44(3): 1125–1132.

Maldjian, Joseph A., Laurienti, Paul J., Kraft, Robert A., and Burdette, Jonathan H. (2003). An automated method for neuroanatomic and cytoarchitectonic atlas-based interrogation of fMRI data sets. *NeuroImage* 19(3): 1233–1239.

Nettekoven, Charlotte, Reck, Nicola, Goldbrunner, Roland, Grefkes, Christian, and Lucas, Carolin Weiß (2018). Short-and long-term reliability of language fMRI. *NeuroImage* 176: 215–225.

Parmar, H. S., Nutter, B., Long, R., Antani, S., and Mitra, S. (2019, March). Automated signal drift and global fluctuation removal from 4D fMRI data based on principal component analysis as a major preprocessing step for fMRI data analysis. *In Medical Imaging 2019: Biomedical Applications in Molecular, Structural, and Functional Imaging* (Vol. 10953, pp. 300–308). SPIE.

Reverberi, Carlo, Kuhlen, Anna K., Seyed-Allaei, Shima, Greulich, R. Stefan, Costa, Albert, Abutalebi, Jubin, and Haynes, John-Dylan (2018). The neural basis of free language choice in bilingual speakers: Disentangling language choice and language execution. *NeuroImage* 177: 108–116.

Rüschemeyer, Shirley-Ann, Fiebach, Christian J., Kempe, Vera, and Friederici, Angela D. (2005). Processing lexical semantic and syntactic information in first and second language: fMRI evidence from German and Russian. *Human Brain Mapping* 25(2): 266–286.

Sahin, Ned T., Pinker, Steven, and Halgren, Eric (2006). Abstract grammatical processing of nouns and verbs in Broca's area: evidence from fMRI. *Cortex* 42(4): 540–562.

Scripture, Edward Wheeler (1902). *The Elements of Experimental Phonetics. Vol. 22.* New York: C. Scribner's Sons.

Setsompop, K., Cohen-Adad, J., Gagoski, B. A., Raij, T., Yendiki, A., Keil, B., Wedeen, V. J., and Wald, L. L. (2012.) Improving diffusion MRI using simultaneous multi-slice echo planar imaging. *NeuroImage* 63(1): 569–580.

Sulpizio, Simone, Toti, Michelle, Del Maschio, Nicola, Costa, Albert, Fedeli, Davide, Job, Remo, and Abutalebi, Jubin (2019). Are you really cursing? Neural processing of taboo words in native and foreign language. *Brain and Language* 194: 84–92.

Tie, Yanmei, Rigolo, Laura, Norton, Isaiah H., Huang, Raymond Y., Wu, Wentao, Orringer, Daniel, Mukundan, Srinivasan Jr, and Golby, Alexandra J. (2014). Defining language networks from resting-state fMRI for surgical planning—A feasibility study. *Human Brain Mapping* 35(3): 1018–1030.

Van de Putte, Eowyn, De Baene, Wouter, Brass, Marcel, and Duyck, Wouter (2017). Neural overlap of L1 and L2 semantic representations in speech: A decoding approach. *NeuroImage* 162: 106–116.

Veltman, Dick J., Rombouts, Serge A. R. B., and Dolan, Raymond J. (2003). Maintenance versus manipulation in verbal working memory revisited: an fMRI study. *NeuroImage* 18(2): 247–256.

Wang, Yapeng, Xue, Gui, Chen, Chuansheng, Xue, Feng, and Dong, Qi (2007). Neural bases of asymmetric language switching in second-language learners: an ER-fMRI study. *NeuroImage* 35(2): 862–870.

Williams, Jeffrey P. (ed.) (2014). *The Aesthetics of Grammar: Sound and Meaning in the Languages of Mainland Southeast Asia.* Cambridge: Cambridge University Press.

Williams, Jeffrey P. (ed.) (2020). *Expressive Morphology in the Languages of South Asia.* New York: Routledge.

Williams, Jeffrey P. (ed.) (2021). Expressives in the languages of Mainland Southeast Asia. In Paul Sidwell and Jeremy Mathias (eds), *The Languages and Linguistics of Mainland Southeast Asia.* Berlin: De Gruyter, 11–824.

Williams, Jeffrey P. (ed.). *Capturing Expressivity.* Oxford: Oxford University Press, 2025.

Zahn, Roland, Huber, Walter, Drews, Eva, Erberich, Stephan, Krings, Timo, Willmes, Klaus, and Schwarz, Michael (2000). Hemispheric lateralization at different levels of human auditory word processing: a functional magnetic resonance imaging study. *Neuroscience Letters* 287(3): 195–198.

Zhu, Linlin, Fan, Yang, Zou, Qihong, Wang, Jue, Gao, Jia-Hong, and Niu, Zhendong (2014). Temporal reliability and lateralization of the resting-state language network. *PLoS one* 9(1): e85880.

Zwicky, Arnold and Pullum, Geoffrey (1987). Plain morphology and expressive morphology. In *Proceedings of the Thirteenth Annual Meeting of the Berkeley Linguistics Society*: 330–340.

11

Learning to learn expressives

Finding cultural salience in linguistic fieldwork

Nathan Badenoch

11.1 Learning expressivity in the field

Sitting on the woven bamboo veranda after a spirit-calling ritual, my friend is approached by a young man who starts speaking quickly, with animation. My friend is the village headman, and the sudden visitor had come to ask for help on an argument between two people in the village. The headman leans to his brother-in-law and says, *ʔaaa ŋʋʋ ʔim cakbrak-cikbrik nʋk, tɛʔ nɛɛw bii ŋʋʋ cʋʋ* 'oh man, he just shows up *cakbrak-cikbrik* like that, what is wrong with him?' After a few moments, I ask, 'What does *cakbrak-cikbrik* mean?' He explains that it is the flustered feeling you get when someone unexpectedly approaches you with a question or a request and then disappears. This word is typical of the semantic, morphological, and pragmatic complexity of expressives in his language. Discussion the next day produced a longer explanation of the movement of the visitor's arrival, the social environment of the veranda when he appeared, the ensuing confusion about what the visitor was talking about, and the feeling of annoyance among those seated after he left. After some elaboration, it emerged that this expressive is about both a sudden movement and a reaction to experiencing it. This was during the early days of my study of expressives in the Bit language, spoken in northern Laos and across the border in southern China by about 2,400 people.

It is widely held that expressives or ideophones are difficult to elicit in linguistic fieldwork, and the difficulty of pinning down expressive meaning has been commented upon since serious work on this phenomenon began. That said, research on expressives, often from an anthropological and ethnographic perspective, has provided many insights on the nature and dynamics of expressive meaning. I follow the South-east Asian tradition established by Diffloth (1976) in using the term 'expressives', sharing the sense that these words represent a mode of language that operates in parallel to prosaic mode in Bit. I have been learning expressives with Souler over the past twelve years at his house, walking through the forest, at gatherings in the village, and more recently over WhatsApp. I have been interested in how my understanding of Bit expressives has been shaped by Souler. Thanks to him and many others in the village, I have been able to uncover the meaning of

Nathan Badenoch, *Learning to learn expressives*. In: *Capturing Expressivity*. Edited by: Jeffrey P. Williams,
Oxford University Press. © Nathan Badenoch (2025). DOI: 10.1093/oso/9780192858931.003.0011

216 NATHAN BADENOCH

more than two thousand expressive forms as recorded in conversation and various forms of oral performance. Through our interactions, Souler has offered metapragmatic insights into what it means to use expressives in Bit. He has taught me how I should learn expressives in order to be able to understand and use them in the context of Bit cultural life. Souler identifies, elucidates, and emphasizes those linguistic elements of expressives that are culturally meaningful to speakers of Bit. This is more than a detailed view on the pragmatics of expressive usage, and I have come to understand our work together as a window on Bit semiotic ideology.

In this chapter I reflect on my conversations with Souler as a consideration of how we learn in fieldwork. In doing so, I engage with previous efforts to bring the people we work with into the reflection with a specific interest in understanding how my own framework for studying expressives has been influenced by people that we frequently call 'consultants' or 'informants'. As suggested by Briggs (2012), ethnographic work should recognize our many 'teachers' along with the important role they play in influencing our thinking at the theoretical level, as 'mentors' with whom we have ongoing relationships of co-authorship. The writing of linguistic ethnography provides much inspiration. For example, Janis Nuckolls has shared her intimate relationship with Luisa Cardono and the impact this strong woman has had on opening up the world of Kichwa ideophones (for example Nuckolls 2010, Nuckolls 1996, and many others). Anthony Webster has taken us through dialogues with his long-time collaborator Rex Lee Jim about the inner works of composing and translating Navaho poetry (Webster 2017, Webster 2015, and many others).

My own work has been directly and deeply informed by the opportunity to take part in elicitation and explication of expressives in Surin Khmer through the discussions between Somruan Wongcharoen and Gérard Diffloth. More recently, I have had the good fortune of working with Madhu Purti and Toshiki Osada on Mundari expressives and reflecting with them (Badenoch et al. 2021a, 2021b). Both 'scholars' encourage their collaborators to lead the way in explaining not only what is correct and acceptable in expressive word use according to their native intuition, but also what is relevant from this work in understanding expressives more generally in their languages. They work through ongoing dialogue, rather than elicitation and response, and both 'collaborators' have a deep and nuanced understanding of their role in the research. Inspired by their work, I share here one angle on the ongoing process of learning from and with Souler about what expressives do in Bit, and what Bit speakers do with expressives in their speech, with a particular interest in how he has guided me through what he deems salient.[1]

---

[1] Souler readily agreed on the idea of a chapter that focused on our expressives work. At the same time he stressed the important role of my many other teachers in the village, reminding me that people use language in different ways.

11.2 Metalinguistic framing of Bit expressives

The Bit language is full of aesthetic play that gives voice to the linguistic culture of its speakers. Through different practices of 'attaching flowers' (*prɟʊk baar*), Bit speakers enhance the communicative-affective impact of words by reduplication of syllables and manipulation of segments. Expressive words are an important part of these everyday poetics in Bit (Badenoch 2021a) and many other languages of South-east Asia (Williams 2021, Williams 2014). Researchers have long pondered the difficulty of eliciting expressives and pinning down expressive meaning, because as poetic language they foreground a gradation of interrelated aesthetics (Mukařovský 1983 [1932]). This is partly because expressive meaning is deeply entangled with culturally specific ideologies of poetics, but it is also related to the fact that each usage happens within a complex social context specific to time, place, and relations. Previously it was generally thought that expressive meaning was vague and that these words did not have morphology. Now we know that expressive meaning is extremely complicated, if perhaps more conventional than originally postulated (Dingemanse 2015), and some languages such as Bit have complex morphology that work only on expressives.[2] It is only recently that expressives and ideophones have come to be considered as a grammatical word class (Dingemanse 2021), and in practice, the tension between formal and functional angles on expressives has made a universally satisfactory definition of expressives difficult to articulate (Williams 2021).

Studying expressives with native speakers asks them to engage in a highly reflexive sharing of linguistic practice. Given the difficulty that has been noted in eliciting and explaining expressives, it is worth considering how our teachers do this specific type of reflection in discussion with us. Diffloth (2021) has described how speakers of Semai characterize use of expressive words as 'shooting', as one would shoot an arrow. Here, expressives are individual acts of language, which cannot be retrieved after they have been 'shot'. Because expressives are so deeply situated in lived experience in specific cultural-ecological settings, it may be difficult for speakers to create abstracted examples of how an expressive can be used. Yet we are able to engage speakers in discussions about their expressives, and the question seems to be: what aspects of expressives do researchers want to know about, and what aspects do speakers talk about? Silverstein (1981) discussed the possibility of limits to speakers' awareness of certain areas of their language. It has been pointed out that salience is not the same as awareness but is the product of the interplay of linguistic elements and sociocultural phenomena (Choksi and Meek 2016). Recently, Zuckerman and Enfield (2023) have proposed that social

---

[2] This work has been inspired on many levels by Svantesson's (1983) work on Kammu, a related Austroasiatic language that is part of the multilingual life of the Bit and is actively used in other areas of linguistic play (Badenoch 2021a).

218 NATHAN BADENOCH

and semiotic limitations, more than cognitive ones, affect what people can identify as salient. They demonstrate how this brings into mutual focus speakers' ability to thematize elements of language and allows us to learn what is salient from the speaker's point of view.

With this shift from pure cognition to entextualized interaction, I can more comfortably explore the picture of cultural salience of expressives as painted by Souler, my main teacher of Bit expressives. He enthusiastically and patiently responds to my questions and prompts, and constantly guides me towards ways of thinking about expressives in the ways he knows. He, like most Bit speakers I have interacted with, has a high awareness of the poetic play that expressives add to speech. People are in agreement that this is serious business, not linguistic frivolity, and are quick to say that without using expressives, one isn't 'speaking Bit like us'. Souler's heightened awareness of his language, not to mention his appreciation of my desire to learn Bit, is accompanied by consistent and systematic thematization of what he knows to be good. In our discussions he frequently uses two words to indicate this 'good' language—*jʊk* 'on target' and *muən* 'enjoyable'. As is the case in anthropological fieldwork in Laos broadly, the notion of 'important' (in Lao *samkʰan*, also borrowed into Bit as *smkʰʊn*) has little cognitive relevance in these discussion, and can create great difficulty in otherwise smooth interaction. More than just a matter of communicative relevance (Sasamoto 2019), Souler's articulation resonates with Drager and Kirtley's (2016) notion of salience as a semiotic dynamic affecting the reflective and reflexive performance of an individual, where the former is a controlled metapragmatic awareness and the latter is an automatic perception or feeling of difference.

11.3 Sites of expressivity: engaging with the linguistic practices

What are the right words to describe how Souler teaches me expressives? He *explains* the meaning using words, he *demonstrates* actions and states using his body and the space around us, and he *performs* emotions and reactions using facial expressions and head movements. He also *involves* me as a learner in his teaching, evoking shared experiences. It is well-known that expressives are multimodal performances, their use comprising not only the sound but also iconic non-verbal language (Dingemanse 2013). We also know that speakers' efforts to demonstrate expressives make ample use of body language and other communicative means (Nuckolls 2020). Expressives are performative in use, so explanation of expressives is necessarily performative and decidedly non-referential.

When Souler, a trilingual speaker of Bit, Lao, and Khmu, explains an expressive, he does it in Bit. The Bit language does not have specific terminology for talking about word classes or the various morphological processes that are involved in producing expressive meaning, but he has little trouble explaining meaning and usage. When I first started learning the language, he would use often use Lao to explain the meaning of Bit words, as well as the social context in which the speech was taking place. This mode of communication shifted quickly to Bit as he understood that explanations in Bit were important for my learning, also reflecting the belief that Bit is the language that *psiiŋ ʔii* 'our (inclusive) people' speak together. This was never the case with expressives, however. From the beginning, he preferred to explain expressive meaning and elaborate nuances of usage in Bit, using gestures, props, and other means. Working with Souler on a Bit expressive always includes discussion of meaning, context, and relationship, always framed in Bit linguicultural terms. His choice to work solely in Bit supports the notion that monolingual fieldwork should be the approach of choice, even if it is not 'necessary' (Everett 2001).

Speakers of Bit use expressives in most aspects of linguistic performance. Aside from ritual language and 'official register', it is common to hear speakers include expressives as they engage in and recount the experiences of a day in their life. One of the most fruitful expressive learning environments I participated in was a week of building Souler's new house. Because house construction is a communal activity, there were many people present, performing different tasks, all involving a wide range of actions, sounds, changes, physical characteristics, and emotional responses. For example, the surface of sawn wood, the falling of sawdust, the bend of a saw blade, the fit of a beam joint, and the sun shining through the trees as it moved across the sky, all provided seemingly endless discussion of expressives.

Children use expressives, learning the fine nuances as their socialization progresses. It was common during our work for Souler's children to intervene with their own definitions, interpretations, and performance of expressives. This was met with enjoyment by the parents, although some information provided by the children was rejected with *ʔah mɛɛn nhəə* 'It's not like that' for more serious discussions. When the work intensified in playfulness, as it often did, a fanciful or irresponsible contribution from the children was met with *tryuut!* '[you're] crazy!' The fact that children were corrected for appropriate meaning, as well as monitored for appropriate performance, shows that there is a degree of convention that guides the use of expressives in linguistic acts.

It is important to note that expressives can be studied directly with speakers of Bit. One particularly productive method consisted of my collecting expressives I had heard in conversations during the day or from recorded narrative texts and asking Souler about their meaning and usage. One important benefit of this approach was that it provided the meaning, context, and relationship information mentioned above as well as expansion into related expressives, either by sound or by meaning. Later, I realized, he was providing a framework of related themes that situate expressives within his linguistic culture. In the following paragraphs I introduce three areas of cultural salience that foreground the social meaning of expressives for Bit speakers: morphological marking of aspect, the psychological

220 NATHAN BADENOCH

implications of space, and iconic depiction of scale-intensity. This is followed by a discussion of how we follow various routes of expansion in our work, highlighting how sound and meaning are mapped to cultural salience in the language.

11.4 Talking about how expressives show aspect

One element of Bit expressives is that they depict aspect with their morphology. This grammatical encoding of the experience of time is unique to expressives in Bit, but is perhaps an important part of expressivity more broadly (Nuckolls 1996). Aspect is marked on Bit verbs with auxiliary words that denote completion or irrealis. Expressive aspect is shown with reduplication. When learning a Bit expressive, the first point of detail that Souler points out is how the depiction is situated in time. From his perspective, the form of the expressive differs depending upon one's participation in the event. There are two basic ways of experiencing a situation depicted by an expressive. First, one can experience a movement, a change in state, or an interaction at the point in time when it happens. This form, I call the punctual. Second, one can experience the result of that movement, change in state, or interaction after the moment when it occurs, which indicates a static form.[3] These distinctions in aspect are encoded directly in Bit expressive morphology.

Sitting in front of his house one evening after dinner, I asked about the word *tbuul*, which I had heard when someone was recounting the day's events. Souler explained that this word is used when something piles up, or appears in a large quantity in one space.

tbuul	[points to a space in front of us]	mee	ɲii	ktanhan
EXP: piling up		2s-M	to see	suddenly
'*tbuul*		you see it all of a sudden.'		

His example was if someone *tbuul* dropped a big pile of clothes on the ground, and we were sitting there to witness it at that moment. A punctual expressive, in its canonical C.CVC form, is introduced by Souler as *ktanhan*, as in *mee ɲii ktanhan* 'you see it suddenly' or *mee ʔal ktanhan* 'you hear (or feel) suddenly' at that moment. This word is a borrowing from Lao meaning 'suddenly', incorporated into the prosaic metalanguage he employs to describe the expressive.

From here, the normal progression of explanation is to provide an example of the second encoding of aspect with the static. 'For example, if you then come along and see' the situation that has resulted from the change or action of the punctual—*tulbuul.*

---

[3] The morphological paradigm for Bit expressives is explained in detail in Badenoch (2021a). The terms 'punctual' and 'static' draw on Svantesson's analysis of Kammu.

tulbuul	[hands open, spread apart, pauses speech for a moment]	mee	ɲii	knriəŋ	ɲoʔ	ləʔ
EXP: things piled up		2s-M	to see	things	to be at	over there

'*tulbuul*   you see the things sitting there.'

The static is formed by copying the rhyme and inserting it within the first syllable; thus, from the punctual *tbuul* [t.buul] he derives *tulbuul* [t<ul>.buul]. The static form he describes as *mee ɲii X ɲoʔ ləʔ* 'you see X sitting there', setting up the experience after the punctual event. In both cases, the relevant form of the expressive is the first part of the explanation. But this is not simply him providing a headword topicalization. He is making use of the syntax of expressives, where the expressive often comes before the verb. Expressives are not overtly linked to any verb or noun reference, so these constructions are at the same time both explanations and usage examples.

The non-verbal cues he uses are also consistent. In the static form, an open hand gesture and slight pause in his speech index the suspended animation implied in the static. Opening the presyllable and filling it with rhyme is an iconic gesture that is being mimicked by his hand gestures and speech pause.

Because aspect is not morphologically marked on Bit verbs, he must create metalanguage to explain the relationships across time. The punctual framing of *ktanhan* draws on his knowledge of the Lao language (Lao *katʰanhan* 'suddenly'), and is used to augment the simple Bit verb references to directly experiencing the moment of seeing (*ɲii*) or hearing/feeling (*ʔal*). Experience of the outcome or implications of the punctual expressive is framed metaphorically through a physical location (*ɲoʔ ləʔ* 'sitting there') that results. For speakers of Bit, this encoding of aspect is one of the most salient pragmatic features of expressives. Morphological foregrounding of aspect may be a key element of expressives and ideophones more generally, as suggested by Nuckolls in her analysis of Quechua ideophones (Nuckolls 1996). Souler links these terms in a metapragmatic staging that focuses on the aspect distinction, but he has never explained the morphology. At one point, I tried to confirm the rhyme copy-infixation and he responded simply, *ʔəə nhəə səʔ* 'yeah, something like that'.

11.5 The emotional implications of space

Simple reduplication of an expressive produces the iterative, indicating repetition. For example, in explaining *psɔɔl* 'small puff of smoke wafting up' on a different occasion, he explained,

mee ɲii ʔʋy ktəʔ ʔɔɔk psɔɔl- psɔɔl
2s-M to se steam smoke to go out EXP: small puff of smoke REDUP

'You see the smoke coming out *psɔɔl-psɔɔl*.'

He emphasizes the iterative nature of this expressive with *psɔɔl-psɔɔl pen baat pen tiə* [EXP-COP-instance-COP-occurrence], loosely translated 'once and again'. If the expressive has semantics of motion, the iterative denotes movement across space. For example, a large monkey hanging from a tree branch would be depicted as *ldiəw*, and when the monkey brachiates through the forest, one may hear:

waa ldiəw- ldiəw waʔ
monkey EXP: swinging by the arms REDUP to go

'The monkey went *ldiəw-ldiəw* [through the forest].'

In this example, the iterative *ldiəw-ldiəw* depicts the movement of a single monkey in a single trajectory, moving smoothly in an area with many branches to grab in the desired direction. If, however, the monkey brachiates in multiple directions, one would hear:

waa ldaaw- ldiəw waʔ
monkey ECHO EXP: swinging by the arms to go

'The monkey went *ldʋʋw-ldiəw* [through the forest].'

Here, the first element is a reduplicated echo element that undergoes vowel mutation to form the expansive, depicting a distribution of the motion more broadly across space. Moving *ldaaw-ldiəw*, the monkey will be swinging left and right, forwards and backwards in search of branches to grab. The expansive form may also encode the speaker's reactions to these sensory perceptions. Here, the monkey's movement could be perceived as abnormal in some way, perhaps rushed as it escapes from a predator. It seems probable that the reversal of the order of the base and reduplicated forms has some sort of playful iconic affect.

Returning to our discussion of *tbuul* 'objects piling up', Souler shifts to emphasize how the expansive *tbaal-tbuul* depicts emotion connected to the motion. First, he gives the spatial element,

smut daa ɲii tbaal- tbuul knriəŋ tnlih
for example 2s-D to.see ECHO EXP: things piling up things to fall
laay bɔɔn
many place

'For example, if we see *tbaal-tbuul* things fall to the ground in many places'

The punctual *tbuul* is reduplicated with /aa/ replacing the original /uu/, to indicate that it is happening in more than one place. In this way, dissimilation of the vowel creates a semantic distinction, with the iterative *tbuul-tbuul* 'repeated piling up in one place'.

He then indicates, looking here and there, the things that are hypothetically dropping into sight, then looks at me and says with a smile and raised eyebrows,

klɒhwɒh!	səʔ	ʔɨm	laa	tii	knrɨəŋ	həə?
EXP: confused awe	like that	to come	from	where	things	that

[confused surprise] 'So where did all these things come from then?'

Here he continues the explanation with *klɒhwah*, an expressive that indicates a confused state of shock or awe that evokes imagery of silence or stillness (Badenoch 2021). This expressive is almost never syntactically linked directly to other words in an utterance, but occurs rather as an emotional summary of the preceding speech, spoken alone after a break. It usually evokes smiles, if not laughter, and seems to be one of the expressives that most directly evokes an active response from listeners. The use of *klɒhwɒh* can be understood as a pragmatic gesture, foregrounding the emotional response. Nuckolls (2020) suggests that ideophones depicting visual and motion semantics are frequently accompanied by physical gestures. In this final sentence of Souler's explanation, the emotional content of the expansive expressive is augmented by his playful questioning where the suddenly appearing things could have come from with an expressive and physical gesture.

Souler consistently employs the same terms to explain the linguistic salience of vowel alternation in these reduplicated forms; the iterative repetition of the same phenomenon (*lɛʔ laay tɨə* 'happens many times') or a linear progression through space (*khɨənway* 'moves with purpose'), and the expansive form occurring with spatial distribution (*lɛʔ laay bɔɔn* 'happens in many places'. In this example, he underscored the emotional elements of the expansive by using another expressive that depicts surprise, together with head movements and raised eyebrows in multimodal gesture. In doing so, Bit expressives function in an affective mode of special deixis.

11.6 *raam doʔ*: 'rather small' and the iconic scale of intensity

After a break in the session of discussing how *tbuul* is processed through this morphological template, Souler tells me that there is also a word *tbool*, but specifies that those things piling up are *raam doʔ* 'rather small'. The vowels of Bit expressives are fluid, but not without systematicity. This is where Bit speakers use iconicity to elaborate on the scale or intensity of the expressive. Souler commonly comments upon how a change in vowel affects what is understood by an expressive.

Speakers of Bit make full use of the language's vowel space to specify more or less intensity. This is done by sliding the vowel along the scale of vowel height, typically within the series of vowels of the same front-back position. Bit has a system of ten vowels, all with length contrast, and four diphthongs (one /ai/ occurs only in Tai borrowings).

intensity

iə	ɨə	uə	more
i	ɨ	u	
e	ə	o	
ɛ		ɔ	
a	ɒ		less

For one expressive base, the number of derived vowel-alternations possible varies. It is common that three variations are commonly used, but again, only vowels within the same series are available as iconic scaling. For the expressive *tduur* 'protruding and bending down' (like the end of a tree branch bearing a weight), I recorded four forms, ranging from larger to smaller: *tduər > tduur > tdoor > tdɔɔr*. Here, we find a diphthong depicting the largest on the scale, and this is generally the case, but of the three native diphthongs /uə/ and /iə/ are more common than /ɨə/. The fourth diphthong /ai/ is borrowed from Tai and does not appear in this expressive phonotactic landscape. Other common examples of [larger > smaller] include *piɲsiəɲ > peɲseeɲ*[4] 'single red light shining', *rwic > rwec* 'worms wriggling' and *liəʔɲiəʔ > lɛʔŋɛʔ* 'head cocked to the side'.

Because this operation is a subjective matter of *raam* 'rather' intensity, there is some variation among speakers. One complication is that speakers are often not comfortable making a decision about which is the 'normal' form. The implication is that sometimes an /u/ form will be described as *raam kdiiŋ* 'rather large' and sometimes the /o/ form will be described as *raam doʔ* 'rather small'. These three iconic axes intersect with another variable that affects size, vowel length. Contrast in vowel length is less common and less predictable, but the principle of iconic specification in the vowel space is clear. When I have learned a new expressive, I ask Souler about the vowel shifting potential, trying out contrasting vowels with varying degrees of articulatory distance. There is some range of individual variation here, in terms of 'what would you say about the small one?', but the principle of iconicity along the three axes of vowel space holds solid. Often, Souler will offer a form for the larger or the smaller.

The Bit vowel iconicity scale is noteworthy because it supports Diffloth's finding that /i/ is larger than /a/ in Bahnar, another Austroasiatic language, breaking what was long considered to be a universal of iconicity stating that /a/ is above /i/ on a scale of intensity (Diffloth 1995). Because the Bit scale works on three axes of vowel position, we have three sets of data in support of this possibility. It should be mentioned that the three distinct scales of intensity are principles, and

---

[4] The reduplicated vowel is shortened in the minor syllable, which means that diphthongs get reduced, unless the base has a final -ʔ.

one does occasionally hear Bit speakers cross the lines of front-back vowels, particularly when there are diphthongs involved. However, the implications of vowel height are consistent, providing a solid foundation for the system. When giving the alternative scale forms, providing examples of what 'types' could be associated with *raam doʔ* 'rather small' or *raam kdiiŋ* 'rather large'. Because there is scope for subjectivity in the vowel space and individuals may do slightly different things in creating the vowel dissimilation, Souler consistently uses this word *raam* to underscore the fluid space within the larger semiotic boundaries.

Souler does not, however, comment upon what certain consonants in initial or coda position might mean as part of a larger architecture of iconicity. For example, several expressives depicting the objects rubbing against each other have final /-c/: *ɟriəc* 'hard, heavy objects rubbing together, like two pieces of wood', *kriəc* 'light, dry objects rubbing together, like mouse claws on a house beam', and *cʰɒɒc* 'light sounds of dry things brushing against each other, like dry, calloused hands'. I know from comparative analysis that initial /ɟ/ often entails heaviness and often wetness, and the aspirated /cʰ/ is a marked sound because there are no aspirated stops in native Bit words, yet we find them in expressives. When I rubbed the case of my camera back and forth on the wooden floor, Souler said *kruət-kruət* but did not offer any ideas about how this might be related to *kriəc* or any others. However, my efforts to discuss any possible iconic significance of these contrasting segments have not been met with the same enthusiasm that vowel variation in the scale of intensity has. The dynamic vowel space represents an area of iconicity that is salient for expressive affect for Souler, because these are the elements that people can actively manipulate in their linguistic depictions.

11.7 Following threads of expressive depiction

In the story of The Elephant, a widow is forbidden from farming because she was not able to pay the head tax to the local governor (*caw miəŋ*). Without access to her fields, and with nothing to eat, she decides to transfer soil to a 'large rock'. She plants her rice in the small beds she made, but shortly after, an elephant comes by and eats all her rice plants. Desperate, she sets off after the elephant, vowing to kill him. Along the way, she drinks water from the footprint of the elephant, becomes pregnant, and after three years gives birth to an elephant son. The boy then sets off in search of his father, and in the end defeats the governor and takes his position of power and prosperity. The 'large rock' in the text was a phrase containing the expressive *ripciəp*, which I was not familiar with:

luəŋ   kdiiŋ   ripciəp
rock   big   EXP: ??

'large rock' [NB: with some special features that are important for our understanding of what will happen there]

226 NATHAN BADENOCH

The form *ripciəp* is in the static form, derived from *rciəp* with a copy-infix of the main syllable rhyme into the minor syllable. As a static expressive form, *ripciəp* emphasizes the fact that it is the result of some change that had happened, but was witnessed only after that change had occurred. When analysing the story, I did not always have access to the storyteller, so Souler provided explanations. I asked Souler what the meaning of *ripciəp* was in this case, and the answer was typical of the way in which he has taught me expressives. He uses other expressives in his explanations of expressive meaning, providing comparisons and expansions to highlight the temporal, spatial and emotional nuances. It is common to record multiple 'new' expressives in the course of discussing one term. The following exchange illustrates how Souler provides linguistic clarity and cultural salience in his explanation of expressives. In addition to the points introduced above, we also see how he clarifies less commonly used morphology. My questions were in Bit, but are given here in English for simplicity. The expressives are given only simple glosses in the transcription of Souler's explanation, and expanded in the analysis that follows in order to highlight how the meaning unfolds as he talks.

NB:

When Sone says *tlaar kdiiŋ ripciəp*, what is *riciəp*?

Souler:

mɛɛn	luəŋ	tlaar	trdʋʔ		dee	lɛʔ	laay	san
COP	stone	rock face	to be stacked		REFL	to have	many	layer

mee	waʔ	mih	bɛwaa	səək-səən	brciip
2S-M	to get	to look	means that	EXP: piled up	EXP: layered

'It is rocks in a rock face that are piled up on each other, with many layers. If you went to look at it, you would see it's like *səək-səən brciip*.'

First, he identifies the 'rock' as *tlaar*, which is a large rock face that is usually located near a waterfall, either an upright structure or a flat rock formation. Encounters between human, animal, and spirit beings often happen at *tlaar* in Bit stories, and these rock forms are often a liminal point between the natural and sacred worlds. Here, the *tlaar* is first described with a prosaic word, *trdʋʔ dee* 'stacked on top of each other', with many layers. He tells me that if I went to look it would appear *səək-səən* and *brciip*. It is not uncommon for him to use two or more expressives in sequence like this in his explanations, and one finds expressives serialized in natural conversation and narrative discourse as well. The first term *səək-səən* 'layered' is one of a few expressives that does not take expressive morphology, but is reduplicated in a way that is phonologically distinct from prosaic nouns and verbs with coda replacement. I had already learned this term, but *brciip* was new to me. Because of the main syllable /ciip/ I suspected it was related to *ripciip* '(appearance of things) stacked or piled unevenly'.

NB:

I know *ripciip*. Is *brciip* different from *ripciip*?

Souler:

ripciip	ʔaac caʔ	lɛʔ	mət	ʔan	mət	bɔɔn
EXP: layered	might	to have	one	thing	one	place

brciip	ʔaac caʔ	lɛʔ	laay	bɔɔn	hee
EXP: layered	might	to have	many	place	this

ləʔ	kɔɔ	lɛʔ	rʔəə	kɔɔ	lɛʔ
over there	also	to have	up there	also	to have

'*ripciip* probably has just one thing in one place, but *brciip* probably
has it in many places like this—there is one over there, one up there.'

Here, he confirms the connection between *brciip* and *ripciip*, both derived from
the punctual form *rciip*. The b- form is less commonly heard, and it is not easy to
glean the specific nuances in contrast to the punctual and static forms. He provides
detail on the difference between the b- form and the static *ripciip* form, indicating
how b- depicts the piled layers as composed of more than one layer located close
to each other. He uses spatial deictics *ləʔ* and *rʔəə* to indicate the same amount
of distance from the speaker (/ə/ vowel), but with varying height (/l/ 'level of
speaker' and /r/ 'higher than speaker'). Still not sure of the details, however, I
ask another question based on my general knowledge of how the morphological
paradigm works.

NB:

If you say *rapcaap-ripciip* does that mean it is in many places?

Souler:

rapcaap-	ripciip	bɛɛp	bŋʔəən	mee	ʔiim	ɲii	lɛɛ
ECHO	EXP: layered	way	by chance	2s-M	to come	to see	CMPL

spʰaap	nhəə	mee	haaŋ	ɲii	tʰam ʔit	rapcaap-	ripciip
condition	like that	2s-M	just now	to see	first time	ECHO	EXP: layered

mee	ɲii	ʔooo	lom	ləə	kee	ʻɲii	yɔɔ	ʔɒɒ	həə
2s-M	to see	oh	to talk	to	3P	to see	1s	NMLZ	that

rapcaap-	ripciip'
ECHO	EXP: layerd

'*rapcaap-ripciip* is like if by chance you arrive and happen to see something
in that condition, you have just seen it for the first time, *rapcaap-ripciip* you
see it. Then you tell them, 'Oh, I saw it *rapcaap-ripciip*.''

As discussed above, the expansive form with vowel dissimilation can generally
have two senses—one of spatial distribution, one of surprise. I assumed that the

salient point had to do with space, because of the discussion above of 'one place' and 'many places'. However, it turns out that it is the psychological context in which the reduplicated vowel dissimilation form is used here. He provides other clues, such as 'by chance' and 'first time', showing that there was no intention in the seeing of the conditions that existed. In his example he quotes my hypothetical statement to some others that I just happened upon it. He continues with these psychological contextualization theme with another unrelated example:

Souler:

bah	taaŋ	ɲok	tyaaŋ	kee	cəə	boh	kee	nɒʔ
NEG	to differ	to raise	example	3P	LOC	village	3-s	to like

laʔ	nəŋ	mee	bacɲaac-	bocɲooc	bɛɛp	həə	səʔ
to say	toward	2s-M	ECHO	EXP: large, tall	like	that	like that

psiiŋ	suuŋ	kdiiŋ
person	tall	large

'It's not that different from, for example, the people in our village they like to say about you *bacɲaac-bocɲooc*, like that, a tall, big person.'

In the same way, the expansive *bacɲaac-bocɲooc* 'large, heavy body moving around' form here could refer indirectly to me moving around the in the village in different places, but drawing on the cognitive link he has made with *rapcaap-ripciip*, we understand that more important to this utterance is their noting of my 'abnormal size' among the village people (I am 180 cm and just short of 100 kg). I should note that I had not heard that expressive before, and although I have heard many expressives used to depict my presence in the village, they often had to do with my comings and goings (because I was researching in several villages and had to stay mostly in the province town, they saw me in motion very frequently) rather than my physical characteristics. It is likely that this influenced my initial assumption about the meaning of *bacɲaac-bocɲooc*. Souler continues,

Souler:

brciip	həə	mɛɛn	mee	ɲoʔ	cmɔɔ	mee	ɲii
EXP: layered	that	COP	2s-M	to be at	to look	2s-M	to see

yoʔ	bɛɛp	laksanaa	mee	ɲii	waʔ	mih
EMP	like	characteristic	2s-M	to see	to go	to look

ləʔ	kɔɔ	lɛʔ	rʔəə	kɔɔ	lɛʔ	laay	ʔan
there	also	to have	over there	also	to have	many	thing

'*brciip* is if you are there looking at something, then you go and see that there is some there, some here—many things.'

Returning to *brciip*, he uses the word *cmɔɔ* 'to look at', which has a clear nuance of intention, especially in a situation in which you specifically go to look at something in order to understand what is going on; for example, watching over a child or a sick person. In more poetic language, one hears *mih cmɔɔ* 'to look over, to take care of', so his selection of the second element is to inject the intentionality of the looking, so as to emphasize a more unemotional observation of the layered rocks. Moreover, he states that if I walked over to it after seeing it, I would recognize that there were many layers closely piled up here and there.

Souler:

ʔɛɛ	mee	lom	ləə	kee	bŋtiə	mee			
if	2s-M	to talk	with	3s	maybe	3s-M			

laʔ	ʔooo	ɲoʔ	ɲoʔ	ləʔ	ləʔ	brcaap-	brciip		lɛʔ
to say	oh	to be at	to be at	there	There	ECHO	EXP: layered		to have

laay	ʔan'	ɲoʔ	leʔ	brcaap-	brciip'		laʔ	ʔᴅᴅ	mee
many	thing	to be at	here	ECHO	EXP: layered		to say	3s-INAN	S-M

'if you are talking with someone and say, 'Oh, over there *brcaap-brciip*, there are many of them, over here, over there'. You would say *brcaap-brciip* about it.'

The spatial element is clearly brought into the sight with a vowel dissimilated reduplication of the *brciip* form. The clue here is use of the word *ɲoʔ* 'to be at, to sit', which indicates separate places in which the rock forms are seen. The deictics *leʔ* and *ləʔ* indicating things (*laay ʔan*) distributed on the same level across a space, showing that this form lacks the emotional element of *rapcaap-ripciip*. He then returns to *ripciip* to emphasize the spatial element.

Souler:

ripciip		mɛɛn	ɲok	tyaaŋ	waa	psiiŋ	siə	koʔ	yoʔ
EXP: layered		COP	to raise	example	that	person	drunk	alcohol	EMPH

siə	koʔ	ŋᴅᴅ	ɲok		tɛʔ	ləʔ	cukŋuk	
drunk	alcohol	S-M	to bow head		to do	there	head drooping	

mət	khon	cukŋuk		ŋᴅᴅ	
one	person	EXP: head drooping		S-M	

'*ripciip* is, for example, if someone gets drunk. A guy is there with his head drooping forward there *cukŋuk*. One person, he is *cukŋuk*.'

In this expansion, he sets up a comparison with a simple expressive that I know well, *cukŋuk* 'slumped over, motionless'. Then, he provides the b- prefix to show in parallel how the spatial dynamics play out.

Souler:

lɛɛ	brcaap-	brciip	ɲok	tyaaŋ	kee	leʔ	laay
and	ECHO	EXP: layered	to raise	example	3P	to have	many

kʰon	ɲok	kee	laʔ	bcɲak-	bcɲuk		siə
person	to bow head	3P	to say	ECHO	EXP: hanging head		drunk

ko?   ŋok
alcohol to bow head

'And *brcaap-brciip*, for example, there are many of them with their heads drooping, you say '*bcŋak-bcŋuk* they are drunk with heads drooping forward.''

Thus, the b- form has both a 'plural' and 'spatially distributed' sense, offered as an observation of a situation where the context is easily understood. In this hypothetical case, it would not be surprising to see people in this position if there was a celebration. If he wanted to add the emotional element, to say perhaps that it was not the people that were supposed to be in the room, or they were people who never drink, then he could say *cakŋak-cukŋuk* with the reduplicated form undergoing vowel dissimilation.

The explanation ends here. It has not been stated explicitly, but it is clear that the original *ripciap* is related to *ripciip*, where the form with a diphthong indicates the highest intensity of degree—in this case, a larger rock formation than *ripciip*—according to the principles of vowel iconicity in Bit expressives. But Souler thematizes the more important element, which is the microsemantics of the b- prefix on this expressive, because the physical impression of the rock formation is what gives it cultural salience in the story. If the *tlaar* was not *ripciap*, the woman would not have been able to plant her rice beds, and would not have encountered the elephant.

Because this phrase comes at the beginning of the story, he provides the simple static form of *ripciap* without any spatial or emotional detail, at this point focusing on the expressive affect linking *kdiiŋ* 'large' with the /iə/ vowel denoting the highest intensity. The size is the issue, as we find out several lines later, when the elephant appears as *saaŋ rmis kdiiŋ* 'a large bull elephant'. Souler has read into the deep cultural meaning of the expressive use, based on his knowledge of the story, but moved out of that specific context to provide a broader explanation of how expressives work in different situations.

In his response to my question about the meaning of *ripciap* in the context of this story, Souler took me on a walk through a morphosemantic landscape that pointed out meaning, aspect, space, and emotional formations. When we returned to this discussion later, he pointed out that *rapcaap* was *?ʋʋ raam do?* 'a rather smaller version', confirming the appropriateness of using /ɨɨ/ and /iə/ with the rock face *tlaar* to depict the 'largeness' and enhance the affective stance of the usage. In this session he expanded the semantics further, emphasizing an aesthetic judgement with the forms *rah?ah-rɛh?ɛh* 'small things layered in an uneven and unattractive way' and *rah?ah-rih?ih* 'larger (*raam kdiiŋ*) things layered in an uneven and unattractive way'. The semantics of this alternative re-emphasize the cultural power of the original depiction of the rock face.

In this section I have shared how the flow of discussion moves in a process of expansion along semantic and morphophonological lines, indicating how different aspects of expressive usage are linked in Souler's linguistic map of cognitive-cultural salience (Figure 11.1).

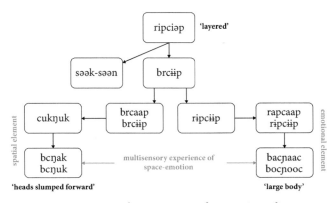

Figure 11.1 Mapping thematization of expressive salience

Clusters of sensori-semantic meaning (Nuckolls 2004) are loosely delineated by networks of sound and sense activated in the specific social situation where the discussion between researcher and mentor happens. (Badenoch 2021b). Asking the question 'When so-and-so said x-expressive, what were they saying?' produces a cascade of information, including explanations, enactments, derivative forms, comparative examples, and new words. From a slightly different angle, at times I will give Souler an expressive in isolation to see what directions his explanation will take. This is another productive way to triangulate the iconic, semantic, and pragmatic nuances of expressive uses. Because of this productive flow, my field notes are often more like mind-maps such as the simplified one introduced above. It is near impossible to discuss an expressive form in isolation, because the points of salience link across linguistic forms and social settings. This parallels the common practice of expressive concatenation in narrative.

11.8 The limits of creativity in expressive performance

The aesthetic practice of *prɟʊk baar* 'attaching flowers' is a central element of Bit linguistic performance. The grammar of expressiveness offers a range of ways for speakers to enhance their interactions. This grammar contains elements that are structurally well-defined as well as those that are open to creative manipulation. The morphological paradigm offers a highly nuanced set of spatial and temporal specifications that are less subject to personal variation. The vowel gradation of intensity is a phonologically defined system, but allows speakers to play within the vowels' space to depict impressions of and reactions to differences in size, speed, and other sensory perceptions. Because expressive meaning is a network of sense elements and psychological-emotional positions, speakers can draw on a wide range of possible semantic applications in their use of expressives. In some cases this may be akin to metaphor, but it is perhaps more accurate to think of speakers foregrounding different elements of meaning as they depict certain actors, experiences, and outcomes in their narration.

Metalinguistic discussion of expressive meaning in actual language use produces clear patterns of thematization. In my experience, Bit speakers share a common understanding of the details of expressive meaning. If I provide an expressive word that I have heard used in one household to someone from another household, I generally get explanations that map closely to each other although the layers of nuance may be revealed over the course of multiple conversations. It is not uncommon to hear similar examples of how the expressive can be used. Considering how 'conventional' expressive usage is in the speech community is a way to think about how much creativity an individual speaker can bring into their expressives. There is certainly variation in expressive use among speakers in the community where I work. Minor phonetic details and contexts of usage are the most common. In most cases, these do not cause communicative problems, and serve to create an individual style. More generally, it is recognized that some individuals use more expressives than others. These all contribute to the idea of *muən*—the feeling of aesthetic satisfaction that exists at the intersection of fun, relevance, appropriateness and meaning—in speech.

Recalling the elaborate phrase for speaking, *tɛʔ buəs tɛʔ tɔɔy* 'doing language, doing words', we can begin to understand the edges of conventionality in Bit expressive use. Expressives are both *tɔɔy* 'words' and *buəs* 'language' for Bit speakers, but people will evoke the notion of *buəs* when they believe that expressive use has departed from the realm of recognized practice. This is particularly common when analysing the speech of different dialect subgroups. One storyteller exercises some poetic licence with his expressives, leading Souler to comment *ŋʋʋ lɛʔ baŋtiə ʔii bah ban, buəs ŋʋʋ hak lɛʔ* 'sometimes he has things we don't understand, but his language has them'. Categorizing an expressive one does not recognize as *buəs ŋʋʋ* 'his speech' suggests individual variation, while *buəs kee* 'their speech' implies a heavier cultural boundary between speech sub-communities. Here, it is more helpful to consider *buəs* in its broader sense of 'logic, thinking' where individual usage and collective convention are negotiated.

This commentary recognizes the possibility of different expressive language practices, recognizing different elements of salience within a semiotic ideology (Keane 2018). As mentioned above, I have heard people comment on adults' expressive use as *tryuut* 'crazy', sometimes falling within the realm of *buəs biət* 'speech of spirits'. This is where the conventions of expressive language use have broken down and expressives cease to be *tɔɔy* 'words' that form the foundation of human language. This discourse is situated within ideologies of cultural differentiation that go beyond language use, showing how expressive use that moves out of the realm of shared cultural logic can be a powerful indicator of internal social dynamics in the community. What Souler explains in our discussions represents a cognitive-cultural map of what is salient within the shared practice of expressive use. Because linguistic and cultural systems of expressivity vary widely across the globe (Williams 2021), it is essential that descriptive and theoretical work strive to reflect the metalanguage of thematization that is used by native speakers.

11.9 Cultural salience and the interpretation of expressiveness

The study of expressives I have introduced here is a dialogic exploration of a special area of language used by Bit speakers in their daily lives. Extended conversations about expressives lead to nuanced commentary on how dynamics of time, space, and mental state are interwoven into speech in ways that are fundamentally different from 'prosaic' grammar. The fact that the Bit morphological paradigm enabling this works only on expressives and not on verbs or other statives suggests that there is a different principle of *buəs*—word, language, logic—at work. This fact also suggests that expressives are a distinct class of words in Bit. The things the Bit find *important*—to use a term from my Western ideology of language—are embodied in a special grammar. We know that in other areas of Austroasiatic, such as the Asian languages, similar morphology is a basic part of the grammar of verbs and nouns (Kruspe 2004). This suggests that this aesthetic grammar is old, but in the history of Bit it has come to index a separate realm of intersubjectivity.

The points of aesthetic grammar that Souler explains with a set of metalinguistic tools he developed in the course of our work—ways of speaking about Bit ways of speaking (Sherzer 2001)—outline the cultural salience of this word class in the Bit language. In this work, folk definition (Dingemanse 2015) becomes a form of field discourse that can inform our theoretical thinking, based on a monolingual framing that confirms our mutual commitment to walking the rugged terrain of expressive semantics together. The cultural salience of expressives is part of a semiotic ideology that reflects heightened awareness of time and space, as well as the mental and emotional states that frame these words in speech. In our discussions, Souler thematizes the salience of expressives in the Bit cultural framework. He does not comment directly upon aspects of expressives that are not salient to him, for example the details of how the static *tulbuul* is derived from the punctual *tbuul*, or how the expansive *talbaal-tulbuul* is derived. He has never touched upon the notion of reduplication either. These elements of the morphology lie outside the immediate scope of salience for him, but the metalinguistic references he uses—suddenly, sitting there, many times, surprising—convey the complexities of aspect, space, and emotion. His explanations keep the expressives within an intimate conversation—his examples and descriptions frequently employ *yɔɔ* 'I' and *mee* 'you', as well as *daa* 'we (dual)'—while he recreates a hypothetical but shared field of experience. This type of metacommunicative framing (Sherzer 2001) helps to orient us in relation to the expressive we are discussing. When he leads the discussion, we follow his networks of sound and meaning that are linked by points of salience. He is doing micro-ethnography in his explanations, collapsing the disconnect between speech event and recorded event (Nuckolls 2003) to capture expressivity and providing insights into what a Bit theory of 'markedness' might look like. Expressives abound in the language, and from this perspective, there is nothing strange about them at all. In my attempt to present an ethnographic account of his micro-ethnographic discourses on expressives, I suggest that the salient features that Souler stresses show how these words contribute to the linguistic culture of the Bit, constituting a central area of their semiotic ideology.

References

Badenoch, Nathan (2021a). Silence, cessation and stasis: animating 'absence' in Bit expressives. *Journal of Linguistic Anthropology* 32(1): 94–115.

Badenoch, Nathan (2021b). Sticky semantics: expressive meaning in Mundari'. In Nathan Badenoch and Nishaant Choksi (eds), *Expressives in the South Asian Linguistic Area.* Leiden: Brill, 17–34.

Badenoch, Nathan, Choksi, Nishaant, Purti, Madhu, and Osada, Toshiki (2021a). Performance in elicitation: methodological considerations in the study of Mundari expressives. In Shailendra Mohan (ed.), *Advances in Munda Linguistics.* New Castle upon Tyne: Cambridge Scholars Publishing, 131–141.

Badenoch, Nathan, Toshiki, Osada, Purti, Madhu, and Onishi, Masayuki (2021b). Expressive lexicography: creating a dictionary of expressives in the South Asian linguistic area. *Indian Linguistics* 82(1–2): 25–40.

Briggs, Charles L. (2021). *Unlearning: Rethinking Poetics, Pandemics and the Politics of Knowledge.* Louisville: University Press of Colorado.

Choksi, Nishaant and Meek, Barbra A. (2016). Theorizing salience: orthographic practices and the enfigurement of minority languages. In Anna Babel (ed.), *Awareness and Control in Sociolinguistic Research.* Cambridge: Cambridge University Press, 228–252.

Diffloth, Gérard (1976). Expressives in Semai. *Oceanic Linguistics Special Publications* 13, Austroasiatic Studies Part I: 249–264.

Diffloth, Gérard (1995). i:big, a:small. In Leanne Hinton et al. (eds), *Sound Symbolism.* Cambridge: Cambridge University Press, 107–114.

Diffloth, Gérard (2021). Foreword. In Nathan Badenoch Badenoch and Nishaant Choksi (eds), *Expressives in the South Asian Linguistic Area.* Leiden: Brill.

Dingemanse, Mark (2013). Ideophones and gesture in everyday speech. *Gesture* 13(2): 143–165.

Dingemanse, Mark (2015). Folk definitions in linguistic fieldwork. In James Essegberg et al. (eds), *Language Documentation and Endangerment in Africa.* Amsterdam: John Benjamins Publishing, 215–238.

Dingemanse, Mark (2021). Ideophones. In Eva van Lier (ed.), *Oxford Handbook of Word Classes*. Oxford: Oxford University Press, 466–476.

Drager, Katie and Kirtley, M. Joelle (2016). Awareness, salience, and stereotypes in exemplar-based models of speech production and perception. In Anna Babel (ed.), *Awareness and Control in Sociolinguistic Research*. Cambridge: Cambridge University Press, 1–24.

Everett, Daniel L. (2001). Monolingual field research. In Paul Newman and Martha Ratliff (eds), *Linguistic Fieldwork*. Cambridge: Cambridge University Press, 166–188.

Keane, Webb (2018). On semiotic ideology. *Signs and Society* 6(1): 64–87.

Kruspe, Nicole (2004). *A Grammar of Semelai*. Cambridge: Cambridge University Press.

Mukařovský, Jan (1983) [1932]. Standard language and poetic language. In Vachek (ed.), *Praguiana: Some Basic and Less Known Aspects of the Prague Linguistic School, An Anthology of Prague School Papers*. Prague: Academia.

Nuckolls, Janis (1996). *Sounds like Life: Sound-Symbolic Grammar, Performance, and Cognition in Pastaza Quechua*. Oxford: Oxford University Press.

Nuckolls, Janis (2003). To be or not to be ideophonically impoverished. *Texas Linguistic Forum* 47: 131–142.

Nuckolls, Janis (2010). *Lessons from a Quechua Strongwoman: Ideophony, Dialogue, and Perspective*. Tucson: University of Arizona Press.

Nuckolls, Janis (2019). To be or not to be ideophonically impoverished. In Kimi Akita and Prashant Pardeshi (eds), *Ideophones, Mimetics and Expressives*. Amsterdam: John Benjamins, 167–198.

Nuckolls, Janis (2020). How do you even know what ideophones mean?: Gesture's contributions to ideophone semantics in Quichua. *Gesture* 19(2/3): 161–195.

Sasamoto, Ryoko (2019). *Onomatopoeia and Relevance: Communication of Impressions via Sound*. London: Palgrave Studies in Sound. Palgrave Macmillan e-book.

Sherzer, Joel (2001). *Kuna Ways of Speaking: An Ethnographic Perspective*. Austin: University of Texas Press.

Silverstein, Michael. (1981) "The limits of awareness." Sociolinguistic Working Paper No. 84. Southwest Educational Development Laboratory, Austin, Texas.

Svantesson, Jan-Olof (1983). *Kammu Phonology and Morphology*. Travaux de l'Institut de linguistique de Lund, 18. Lund: University of Lund.

Webster, Anthony K. (2015). *Intimate Grammars: An Ethnography of Navajo Poetry*. Tucson: University of Arizona Press.

Webster, Anthony K. (2017). 'So it's got three meanings dil dil': Seductive ideophony and the sounds of Navajo poetry. *Canadian Journal of Linguistics/Revue Canadienne De Linguistique* 62(2): 173–195.

Williams, Jeffrey P. (2014). *The Aesthetics of Grammar: Sound and Meaning in the Languages of Mainland Southeast Asia*. Cambridge: Cambridge University Press.

Williams, Jeffrey P. (ed.) (2021). *Expressivity in European Languages*. Cambridge: Cambridge University Press.

Williams, Jeffrey P. (2021). Expressives in languages of mainland Southeast Asia. In Paul Sidwell and Matthias Jenny (eds), *The Languages and Linguistics of Mainland Southeast Asia*. Berlin: de Gruyter Mouton, 811–824.

Zuckerman, Charles H. P. and Enfield, N. J. (2023). The limits of thematization. *Journal of Linguistic Anthropology* 33(1): 1–30. doi: 10.1111/jola.12399

Index

Aaltola, Elisa 124
Abbi, Anvita 192
aesthetics
  aesthetic component of language 10–11, 190, 202
  aesthetic functions of ideophones 56
  aesthetic value for art 202
  Bit language, of 217
  expressives as aesthetic part of language 204, 217, 230, 231, 232
  grammatical aesthetics of expressivity 1, 233
  visual media, of 131
Akita, Kimi 8–10, 93, 174–175, 177–180
Alcover, Antoni M. 110–111
Amazonian Kichwa (Quichua) dialects
  authors' approach, in this book 9, 88, 89, 122–124, 143
  authors' personal interests in 131–137
  authors' relationships with Kichwa participants 129–131, 216
  authors' research methodology 124–129
  cultural context for ideophones 122
  direct, and indirect, research methodologies 137–143
  empathetic use of ideophones 123–124
  indirect and direct research methodologies 137–143
  Kichwa Realwords 93, 95, 97
  Pastaza Kichwa ideophones, meanings of 91–93, 100, 122
  polysemiotic representations 91–93
Ameka, Felix 84
anthropology
  anthropological linguists 3, 6, 124
  ethnography and 215
  expressives 215
  fieldwork 10, 218
  interpretive 1
  sociocultural 135
art
  aesthetic value for 202
  art schools 131
  literary power of 136
  verbal art 78
Asano, Tsuruko 172
Asari, Tomoki 201

audio *See* hearing
Azkue, R. M. 58

Baba, Junko 180
Badenoch, Nathan 10–11, 87, 89
Barrett, Rusty 3
Berlin, Brent 81
Bit expressives *See also* expressives
  affective function of 223
  aspect depiction by 220–221
  classification 233
  class of 233
  explanation of 218–219
  expressivity and 220
  iconicity of 230
  meanings of 215
  metalinguistic framing of 217–218
  poetic expression of 11
  presence of 225
  purpose of 216
  study of 215, 233
  terminologies 215
  use of 216, 218–219
  vowel iconicity within 230
  vowels of 223
Bit language 11, 215, 217, 218, 233
brain science of expressives 203
Brandstetter, Renward 2
Briggs, Charles L. 216
Bühler, Karl 2
Burma *See* Myanmar

Cadena, Luisa 125–127, 131–133
Chan, Rodrigo Petatillo 9, 162–163
Childs, G.T. 53
China 3, 5, 33, 172, 215
classification
  Bit expressives 233
  expressives 5, 44, 116, 118, 233
  ideophones 5, 24, 64
  mimetics 172–173
  prompts/stimuli 63
  semantic 173
contexts *See* ideophones
corpora
  Japanese mimetics 173–175, 178–180

INDEX 237

limits of corpus-based research 179–180
multimodal corpora 178–179
Yucatec Maya natural conversations 164–165
Cruse, D. Alan 3
culture
  cultural context for ideophones 122
  cultural knowledge as to expressivity 202
  cultural salience of expressiveness 233–234
  cultural salience of expressives 233
  cultural systems of expressivity 233
  expressivity as to cultural knowledge 202
  sociocultural anthropology 135

De la Vergne de Tressan, M. 19
detection/identification
  Bit expressives 216
  expressives 108, 112, 116
Diffloth, Gérard 6, 10–11, 36, 53–54, 108, 169,
    190, 215–216, 217, 224
Dingemanse, Mark 8, 42–43, 58, 89, 98–99, 125,
    146, 170, 177–179, 181
Doke, Clemens 5, 17, 20, 30
Dols, Nicolau 8, 110, 116
Drager, Katie 218

empathy
  definition of 124
  empathetic approach to ideophones 124,
    125–126, 129
  empathetic use of ideophones 9, 123–124
  evocation of empathetic experiences 143
  expression of 135
  expressivity and 6
  ideophone research, and 124, 125–126, 129
  natural world, for 135
Enfield, N.J. 156, 217
Erremundeguy, Ihintza 63n5
ethnography
  anthropology and 10, 215
  communication/speech, of 164
  ethnolinguistics 6, 142, 216
  ethnomusicology of expressives 33
  expressives 215
  expressivity research, and 11
  Kichwa (Quechua) Real Words, and 136
  language learning, and 162
  micro-ethnography 234
  multimodal ethnography 165
ethnomusicology of expressives 33
expressiveness 59, 108, 178, 231, 233–234
'expressive onomatopes' See expressives
expressives
  absence of 193, 195, 202, 210

aesthetic part of language, as 204, 217, 230,
    231, 232
anthropological approach to 215
appearance of 2
Bit expressives See Bit expressives
categories of 42–43, 189–190, 193
characterization of 8
classification 5, 44, 116, 118, 233
classification of 116
complexity of 215
contents of 43–45
cultural salience of 233
detection/identification of 108, 112, 116, 216
differences between 198
ethnographic approach to 215
examples of 190–193
'expressive onomatopes' 19
expressivity and 1, 190–193
forms of 1, 2, 4
iconicity of 225, 230
ideophones, distinction from 3, 4, 5–6, 9, 93
interpretation of 11, 190
Kammu expressives See Kammu language
learning of 215–216, 218, 226
linguistic/ethnomusicological approach to 33
meanings of 1, 33, 108
mimetics, distinction from 4, 53
morphology of 34
nature of 4
neurological effects of 203
non-expressives 9, 11, 193, 195, 197, 198, 201,
    202, 204, 207, 208
part-completed research on 173
perception of 10, 11, 196, 201, 202, 204
performances, as 6, 218
pitch differential, relationship with 116
plentifulness of 234
presence of 193, 202, 203, 210
processes of 4, 193
processing of 11, 195–196, 201, 204
production of 11
purpose of 4, 45, 190–191
'quasi expressives' 19
research as to 2, 3, 11, 195, 215, 216, 233
response to 195, 197, 198, 208, 223
scarcity of 202, 203
selective analysis of 116
song, within 33, 38–42
terminologies of 215
translation of 202, 203, 204
types of 116–118
uses of 226, 228, 230, 232
working with 9

238 INDEX

expressivity
  approach to, by current book 12
  Bit expressives, and 220
  capturing of 234
  characteristics of 6–7, 11–12
  cultural knowledge as to 202
  cultural systems of 233
  definition of 1
  documenting of/engagement with 7–11
  exponents of 5–6
  expressiveness, and 178
  expressives, and 190–193
  grammatical aesthetics, and 1
  grammatical aesthetics of expressivity 233
  histories of 2–3
  human language, within 1
  humour, in 137
  ideophones/mimetics, in 19–21, 169, 179
  Japanese language/research, in 169, 178–179,
    181–182
  learning of 215–216
  linguistic systems of 233
  modern linguistic theory, within 1
  narratives/storytelling, in 137, 164
  Principle of Expressivity 2, 190
  role of 6
  sites of 218–220
  terminologies of 3–4
  typological study of 182

Flaksman, Maria 96
Fortune, G. 19–20

Garau, Pere 8, 120
Gärdenfors, Peter 6
Geertz, Clifford 6
Goenaga, Patxi 58
Gomi, Taro 92
González, Pérez 154
grammar
  aesthetics of 1
  grammatical aesthetics of expressivity 1, 233
Grimalt, J.A. 111
Guiscafrè, Jaume 111
Gutzmann, Daniel 3

Hamano, S. 53, 96, 169, 172
hearing See also narratives/storytelling
  auditory stimuli 162
  orally based culture See culture
  pitch differential of expressives 116
Henderson, Robertson 3
Hirata-Mogi, Sachiko 177
Holmer, Arthur 34, 36

Hualde, Jose Ignacio 58
humour in expressivity 137

Ibarluzea, Miren 63n5
Ibarra, Usoa Wyssenbach 63n5
Ibarretxe-Antuñano, Iraide 7
iconicity
  Bit expressives 225, 230
  Yucatec Maya language 154–155
identification See detection/identification
ideophones See also mimetics
  aesthetic functions of 56
  classification 5, 24, 64
  definition of 122
  empathetic approach to 124, 125–126, 129
  empathetic use of 9, 123–124
  expressives, distinction from 3, 4, 5–6, 9, 93
  expressivity, in 19–21, 169, 179
  Japanese See Japanese mimetics
  Kichwa language See Amazonian Kichwa
    (Quichua) dialects
  semantic multimodality of 155–161, 166
IdEus-Psylex stimulus kit
  Basque language fieldwork, use in 55–58
  challenges for Basque ideophone
    research 58–61, 64–65
  choice of stimuli 61
  contribution to ideophone research 65
  creation of 61
  descriptive overview of 62–64
  ideophones, preconceptions as to nature
    of 64
  improvement of 65
  introduction of 7–8
  materials included in 62
  procedure for use of 63
  stimulus-based elicitation 53–55
  study participants, choice of 61
  study participants, variables relating to 62
  use of 63–64
Imai, Mutsumi 169, 180
interpretation
  expressives 11, 190
  interpretive anthropology 1
Itô, Junko 169

Jakobson, Roman 2–3
James, William 135
Japan 172, 177
Japanese ideophones
  areas for future research 100
  author's approach, in this book 9–10
  author's research methodology 75–77, 100
  collecting of 77–80

detailed lexical entries for 95–97
distinctiveness of 140
expressivity, in 169, 178–179, 181–182
lexicographical representation 90–91, 100
meaningfully structured interfaces of 97–99
meanings of 28, 74, 78, 86–90
paraphrasing of 74–75
polysemiotic representations 91–95, 100
targeted research techniques 80–86
Japanese mimetics
author's approach, in this book 169
corpora of 173–175, 178–180
descriptive overview of 170–172
dictionaries of 172–173
experiments with 180–181
expressivity research, within 169, 181–182
history of 169
limits of corpus-based approaches
to 179–180
multimodal corpora of 178–179
phonology of 174–175
semantics of 174–175
study of 9–10
syntax of 174–175
use of 4, 20–21, 140
variations in 175–178
Japardi, Kevin 202

Kakehi, Hisao 170, 173, 175
Kàm Ràw 5, 33, 36–37, 44–45
Kay, Paul 81
Kilian-Hatz, Christa 5, 17, 21
Kirtley, M. Joelle 218
Kita, Sotaro 20–21, 169
Kobayashi, Takashi 177
Koulifa, S. Pierre 20
Kunene, Daniel P. 20, 24

Lahti, Katherine 3
language
aesthetic component of 190, 202
Bit language 11, 215, 217, 218, 233
corpora See corpora
expressives as aesthetic part of 204, 217, 230, 231, 232
Laos 5, 33, 36, 215, 218–219, 220, 221
learning
expressives, of 215–216, 218, 226
expressivity, of 215–216
language learning, ethnography and 162
Le Guen, Olivier 9, 145, 148–149, 152, 162–163, 166
Lennes, Mietta 111–112
Lindell, Kristina 36

linguistics/linguistic research
anthropological linguists 3, 6, 124
ethnolinguistics 6, 142, 216
linguistic/ethnomusicological approach to
expressives 33
linguistic systems of expressivity 233
metalinguistic framing of Bit
expressives 217–218
modern linguistic theory, within
expressivity 1
Lundström, Håkan 5, 36–37
Lyons, John 24

Majid, Asifa 84, 98–99
Malinowski, Bronislaw 6
Marron, Tali R. 202
Matsumoto, Yo 180
Maya language See Yucatec Maya language
McLean, Bonnie 8, 12, 181
media, aesthetics of visual media 131
Medin, Douglas 85
Mester, R. Armin 169
Mihas, Elena 89, 156
mimetics See also ideophones
classification 172–173
expressives, distinction from 4, 53
expressivity, in 19–21, 169, 179
Japanese See Japanese mimetics
Miyazawa, Kenji 174
Moll, Francesc de B. 110
musicology of expressives 33
Myanmar 5, 33

Napo Kichwa See Amazonian Kichwa (Quichua)
dialects
narratives/storytelling
expressivity in 137, 164
literary power of art within 136
Yucatec Maya language 164
neurological effects of expressives 203
Noji, Junya 178
non-expressives See expressives
Nuckolls, Janis 3, 9, 88–89, 91, 93, 130–133,
137, 140, 156, 166, 216, 223

Oehl, Wilhelm 2
Ogura, Tamiko 180
Ono, Masahiro 173
onomatopoeia, 'expressive onomatopes' 19
orally based culture See culture
Ortiz de Urbina, Jon 58
Osada, Toshiki 216

240 INDEX

Parmar, Harshit 10
Pastaza-Upper Napo Quichua *See* Amazonian
 Kichwa (Quichua) dialects
perception of expressives 196, 201, 202, 204
performance
 Bit expressives 218
 expressives as 6, 218
Petatillo, Rodrigo 9
pitch differential of expressives 116
poetic expression of Bit expressives 11
Potts, Christopher 3
processing of expressives 195–196, 201, 204
prompts *See* stimuli
Provoost, D. Pierre 20
Pullum, Geoffrey 3
Purti, Madhu 93, 216

'quasi expressives" *See* expressives
Quichua *See* Amazonian Quichua dialects

response of expressives 195, 197, 198, 208
Rhodes, Richard A. 27

Saji, Noburo 180
Salaburu, Pello 58
Samarin, W.J. 53, 96
Sarasola, Ibon 58
Saussure, F. de 54
Schuchardt, H. 58
Scripture, Edward Wheeler 191
semantic classification 173
semantic multimodality 155–161, 166
semiotics, polysemiotic representations 91–95,
 100
Sherzer, Joel 3
Sicoli, M. 165
Silverstein, Michael 217
Smalley, William A. 36
song, expressives within 33, 38–42
stealth words 161, 162, 167
stimuli
 auditory stimuli 162
 classification of 63
 IdEus-Psylex *See* IdEus-Psylex stimulus kit
 stealth lexicon, and 162, 167
 stimulus-based elicitation 8, 75, 81–86, 88,
 93, 95, 166, 181
 visual stimuli 166
storytelling *See* narratives/storytelling
Svantesson, Jan-Olof 5, 34, 36, 37, 43

Swanson, Tod 9, 122, 128, 130, 135–138, 142

Takamaru, Keiichi, 177
Tamaoka, Kazuo 174
terminologies
 Bit expressives 215
 expressivity 3–4, 215
Thailand 5, 33, 36
Toratini, Kiyoko 174
translation of expressives 202, 203, 204
Tsujimura, Natsuko 140
Tufvesson, Sylvia 191

Urtel, H. 58

vision
 aesthetics of visual media 131
 visual stimuli 166
vocal performance *See* performance
Voeltz, F. K. Erhard 21

Webster, Anthony K. 3, 216
Westermann, Diedrich 17
Williams, Jeffrey P. 3, 10, 108

Yamaguchi, Nakami 172
Yùan Kammu dialect *See* Kammu language
Yucatec Maya language
 author's approach, in this book 9, 146
 author's research methodology 161, 162–163,
 166–167
 corpus building of natural
 conversations 164–165
 iconicity 154–155
 ideophone occurrence 163–164
 ideophone research 145–146
 ideophones derived from existing word
 roots 148–149
 ideophones within 146–148
 narratives/storytelling 164
 semantic multimodality 155–161, 166
 stealth words 161
 stimulus-based elicitation 166
 suffixation 151–152
 templates 152–154
 vowel derivation 149–151

Zamarripa, P. 58
Zlatev, Jordan 78
Zuckerman, Charles H.P. 217
Zwicky, Arnold 3